A LIFE DERAILED

MY JOURNEY WITH ALS

NATE METHOT

ONION RIVER PRESS

Burlington, Vermont

Onion River Press
191 Bank Street
Burlington, VT 05401

Printed in the United States of America

ISBN 978-1-957184-02-9 (*paperback*)

Library of Congress Control Number: 2022903694

Book cover design by Marko Markovic, 5mediadesign
Book cover photo by Torrey Valyou

To my mom, who has done everything for me.

CONTENTS

PREFACE

I never thought I'd write a book. I never imagined that stories from my life would be interesting or meaningful enough for anyone to read. But that's changed over the years. I'm no longer normal in any sense of the word. Enough time has passed since my second life started that I've had the opportunity to reflect. I've had more than enough time.

I was forced to move in with my parents in 2019. No longer solely responsible for life's daily tasks, I had more time to focus on writing. About a year into my new cohabitation, COVID-19 forced still more time in the house. Without a complete picture of what might result, I began writing stories from my long-running battle.

I'd thought about a lot of them for years. At the very least, I'd write them down for my own eyes, if no one else's. That's all the purpose I needed to get started.

As the stories piled up, a framework began to take form. I had to go back to the beginning and, with each step, move closer to the person I've become. I wanted the reader to come along on my journey and take up a chair in my head. I'd try my best to explain what it was like.

It's been ten years since that Wednesday morning at the hospital. I was diagnosed with amyotrophic lateral sclerosis (ALS, Lou Gehrig's disease, motor neuron disease) in August of 2011, a month after my twenty-seventh birthday. It feels like more than a lifetime ago.

It may seem like everything changed in one day, but that isn't the truth. I'd been navigating a not-so-steady stream of changes long before they had any label — from my first inkling to my first doctor's visit to the day I got my first wheelchair to everything yet to come. My story is about change more than anything.

I'm repeatedly broken in the pages of this book. I gradually succumb to a physical enemy and emerge from each fight a new person. I grow into an adult, if only in my own head. All of my struggles bring mental maturity.

What follows is a collection of stories relating to my diagnosis, mixed with a number of thoughts and feelings to better fill out my experience. The narrative is organized broadly by subject — chapters often overlap chronologically. I jump between the past and the present in order to provide a description of events from my perspective in the moment, reflect on those times, and demonstrate the far-reaching changes I've gone through. I touch on memories from my childhood, school years, and twenties to provide a more well-rounded picture of myself.

It may seem a sensitive subject, my journey with ALS, but few tears were wept in the process of writing. I've been slowly and gradually worn down by this life. I often find myself emotionally numb.

I did not interview anyone for this book. Any outside input I received from the story's participants was limited to correcting a few factual details. The way others may have seen things is hardly the point. Whether or not it is entirely accurate, this is my reality.

CHAPTER 1

TRYING TO FIND THE BEGINNING

It wasn't me doing those things.
I'm only watching someone else's memories.

1.

I sit at my desk in the office and stare at my laptop. That's how I spend most of my days. With the mouse in my left hand, I lean forward in my chair, propping my right elbow on the desk. My left index finger rests on the left click button of a right-handed mouse, never straying from its spot. I don't use the scroll wheel or the right-click button because, realistically, I can't. Doing my work and writing my thoughts and stories — even pushing my laptop away to make room for a book — are balanced with repeatedly scrolling a handful of sites and evenings of streaming entertainment. The onset of winter, and ongoing pandemic, have combined to narrow my world even further.

In 2019, almost fifteen years after I signed my first lease, I moved back in with my parents. It's a different house, in a different town than the one I left midway through college. Very little remains from our lives in those days.

I was twenty years old on the first day of 2005. I'd spent the past two years shuttling back and forth between dorm rooms and my parents' basement, getting my first taste of freedom in that opaque space between childhood and adult life. I'd been feeling optimistic; I was getting an apartment. I was finally ready for things to get better.

Our lives had changed tremendously in the short time since I'd gone off to college. The house I grew up in — the holidays, the family dinners, and every nagging moment — was perpetually quiet and empty. There was an unrelenting weight in the air; my family was one person short.

***

Nicholas John Methot was two years my senior. He had fair skin, covered in freckles, blue eyes, and a head full of reddish-brown curls that tightened with age. He was always a head taller than me, but small for his age, nonetheless. In some ways, we looked alike — in our noses and ears, and thick, often wild heads of hair — but mostly, we were different, in both looks and temperament.

Nick was quiet and shy, curious, creative, and introverted. He wore glasses as a child and was, in stark contrast to me, well-behaved — a parenting dream for the most part. We were always together — Nick and Nate, to the neighborhood kids — we rode bikes, caught frogs, and found sledding hills in the winter.

I was always the instigator with Nick. If we didn't have something to do — on a rainy day in the house, torturing our mom with cries of "I'm bored…" — I'd poke the bear. I was such a little asshole. A handful is the polite way to put it. Strong-willed and independent makes me sound like less of a villain.

By the time he went off to college (he attended the University of Vermont ["UVM"] and lived in the dorms), we'd found our own interests. I hardly remember seeing him in the high school hallways. I spent nights and weekends at the family restaurant, bought my own car, and moved my room to the basement. He found a passion in running, hung out at his girlfriend's, and spent his summers doing almost masochistic levels of physical labor for a small-time contractor. (I worked with him for one day, digging a drainage ditch through clay and mixing bag after bag of cement to repair a foundation. It made days at the restaurant seem like a breeze.)

The four of us were back in the house — a postwar ranch on Dumont Avenue by the Burlington International Airport — after my freshman year at Villanova University. I'd already decided not to return, applied and was accepted to UVM, and had a carefree summer ahead. My parents had finally decided to rip out the brown, poodle-haired wall-to-wall living room carpet and have the hardwood floors refinished throughout the house. My mémère (French Canadian for grandmother) was visiting her sister in Manchester, New Hampshire; we stayed at her house around the corner.

Asleep on the foldout (legendary) blue couch in the sunroom addition at the back of the house, as a clock radio alarm continued its call in the background, I was awoken to screams from the bedrooms. I'd never heard such a sound. In the morning light of Friday, June 6, 2003, we discovered my brother — half slumped off the bed, an open book by his side, his face blue and cold. His heart had stopped beating after the house went dark for the night.

***

My laptop is a touchscreen model with tablet mode, though I've never used it that way. My gradual loss of finger strength, dexterity, and coordination almost perfectly coincided with the proliferation of touchscreens. Perpetually corded and unmoving, it sits atop an old Bostonian shoebox that I recently learned, to my surprise, contains an all-but-new pair of cordovan leather shoes. Its screen falls just below eye level, a vast improvement over its natural, neck-pain-inducing placement on the desk. I also don't use the keyboard. With the assistance of a factory on-screen keyboard equipped with an auto-fill function (a standard feature of Windows), I point and click my way through every sentence. It's tedious but reliable — far more than any talk-to-text function paired with my weak, often unintelligible voice. For several years, it's been my only real option.

I sit on a Purple brand cushion on a well-worn high-back wooden chair that once served to seat my pépère (French Canadian for grandfather) at the top of the booth he built in the family's kitchen. The desk is, in fact, a 9-by-2 ½-foot live-edge slab of butternut resting on twin file cabinets. To my left is my cell phone and propped open to page 323, *The Tender Bar*, a memoir by J. R. Moehringer. To my right is a 500 milliliter Cuisinart immersion blender base that I use as a water glass and a plate of food my mom sets out after dinner. Each night since I moved in, she makes me a fourth-meal — of fruit, cookies, cakes, breads, nuts, granola bars, bowls of pudding, ice cream cones, or anything else in the house. Tonight, I have a banana, granola bar, and a coconut and maraschino cherry Christmas cookie from the freezer. We're trying to keep my weight up.

My 370-pound, battery-powered Permobil M3 wheelchair rests quietly behind me. If I need to leave the room — to use the bathroom a few steps across the hall, to go to the kitchen for dinner, or my bedroom at night — I stand, slide my stocking feet on the hardwood floor, and plop down in the chair. Using my heel, I push down the folding footrest — usually only the right one for short trips — and use it to reposition myself in the chair. They're not so much footrests as anchors. Pushing against them keeps my body from falling forward.

I've had plenty of time to get used to this life. It's been a slow, almost unnoticeably gradual decline. I haven't kept track of the signposts; I didn't record each of my losses. It's been tough to see how it matters where I am on the journey.

2.

Lenny and Laura were married in the fall of 2009 — I was in the wedding party. They were the first of my friends to be married. It was all things that a wedding should be: a special group of people, a beautiful location, and endless dancing and drinking; it was a joy. And I was at the center of all of it, drinking too much, dancing wildly, and creating stories for a lifetime.

I was living at my mémère and pépère's former house, 6 Patrick Street, a pint-sized ranch across the street from the Burlington International Airport. A few months after the wedding, I threw a New Year's Eve party. On a Thursday after work, I drove to Beverage Warehouse and inquired about a keg. The owner, on the floor trying to keep things moving on the busiest night of the year, couldn't help but laugh in my face.

"You know it's New Year's," she replied. She walked me to the cooler and showed me what she had left. It was nearly empty, a handful of kegs in a big open space. I walked around and checked out the labels. One of them was Switchback; I took it.

I lifted the 124 pints of beer into my back seat and headed home. I felt I needed something to keep the beer cold — this wasn't college, after all — though I knew that it would be gone in a matter of hours. I grabbed a big plastic garbage bin from the garage and filled the bottom with handfuls of snow. I lifted the keg onto the stoop, dragged the barrel alongside, and from my elevated position, lifted the keg into the barrel. I packed some more snow around the keg and slowly, one step at a time, pulled my beer-filled trash can into the house.

An hour or so later, my friends started to show up and before long, the little, basement-less ranch was packed full of people. I felt no signs that things weren't right. Through all the beers, the champagne, and the ill-conceived batch of Irish coffees I made around eleven — to quote the excellent motion picture *Beerfest* — it felt "Just like college!"

I don't know when things started to change. I have memories of nights out drinking, thinking something felt different, and wondering why. Mostly, I brushed those thoughts aside. So, I couldn't drink like I did in college. That's probably normal. But in a small corner of my brain, on those nights and the days after, I felt something was wrong.

I was never one to fall down drunk or lose my balance. I knew guys like that, guys who got so drunk they couldn't get up off the floor. That was never me. Even at blackout levels — which of course, I don't remember — I never had an issue walking, or running, or with stairs. Physically, drinking never seemed to affect me that much.

At some point, I felt that changing. A little voice began to creep in: *Something has changed; things are different.* My only evidence was alcohol-induced; maybe that was it. Maybe I'd developed some sort of allergy; maybe I was just getting older. Maybe it was all in my mind.

I still don't know when it started. I look through Facebook — with each picture, I assign a *yes* or a *no*. I know the times that things felt wrong; I have to go back a long way before I'm sure I felt right. There are gaps in the pictures: *I definitely felt alright here, but six months later, in this one, I don't think I did.*

3.

In 2009 and 2010, in the National Life building on the hill in Montpelier, I worked in a four-desk pod by the fourth-floor window. At some point, typing at my desk, I began to feel a change in my fingers. What had been second nature felt a little more deliberate. One day, I noticed my fingers weren't flying so freely.

The three of us (the fourth desk was empty) played Scrabble at our desks, each taking a couple of turns each day. Seemingly out of nowhere, placing the tiny plastic pieces on the board became frustratingly challenging. Something had to be wrong; I didn't know what to do. I made every effort to ignore it.

I started to notice all sorts of things; they piled up at the edges of my mind. My fingers were cold and weak in the morning — I could barely tie my shoes. I tried to put on my baseball mitt — my fingers wouldn't stay straight; I could barely get my hand in. I threw a tennis ball and chased my parents' dog around the yard — my shoulder felt weak, my body tired. I threw rocks in the lake and wondered when my arm would fall off. We rode bikes late at night, highly intoxicated, and I couldn't keep up, fell off, and got lost. We played Wiffle ball in a field — truly my comfort zone, with my entire childhood as practice — and like a drunken has-been, I repeatedly swung hard and missed. I watched helplessly as my belly grew larger. It seemed like I'd aged thirty years overnight.

Everyone probably thinks it was 2011; that's the year everything changed. But it was 2010. As I see now, it couldn't be clearer.

4.

I picked up the alto saxophone in seventh grade, a year after starting on the clarinet. For about three years, I was obsessed. No one needed to tell me to practice; on my first day with my new sax, before I even had sheet music, I was making up riffs in the basement. I had a blast in the jazz band, showing off a loud, brash style that caught everyone's attention.

As I got a little older and other interests came into my life (sports, jobs, girls, cars, friends), I spent less time with my saxophone. I still loved playing, and I loved a lot of the music — some real head-boppers like James Brown's *I Got You (I Feel Good)*, the Tower of Power's *What is Hip?*, and a number of Latin jazz songs whose names I've long forgotten — we got to play, but as I moved through high school, I lost that single-minded focus. I'm not obsessive by nature; I get bored and move on. My saxophone was a small piece of my high school life, not all of it.

I took my sax to college but didn't pursue any music classes or do much playing. In the summer of 2004, working together at my parents' restaurant, Vin told me about his band and asked me to come to a practice. I'd been awed by his guitar skills before; I knew his band would be no joke.

I was really impressed with their talent and original songs (but not by their name — F2 was meaningless). With Vin on guitar, Lenny on bass, Tyler on drums, and Tom writing and singing the vocals, I tried to layer on some alto and tenor sax. Jamming in the basement and relaxing on the back deck, I thought they were the goofiest group of guys I'd ever spent time with.

When summer turned to fall, it was hard to find time to play music. For five guys in college, living in dorms and apartments, with classes, part-time jobs, and girlfriends, the band had to take a backseat for some of us. When Vin moved to Boston, though we may not have recognized it, our time as a band was effectively over.

Almost five years later, Tyler asked me to play on a song or two with his punk rock group, Husbands AKA. I jumped at the chance; I hadn't played with anyone in years. After a couple of limited practice sessions in my living room, I was deemed ready to go.

I stood in the crowd, pint glass in hand, but this wasn't just another night of drinking at Nectar's (the iconic music venue on Main Street in Burlington). For the last two songs of their set, they brought me on stage, and I did my thing. Feeling the adrenaline of the stage lights and crowd, I ripped off a couple of the attention-grabbing improvised solos I'd fallen in love with from the first time I picked up a sax. I think it went pretty well. The crowd cheered wildly; the band seemed to approve.

A couple of months later, they asked me back for a show at The Monkey House in Winooski. I got my sax ready before they took the stage, but something had changed; my fingers felt different. I was on my second bottle of Budweiser and, as I stepped through the crowd to retrieve my saxophone from its stand, I felt strange — nervous, sweaty, and slightly off balance. The confidence I should've felt — from my practice, from the last time — was gone.

Why did I have anything to drink? I'm at The Monkey — that's what I do. I can't drink anymore. Why can't I drink anymore? What's happening to me? Will this ever go away?

I stood on stage in a room full of energy and flailed around on the keys. It wasn't that I hadn't practiced enough; my fingers wouldn't do as I expected. The connection between my brain and my fingers seemed to have withered. The muscle memory, the dexterity I needed, was gone.

They never asked me to play with them again. Frustrated and confused, I tried to put it out of my mind. Over the summer, a few times in the garage by myself, I broke out my Charlie Parker Omnibook and played some old favorites. I couldn't seem to practice and get better — my mouth and tongue felt weak, and my hands had grown worse. But I knew it was more than only the saxophone; the signs were beginning to gather in my mind. I felt embarrassed and defeated; I wanted to curl up in a ball in the corner. I didn't want to try anymore. I put my saxophone away; I didn't know it'd be the last time.

There are a lot of things I let go of over the years, things that I never intended. I didn't recognize the value of so many pieces of my life, and I let things get lost over time. I'm not alone in any of this, but I can't go back. I can't take out my sax and start new at forty. I have no sense of possibility. All those opportunities I gave up long before I had to — they're gone. Playing music is gone. I wish I'd played more.

NO PARKING

For years, I've kept a red and white "No Parking" sign from the Vermont City Marathon ("VCM"). I moved into my first apartment in January of 2005, and it was there, taped in the window of the back door. I had seen them before, lining the streets on Memorial Day weekend, but I stopped and took a closer look. Its temporary paper date read May 25, 2003.

In May of 2003, I had just returned home from Villanova and had never participated in, or watched, the VCM. Running a marathon was unfathomable to me, but when I found out my brother planned to run his first, I had no doubt. I hardly gave it a thought at all. Running wasn't my gig; I didn't know much about it, but it didn't take much thought to know that Nick would not fail.

Now, when I find out someone is running a marathon (and especially their first), I am impressed. It takes a strong will and commitment to both prepare and succeed on race day. I feel pride for them.

In 2003, I thought, "Oh, you're running the marathon? Cool. That's not for me."

I've watched several marathons and seen many a familiar face battle through, most reaching the finish line. But I didn't go in 2003. I don't know what I did that Sunday, but I didn't make it downtown.

To no one's surprise, Nick finished the race. He ran the 26.2 miles in a time of 2 hours 46 minutes and 21 seconds. He came in 19th overall, 22 minutes behind the winner. He was the 5th Vermonter to finish and, a month after his 21st birthday, placed 3rd in his age group.

I never asked him what it was like, never showered him in praise, and I wasn't there to greet him at the finish. I'm not even sure I was impressed. "Nick did well in the race," was not a story to me.

Twelve days later, I woke up, and he was gone. I'd no longer have an automatic best friend. My partner in life had been taken.

5.

I was never a serious runner; I never felt competitive about it. I'd get out for runs because it made me feel good, refreshing my mind and creating that satisfied feeling. I ran a few 5Ks over the years, but most races felt like a drag. On Memorial Day weekend 2007, sandwiched neatly between college and a career, I ran the 6 ½-mile, third leg of the Vermont City Marathon. Though I don't know my time or even recollect how our five-member team fared, I remember that as my best race.

Three short years and a lifetime later, I was preparing to run my third Corporate Cup 5K in downtown Montpelier. As its May 20 date approached, I got out for a few runs around South Burlington. I hadn't run since the fall; I felt sluggish that spring. I felt tired when I finished, but not in the usual way. My muscles felt sluggish, almost like I was sick, my energy drawn low. I tried to brush it off: surely it would take time to get back into shape after winter.

I tried a few times on the treadmill. It seemed fine; I felt good. But as the date drew nearer, running the bike path on Kennedy Drive — pushing forward in a way the treadmill didn't require — things weren't improving. *How am I supposed to run a 5K? I feel like shit. I can't not run the race. I'm not a quitter; what would I say? Maybe I'll feel better; maybe it'll be fine.*

A group of friends came down to Montpelier for the race; Lenny had agreed to take the place of a coworker on our three-person team. I wasn't looking forward to running, but mostly I thought it'd be fine — it was only a 5K. Having changed in the event's makeshift parking lot after work, I sat in the grass with my group. Laura and Tom, both UVM Cross Country veterans, suggested we get out for a warmup.

Five of us started out down a side street, and immediately I was at the back of the pack. After only a few hundred yards, I wanted to stop; I needed to conserve my energy. *Fuck! What is wrong with me?! This is awful.* Before the race had even started, I was wiped. There was no spring in my step; it felt like my feet were pushing through sand. I looked at my friends, gracefully gliding along, completely carefree. I felt like I was entering a war zone, only I was alone in my torture. I couldn't explain what was happening. *How could I be this out of shape?*

I started the race with low expectations: I only wanted to finish; this would be a three-mile jog. For much of the race, I wasn't moving as fast as I would've liked, but I was still ahead of much of the crowd. (It was a weekend warrior event, for the most part. There were some serious runners, but much of the crowd — the basketball-sneaker, or even cargo-shorts-wearers, and the overweight desk-jockeys — were merely trying to muddle their way through.) With about a mile left to go, it felt like everything changed.

I was running down a long straightaway, and I knew it wasn't hot, but I was boiling. I could feel my heart pounding; my legs had the strength and stability of a bowl of Jell-O. Getting passed by everyone, struggling only to keep going, I'd moved past cursing myself out. I was an utterly exhausted marathoner trying everything just to reach the finish. I watched in agony as the slower of my two teammates — running with his ridiculous upright, high-knees form — left me behind.

Finally, mercifully, I reached the finish. I was embarrassed to find my friends afterward. I imagine they thought what I wanted to believe: I was woefully out of shape, the victim of a sedentary career. No one said a word of what seemed impossible to overlook. I was screaming on the inside: *What's happened to me? Where am I?*

That was the day it really started for me. I had my first undeniable evidence. I couldn't confront it; my fears ran too deep.

WILLFUL IGNORANCE

Once you admit there's a problem, there is only one way to react: with fear. The fears are wide-ranging: of the unknown and of finding out, of the lack of an answer and of what the answer might be. From the first sign, the most natural, easiest, and most childish thing to do was to avoid the problem, whatever it was. I spent my days in willful ignorance and my nights trying for hope.

Others might be different. They might be on the phone to their doctor and scouring the Internet — spending all of their time in obsession. I never intended to do any of that.

I was too afraid to self-diagnose. My best defense — perhaps the only way to continue living my life as I wanted — was to stay in the dark. Until I knew something real — convinced myself of its reality, and perhaps most importantly, made it known to others — I could go on pretending.

Maybe I was irresponsible. Maybe I was weak. Maybe I chose ignorance for so long only because it was easier. Maybe I could have lived my life differently if I had been stronger. I'm not sure. Actively involved or blindfolded on the sidelines, my life was changing forever.

6.

A week and a half later, on Memorial Day weekend 2010, I played in the Member-Member tournament at Burlington Country Club ("BCC").

I was introduced to golf at about ten. A kid in the neighborhood gave Nick and me two junior clubs. With a handful of golf balls we'd found in the woods behind the same neighbor's house, we walked to Chamberlin (the elementary school we attended, a couple of blocks from our house) and hit back and forth in the field. He was bigger and took the longer 5-iron; I tore up various patches of elementary school grass with the 7-iron.

One day, we heard about a junior tournament where, for the low price of five dollars, we could play eighteen holes at Kwiniaska Golf Club in Shelburne. Having never chipped, putted, or set foot on a golf course, Nick and I, along with a few other kids from the neighborhood, played in a tournament with about a hundred other teens and preteens. In my tiny, black, faux-leather golf bag, I carried a 5-iron, 7-iron, 9-iron, 3-wood, and putter, each of them hand-me-downs from a dark, spider-web-infested corner of the neighbor's garage. I shot a 103 from the ladies' tees, as kids my age were instructed. The highlight came when, choking up on my 9-iron, to the amazement of everyone in view, I holed a forty-yard shot for an underwhelming par.

In 2010, Tom, Rob, and I, in an early attempt at adulting, became junior members at Burlington Country Club. I learned a lot from Rob, who was both more skilled and more experienced, and began to feel like the kind of golfer who could play with anyone. That is to say, I would no longer embarrass myself — with "worm-burner" tee shots, uncontrolled cursing, club throwing, or any other eye roll-inducing behavior.

I finally rid myself of the weekend-hacker power-fade that, for as long as I could remember, had me aiming left on every shot. Thanks in part to BCC's bunkers and their actual golf-course sand — rather than the densely packed dirt found on many Vermont courses — I finally gained confidence in the trap. And, with help from the beautifully groomed greens and Rob's no-gimmes policy, I learned how to putt without fear. (If you want to know what that looks like, watch old clips of Tiger Woods. He's not timid; he's not thinking, *What if I miss?* His ball hits the back of the hole with some serious pace. Indeed, I just compared myself to Tiger Woods.)

On Saturday morning, as the tournament began, I arrived at the course with coffee cup in hand. Rob was hitting balls on the range as I climbed out of my Subaru into the still-cool air. Ordinarily, we were never at the course in the morning; our junior-level memberships carried back-of-the-line tee times. Most of our rounds had me closer to beer than to coffee. This was different; I felt energized.

We were paired with a guy in his forties and his not-quite-old-as-dirt father. With the memory of my struggles at the Corporate Cup at the forefront of my mind, and an ever-present fear creeping in, I played great. We both did. Feeding off each other's energy, we were able to avoid the major pitfalls that could mushroom into round-killing negativity. Rob carded a 78, and thanks to a drive out of bounds on the par-five 18th (my first lost ball of the day) and the resulting snowman — a triple-bogey 8 — I scored an 81.

We could hear the Marathon Sunday cheers as we arrived for day two at the golf course up the hill. With a different and less memorable pairing, we started with three consecutive pars on our scorecard. But the positivity broke down when we both chunked our approach shots on the soggy fourth fairway. With Rob's ball a few yards ahead, and only an easy wedge to the green, I drove the clubhead deep into the sod; the muddy golf ball flew no more than ten yards. I cursed myself out and Rob, afraid to catch my negativity, preached calm. Moments later, I watched as he did the same thing.

The rest of the round was more up than down, but felt like a letdown. I was able to avoid the final hole tee shot from hell and finished with a solid 84. Rob carded an 82.

If I was worried that something had changed, that I'd lost some strength or athleticism, it didn't feel that way that weekend on the golf course. After hundreds of swings, and miles on my feet, I felt fine; I felt strong. Those kinds of days helped my doubts disappear, pushed out of my mind by reality.

It's hard to believe that the best thirty-six holes I ever played — in a club tournament without gimmes or mulligans or any of the crutches relied on by weekend golfers — came after ALS had started to take hold of my body.

7.

In July, six of us drove to Maine for a point-to-point canoe-camping adventure. It'd be four days in the woods, with nothing on our minds but the moment in front of us. We'd have no contact with the wider world. Our phones, unlikely to work anyway, were turned off and tucked away. We'd be living the simple life: waking up with the light and making camp before dark. Every action would serve a purpose as we tracked our progress on a map.

In the morning, there'd be breakfast and packing; our days were spent two-by-two on the water, our evenings making camp, eating a hearty meal, and relaxing around a fire. It'd be four days of physical toil and mental release, four days filled with camaraderie and laughter, free from the real-world stresses of our lives.

That's what I wanted, and that's what I looked forward to. That's what these trips had always been — in all the majesty of the surroundings, a place where I could simply *be*. In the summer of 2010, with a new set of worries beginning to make a home in my mind, that's what I hoped for; that's what I needed.

On a Wednesday after work, three of us met in Montpelier on our way to East Burke to pick up a canoe and a fourth. With my breezy assurances, Johnny — then cutting trees for a living — left his dump truck in the center of the National Life parking lot. I hadn't obtained the necessary parking permit from security, but I was excited, and we'd be back Sunday; I thought (I hoped) it'd be fine.

The rendezvous with our remaining adventurers, somehow delayed in Burlington, didn't go as expected. We sat at a tavern in the Northeast Kingdom watching the clock (and cursing them out) until, just after dark, they finally made it. After a quick stop to strap a second canoe to the oversized roof rack of Bert's Forester, we started our overnight convoy to nowhere.

At an unknown gas station at two-thirty in the morning, we stopped for fuels, both human and automotive. We piled out of both cars in the fluorescent light and marched toward the door, wandering aimlessly, perusing the aisles, in line for the facilities. Standing by the gas pump with an oddly out of place, undoubtedly not-so-fresh cup of coffee, Tom stood ready for his shift behind the wheel. Refreshed and relieved, we got back on the road.

We pulled up to a checkpoint gate in the gentle, gray morning light. We'd reached the southern tip of the 96-mile, dirt-clad Golden Road, built by the Great Northern Paper Company to access its 2.1 million acres of timberland. We paid a triple-digit fee to a man in a booth for our time on their land. From the town of Millinocket, we drove over two hours to our planned starting point.

At the Roll Dam Campground on the West Branch of the Penobscot River, we parked and began to unload: six guys, three canoes, tents, sleeping bags, backpacks, food, clothing, and supplies. Three of us waited while the others made the three-hour round trip to drop a car off at the southern end of the manmade Chesuncook Lake. (Measuring 1-4 miles wide, 22 ½ miles long, and over 25,000 acres, it is the third-largest body of fresh water in Maine.) The plan was to paddle north on the West Branch of the Penobscot until it dumps into Chesuncook Lake, then traverse the lake to its southern tip alongside the aforementioned Golden Road. We'd have to find campsites on the multiday journey. Left waiting for us at the end of our journey would be a twenty-year-old Volvo 240.

We paddled downriver through the afternoon and began to look for a place to stop for the night. At a high bank on a bend in the river, we spotted a set of wooden steps leading to a picture-perfect campsite. We pulled our canoes to shore, unloaded tents and gear, icy coolers of meat, eggs, cheese, and beer, and hauled everything up the staircase built into the hill.

We cooked cheeseburgers in a cast-iron skillet on a gasoline-powered, vintage Coleman camp stove. We drank Sierra Nevada Pale Ale and Long Trail Ale from almost-too-cold cans, passed a plastic jug of Canadian Hunter whiskey, and watched night fall over the campfire. Despite our collective lack of sleep, no one seemed eager to let the night end.

Staring into the fire in the enveloping darkness of the remote wilderness, we heard noises from the river below — it was clearly something big. Somebody grabbed a flashlight, and there he stood, a full-grown moose staring directly into the beam from the center of the river, ten yards from our camp. A little fear creeps in when you see such an enormous animal that close. Once identified, the light was turned out, and the gentle giant shrugged and went back to his business.

We were back on the river in the morning. By midday, we'd turned the corner and glimpsed the vast Chesuncook Lake. Cut out of the endless pines, we came across a group of buildings that made up the tiny Village of Chesuncook, an off-the-grid remote outpost built on logging.

The wind picked up in the early afternoon, blowing down the lake to the southwest, almost the direction we were heading. With three canoes and no sail, a breeze wouldn't do us much good. Johnny, former Eagle Scout and UVM forestry major, suggested we build one.

With two pieces of driftwood, several ropes, and a blue tarp, we tried just that. Johnny, in a tremendous exhibition of rope and knot skills, formed a T with the sticks, and we had our mast. Beginning to see the plan take form, we dragged the canoes together and tried to create a base for our sail. Using every last inch of our rope, Johnny fastened the tarp to the T and secured the parallel boats to each other. We placed the mast between two coolers at the center and ran lines to all four corners of our three-wide vessel.

Satisfied with our ingenuity, ready to pat ourselves on the back, we nudged our new conveyance into the water and paddled away from the shoreline. It worked better than we could've imagined. The sail caught the wind; water splashed in the crevices between the boats; a sturdy paddle at the rear was the rudder. Steadily cruising on open water amongst sizable waves in the center of the lake, we began to pass the Canadian Hunter in the afternoon sun. Besides Johnny the rudder man in the rear center seat, we all sat back and enjoyed the ride.

A couple of hours into our sailing experiment, despite every effort to keep us moving down the lake, we began to approach the opposite shore. *This might be the end of our leisure.* We discussed our next move, and before reaching land, made an ambitious decision. We'd break down our creation, paddle the canoes directly across the lake, reassemble on the opposite shore, and continue our sail to the south.

I thought it was crazy; I thought it would take forever, but that's exactly what we did. With the canoes three again, we set off into the heightening waves. Quickly, the six of us were in a battle to make it across. It was heads-down paddling into the wind.

Halfway through the mile-long sprint, relentlessly paddling from the rising and crashing bow, I was scared. I still wasn't convinced that anything real was wrong with my physical body; more likely, I was unable to admit what had been happening for months. I'd felt a little off the whole trip — everything felt a step slower. Instead of out front and leading, I felt like I could barely keep up. I wasn't especially tired, but when I pulled my paddle through the water, I wasn't sure I had the force of my canoe-mate. In the center of the lake, in the face of the oncoming whitecaps, I felt an unfamiliar vulnerability. The seemingly ever-present invincibility of my youth was no longer part of my being.

With the three canoes safely resting on the rocky beach of the western shore, we reassembled our contraption and eased it back into the water. The rope work was a little shoddier the second time — the boats bouncing around more than they had been — but it didn't matter. Once again, we could lay back and let the wind do the work. We arrived on a flat sandy beach on the lake's eastern shore in the early evening.

We unloaded the boats, set up our tents, and gathered up the driftwood that seemed to be everywhere. We drank beers around a roaring fire in the lingering sunlight — the sun-drenched driftwood burned fast. It might've been the breeze, which had all but died by nightfall, or our location by a big lake away from the never-ending pines, but there were no bugs. The entire trip was surprisingly light on airborne annoyances.

Hours after we'd watched the sunset over the flat, pine-tree horizon, Johnny and I were dozing by the fire. "I'm sleeping right here, man," he told me. As much as I liked the idea of spending the night under the stars, lying in the beach sand by the fire, I didn't think I'd be able to fall asleep. I wandered a dozen yards down the beach to my tent. Had I known it was my last chance at such an experience, I would've stayed.

With the wild blueberries we'd harvested from the hill by the campsite, we made pancakes on the grill and cooked bacon over a fire in the morning. Under an overcast sky, we separated the boats and paddled down the lake. In the mid-afternoon, having stopped once along the way, we reached the southern tip of the lake. The sight of the maroon station wagon was in itself a relief. It'd been parked since Thursday morning on a patch of dirt by the only road in the area — it was now Saturday afternoon.

With an extra day to spare, someone suggested we add one more adventure. A short drive down the Golden Road was Baxter State Park, home of Mount Katahdin, the northern terminus of the 2,190-mile Appalachian Trail. At 5,267 feet, it dominates the view from the thousands of square miles of forests, lakes, and streams in every direction. Steep and full of exposed granite, its trails are considered the most strenuous on the AT.

We rolled into the visitor's center en masse and spoke with the rangers to learn our options for trails. Most of them, they told us, would take eight to twelve hours round-trip. The Abol Trail is the shortest, steepest route to the summit. We were advised to start early — it was rated at eight hours.

Confident that the 4.4-mile trail covering 3,982 feet in elevation gain couldn't possibly take four hours each way, we made plans to be on the trail at first light. We'd summit Katahdin on Sunday morning, return and break down camp, and get on the road back to Vermont. We booked a lean-to at Abol Campground and, for the last time, set up camp, made dinner, ate ravenously, and drank beers. Much later than we should have, we retired for a half-night's sleep.

A watch alarm rang out sometime between three and four. We dressed, ate, and packed a few things for the hike — all by the light of a few headlamps. In near-total darkness, we started on the trail. We came out of the woods as the sun began to rise; a seemingly endless staircase of granite lay before us.

In cargo shorts and a T-shirt, with a camera hanging from my neck, without pause, I climbed with the group. On the side of a barren mountain rising to what looked like the peak, the rocks grew bigger, the trail less obvious. I'd fallen a short distance behind, and though I could see some of the guys out ahead, I seemed to have lost track of the trail. Suddenly, I had nowhere to go. Grabbing onto the boulders for balance, I searched for blue dashes around me. I was pressed up against the rock face, using all of my willpower not to look at the steep slope below. For the second time on the trip, I'd lost confidence, felt uneasy. I was scared.

I edged my way along the rock and saw Bryan, a fellow straggler off the trail. We yelled to each other and agreed that we'd drifted too far left. A few minutes later, moving slowly among the boulders, I spotted a blue dash, then another. As I gained the relative safety of the fully exposed and visually arbitrary trail, I saw Bryan a few yards above, feeling his way toward the peak.

Back on the staircase, the trail began to level off as we approached the summit. Walking across the top, I paused to take it all in — and capture the moment. My first photo is time-stamped 5:52 a.m.

I rejoined the group at the summit, keeping my off-trail adventure to myself. A fellow early morning hiker offered to take our picture — I gave him my camera. He captured the six of us amongst the boulders: wispy clouds and blue skies above, rock outline behind us, forests and lakes to the horizon. Gazing at the Knife Edge (a trail atop the ridgeline connecting the mountain's several peaks, said to be as narrow as four feet with 2,000-foot drops on either side), we longed for the time to traverse that mind-bogglingly-insane-looking trail.

We were back at the campsite before most of our neighbors had set out for the day. We took some time just to sit, and eat, and make use of the luxurious on-site facilities. No one was ready to get back in the car.

The over-seven-hour drive was a featureless slog. We arrived back in Montpelier in the early evening to find, sitting in the center of an entirely empty lot, a dump truck awaiting our return. With my Subaru parked in the garage, and each of us with one final leg, exhausted, we parted ways.

Four days in the woods, without complication; the physical journey, alone, leaves me in awe. But it's the mental one that perhaps I miss most: four days in the moment, with nothing on our minds but the here and now. Maybe it's lost to time; maybe it was a vestige of youth, but that's what I long for. I've been on a few camping trips since, and even a couple of hikes, but that was the last time I was just one of the guys. That was the last time I could pull my own weight, that plans didn't need changing for me. In some ways, I might even say, that was the last time I felt truly alive.

WOULD YOU RATHER?

When I was waiting tables in college, some of us played exceedingly dorky, oftentimes gross bordering on disgusting, games of *Would You Rather?* None of the quandaries were ever pinned to reality but mostly served to pass the time with nonsensically humorous one-upmanship. Recently, nearly fifteen years removed from that gross-me-out, middle school level of comedy, I came up with a new, thoroughly realistic one.

Would you rather be able to walk, talk, or use your hands and arms?

There is no definitive answer.

I would love the ability to walk, run, hike, and do stairs — so much that it almost hurts to think about. The personal freedom that it provides — the simplest human act of walking down the street or through the woods — might alone be enough to fill every other hole in my life. I don't think I'd ever get tired of it. I might feel like I could do anything.

I haven't yet lost my speaking ability, though it's certainly been compromised, so I'm sure I don't fully understand its impact. It's hard to imagine not being able to communicate with words, but as my voice has grown weaker, I've gained some perspective. I've lost a significant piece of my identity. I act differently, more quietly. Without total control of my voice, I'm never fully present. Having it back would bring me closer to the people around me, make it easier to have people around me, and undoubtedly make me feel far less alone.

Perhaps last is the outlier, the reality most difficult for most to imagine. What would your life be like without the use of your hands and arms? We've all seen people in wheelchairs, capably performing all sorts of tasks. But your hands?! The hands do everything. If you were to care about your independence in the slightest, you'd need your hands. With full use of my hands and arms, my life would be entirely different.

It's an impossible decision for me. Unlike those old, juvenile hypotheticals, each choice makes my heart ache. How could I settle for just one?

8.

On a Saturday in September, Tom and I drove to the Adirondack Loj in Lake Placid. We'd be hiking Mount Marcy, at 5,344 feet, the highest of the forty-six major peaks of the Adirondack Mountains. From the Adirondack Loj parking lot, the trail gains 3,166 feet. Its summit is a 7.4-mile, "steep, serious climb…making for a very long day," according to lakeplacid.com.

After finding the parking area full, we left Tom's old Outback at the end of a long line of cars on the dirt access road heading up the hill. Walking past the dozens of parked cars, a couple in a Golf with Quebec plates stopped and offered us a ride. Neglecting to tell them why we'd parked down the hill, we hopped in.

The lot was full, and the trail was packed. We were almost constantly passing hikers as we cruised through the early part of the trail just short of running. As we slowly gained elevation on a hot, hazy day, we continued to pass groups on the single-file trail. With more than half the mileage behind us, we both wondered aloud, "When is this going to get steep?"

As we crossed above the tree line and the summit appeared before us, the trail finally became more vertical. We made our way through the rocks, pausing once or twice to allow hikers to descend. A short time, and about a half-mile later, we were walking across the broad summit, taking in the view amongst a handful of groups. I dug out my phone. It was noon.

After a short break, a granola bar and some water, we headed back down. We passed all the groups we'd passed once before on a needlessly breakneck descent. When the trail began to level out, we capped off the day with what Tom might've obnoxiously called a "cool-down run."

Following a few yards behind, drifting smoothly over the downhill terrain, I kicked the ground and fell violently onto my hands. Tom stopped and turned back as I brushed it off. *Must've hit a root or something.*

A few minutes later, it happened again. My feet were falling behind, unable to safely clear the ground on their way forward. Tom once again pressed pause and turned. I offered no explanation; I *had* no explanation. We were almost in sight of the finish — I followed slowly at a walk.

Sweaty, smelly, and exhausted, we fell into the car and began the drive home. I said nothing of the only thing on my mind; Tom kept his thoughts to himself. I hiked fifteen miles at Tom's breakneck pace. It didn't feel like a grind; it was a pleasure. We joked and laughed; it felt familiar. I felt like myself. If only I hadn't tried to run at the end, I might have escaped worry-free.

9.

My parents bought Rick's Pizza in 1998 and later rebranded as Dave's Vermont Pizzeria ("Dave's"). I met Vin at Rick's when we were fifteen — he was my first friend from work. We spent a lot of time cruising around Milton, getting hopelessly stoned in his Subaru. One night we drove out onto the frozen Arrowhead Lake, attended an ice-top, parked-car-surrounded bonfire, and did never-ending donuts at high speeds. On trips to visit him at Keene

State, a number of us met lifelong friends, or in Tom's case, a wife. It was Vin who introduced me to Lenny and Tom and invited me to play in their band. Though he moved first to Boston, then San Francisco, and like so many, we're not as close as we used to be, Vin is family.

The week of Thanksgiving, 2010, Tom and I flew to San Francisco to visit Vin and his then-girlfriend Jess. From their one-bedroom Outer Sunset apartment — where Tom and I shared the pull-out couch — we walked to the beach and to Golden Gate Park. Strolling the blocks in the cool ocean air, I didn't feel right. Beyond the weakness in running and hiking, I was beginning to notice other annoyances from my body. As I walked on the sidewalk in perfectly comfortable sweatshirt weather, my feet were sweating, and my hands were cold.

It wasn't the first time. I'd been experiencing these things for a while. I'd kneel at the door getting ready for work and grab at the laces on my shoes — my inexplicably cold fingers were sluggish and unfeeling. I had trouble just getting them tied. I'd get in the car, five steps from my door, and my feet — wrapped in leather for all of two minutes — were already uncomfortably sweaty. Other times I'd swear I seemed normal and tell myself, *See, there's nothing wrong; you're still the same person.* I was always looking for that confirmation, desperately bending the rules to my will. But all the while, a battle was waging in my mind and the enemy was gaining in strength.

In Golden Gate Park — walking the Frisbee golf course under the trees — my hands simply weren't right. I grabbed the frisbee and tossed it toward the goal — my arm had the strength, my mind had the know-how, but my hands and fingers lacked the finesse. I couldn't hold it like I wanted; I couldn't release it when I needed. My hands were cold and stiff — like they'd been left out in the snow.

The next day, Vin borrowed a car, and the three of us (Jess was working) got out of the city. We drove up to wine country and checked out a couple of vineyards; we visited the University of California, Berkeley, passing a soccer ball between us as we walked its manicured grounds; we took the obligatory pictures at the Golden Gate Bridge; and under a stifling sun that hadn't existed across the bay, we ate burritos in a parking lot in Oakland.

At a freshly watered field at Berkeley, the three of us spread out with a soccer ball. Discounting one summer in the fifth grade, I'd scarcely set foot on the pitch. On that afternoon, it looked like I'd never kicked anything in my life. It felt like another test, and I knew I would fail. That feeling was getting all too familiar; I felt like I was hiding all the time. I couldn't face the changes; I couldn't let anyone see.

I kicked and ran like the others. I looked like a person, but that person wasn't me. I feigned nonchalance — like I was too cool to try — but I was broken inside. There was a new wave of examples every day; my mind couldn't escape. On a soccer field in California, I couldn't let go, I couldn't just be. Silent anxiety was beginning to crush me.

***

The four of us took the trolley to a seafood place for dinner that night. We had a beer or two at the apartment before carefully hiding open pint cans in our pockets as we stepped onto the train. Standing on the bumpy, jostling car, with no more than two beers in my belly — while sneakily sipping another — I felt drunk. Not the familiar drunk that lives in the head. My body felt drunk. I scanned the car around me — disinterest and routine were all that I saw. No one else seemed to think the next corner might throw them to the ground. I was alone on the car.

There was a line on the sidewalk outside the restaurant. Vin and Jess knew — had chosen the place — in part for that reason. Within a few minutes of joining the group, a plump, red-faced Santa Claus handed us four wine glasses, asked "red or white," and returned with a jug of wine.

Before long, we'd had three or four glasses, but with my feet on solid ground — needing only to cross the room to the table — I felt fine. I wouldn't say I felt "normal." Normal would have been completely carefree. I was not; my mind was focused on my physical movements. I was always on watch, carefully monitoring a plethora of indicators. Once I had a full, restaurant-sized meal in me, I sobered and gained confidence. The trolley back to the apartment was nearly empty; we all grabbed a seat, and I forgot about the last time.

Like the mid-twenties tourists we were, Tom and I went drinking the next night. Our first stop was the Rogue Ales Public House — part of the 650 block of Union Street that went up in flames on St. Patrick's Day, 2018. Examining some two dozen varieties of Rogue, we made our choices and were presented with our prize. The bartender kept going to the back, leaving us alone for what felt like forever. The only other patron — a man at a table in the back — walked out the door as we were making our way through pint number two. When the bartender disappeared once again, Tom and I were the only souls in the room.

"How easy would it be to finish these and bolt?" one of us asked.

"Easy," answered the other.

A few minutes later, we downed our last gulps and made for the door. Bursting out onto the sidewalk, we ran up the block and around the next corner. No one followed. If anyone had bothered chasing the $20 bill, I'd have been caught. I lumbered down the sidewalk like an overweight, out-of-shape cop in a chase scene. I wouldn't have made it far before stopping.

With directions from Vin, we found our way to a bar up the street. It was sort of a dive — hot, loud, and full of bodies — with a small stage in the back. A hipster bluegrass band was cranking out the tunes; folks were dancing, drinks in hand in front of the stage. Tom elbowed his way to the bar and yelled an order into the noise. He returned with a couple of whiskeys.

Several hours, bands, and rounds later, we spilled out onto the street. We had a loud, sweaty, drunken time; I breathed in the cool night air and felt refreshed. Tom did not. He was surprisingly drunk and trying to prevent regurgitation. *Didn't we have the same amount to drink?! I feel pretty good. Hmm.*

The four of us spent Thanksgiving in the apartment, cooking, eating, drinking, and enjoying each other's company. We each made a dish and at mealtime had a kitchen full of food. My biscuits — made with my mom's failsafe recipe — came out like crumbling bricks. I blamed (and still blame) the whole-wheat, organic, super-dense flour — and the hosts who provided it. Other than the biscuits, which went straight to the compost, our Friendsgiving was a success, and the four of us ate ourselves into a collective coma. Tom and I flew home the next day.

I started to feel more isolated among friends in San Francisco. I could easily avoid running 5Ks and climbing mountains if my body couldn't do it anymore. But my symptoms, and the sinking feeling that accompanied them, were bleeding into my everyday life. If I couldn't go for a walk or have a few drinks without feeling "different," how could I go on pretending?

MY BODY AND ME

I read that a lack of fat in the face makes people look old. It turns out, a lack of muscle does the same. My face — the skin-on-bone wrinkled forehead and drooping, hollow cheeks; even the narrow bridge of my nose — is looking older all the time.

As I stare at my hands and arms, it's hard to remember how they used to look. The indentations between the bones in my hands, the gaping hole between my thumb and forefinger, have become all too familiar to these eyes. Where once there were Popeye-esque forearms — built on years of swinging baseball bats, hockey sticks, and golf clubs — are a set of bones and tendons wrapped in skin.

I hold my arm above the elbow and squeeze the loose skin where my triceps used to be. They're still there, clinging to the bone underneath, flexing like a mouse in an elephant's body. I curl my arm to check on the biceps. They tremble under the weight.

My shoulders are exposed, their bony shapes unencumbered by muscle. I feel gaps between the bones and shapes I didn't know existed. The collar bone protrudes on display — my chest and neck have eroded.

I lay on my bed and cross one leg over the other — it's much easier than it should be. I used to have thighs — big, powerful thighs — that rubbed together when I walked. I actually felt self-conscious in my baseball pants, legs spread out on the bench. I can't believe I felt shame for my muscles. Now they cross over with ease. There's just so much less of them.

My stomach has gotten bigger; I can feel it protruding in a way I never experienced. Though the scale tells me otherwise, I feel fat. My clothes hang off of me, but my waist has grown larger. I've lost so much weight, but my pants are too tight.

My knees, once square and bulky — the result of years of squatting behind home plate in the backyard — are bony and narrow. My hips and butt have flattened and narrowed — and softened. My calves barely exist; it's hard to tell when they're flexed.

My head looks bigger in every picture — my neck and shoulders no longer fit its proportions. It sits precariously atop my seemingly elongated neck. My head and face almost appear normal. Compared to my body, they are.

It's difficult to look in the mirror. The guy who stares back doesn't match the one in my mind. My body and I began to take different paths long ago. It's still hard to believe they'll never come back together.

10.

I bought a pair of used skis, boots, and poles midway through college. I went to a high school ski swap and splurged on a "Double Major" — the student ski pass that combined Jay Peak and Bolton

Valley. On weekends, when I wasn't working, we'd make the trek up to Jay. In my final semester at UVM, I packed my class schedule into three days, leaving Wednesday and Friday free for a few hours at much-closer Bolton.

I spent a lot of time in the woods, fearlessly pretending I knew what I was doing. I didn't. I hadn't grown up skiing, and though I cross-country skied for three years in high school, I'd hardly been on a chairlift. Once I had a season's pass and my own equipment, I did the only thing that came naturally: I dove in.

By the winter of '10-'11, it had become a routine — I bought a ski pass. I knew deep in my heart that things weren't right with my body, but I didn't have a definitive, factual reason to point to, so I kept moving forward. How could I explain anything else?

I'd been noticing I felt different after a workout. I could run or bike, lift weights or do push-ups, and the next day I wouldn't be sore. I didn't know why — I tried to fix it. If my ankles felt weak, I'd strengthen them; if my wrists were frail, I'd build them up; if I was out of shape, I'd change that.

Over the winter, Rob and I started going to the National Life gym after work. I've never liked gyms, but two or three days a week, we spent an hour or so under the fluorescent lights and drove home in the dark. After a few sessions, I learned a few things. Some of my muscles were strong. I could ride the bike forever, but nothing seemed to improve. I'd run on the treadmill, and every footfall felt awkward — like I didn't know when and where each step would occur. My brain and my body seemed no longer connected.

I woke up to a forecasted dumping of snow on a Monday, texted a friend, and called out of work. We drove up to Jay for the day. Any skier (or rider) would have killed to do the same — it was that kind of day at the mountain.

I carried my skis, boots, and poles through the parking lot — they'd never seemed so ungainly. From the first run, I told myself, *I can do this; I'm OK.*

And I could. But even I — champion of self-serving delusion — couldn't pretend it was the same. I could still make my way down the mountain — even ski the same trails — but I was always falling behind. My mind was full of anxiety. Nothing felt natural; I was off-balance all day. I fell a few times, popped my skis off once or twice, and almost gave up looking for one in a snowdrift. I couldn't ski without fear; I couldn't be me.

I continued to go through the motions for a while. I ended up skiing my own trails alone. I saw the joy all around me — *This is supposed to be fun.* I couldn't keep pretending to have a good time.

At some point, I gave up. One weekend at a time, I made an excuse, sat on the couch, and watched the hours pass. I don't know what my friends thought. One weekend at a time, I lost a major source of joy in my life — I quit skiing.

For the first time in my life, I was spending Saturdays and Sundays indoors — at home. Monday would come, and I'd wonder where my weekend had gone. What had I done? I relied on those days to recharge; sitting on the couch didn't do it.

I tried snowshoeing instead. Snowshoeing is always a bit awkward, even for the strong and highly coordinated. Just getting them on my feet took forever; my fingers didn't work in the cold.

I could walk on flat ground, and going up hills seemed alright, but coming down was entirely different. I had to concentrate on lifting each foot and locking my ankles to keep the front of the shoes elevated. I was convinced there was something wrong with both the snowshoes and my ankles. To keep up with my friends, I tried to run down the trail. I kept digging the front of my snowshoes into the ground and crashing violently forward. They'd left me so far behind, they didn't notice. When finally, I joined them, they saw the snow packed into my zipper and stuck to my hat and knew I had taken a digger. I didn't tell them I'd, in fact, taken ten.

11.

As students at UVM, in our seemingly nonexistent free time, Tom and I played a lot of pick-up basketball at Gutterson Fieldhouse. In the winter of '10-'11, despite having no affiliation with the school, for weeks Tom had been using the gym at Saint Michael's College. UVM had an ID and turnstile system, but Tom assured me that I'd have no problem joining in his charade. Mostly he just walked in the door; no one was there to ask any questions.

The ten-minute drive wasn't enough to warm up the car on that single-digit February night. We walked through the salty parking lot in boots and sweatpants, carrying clean shoes and a basketball. After changing and trying to rub some warmth into my hands, I dribbled across the court. My hands felt like bricks. I had no feel for the ball; I must've looked like a five-year-old, slapping at it clumsily.

My shot felt weak. I needed to rely on my legs, jumping hard just to assure the ball would reach its goal. After a few minutes of shaking the dust off (i.e., warming up), we began a game of "taps." Taps is a game in which one player shoots foul shots while the other "taps" into the basket, any misses. It requires the tapper to jump, catch the ball, and shoot before landing. There was a time when it came as easily as anything, but that time had passed. On my first attempt, I discovered what had once been so easy was now nearly impossible.

I barely had the strength to reach the basket from the foul line without jumping. Watch a basketball game — high school, college, or professional — no one over the age of twelve jumps on a foul shot. But I did. I had to.

We started to play "21," a one-on-one game with foul shots and a three-pointer at the end. I was more than a step slow on defense, and though they'd warmed, my hands still felt disconnected. I just couldn't move the way I wanted; I didn't have the quickness or agility I needed. Dribbling with my right (dominant) hand, I tried to drive to the basket — when I tried to collect the ball for a layup, I couldn't grab it. As if a sneaky defender had stripped it from my grip, my arms went up, and the ball continued onward — out of bounds and into the wall.

I tried to slow the game down, bring the ball into the post, maybe that would work. I backed Tom down, using my body to shield him from my dribble. I leaned in, preparing a series of Kevin McHale post moves and pushing him closer to the basket. Suddenly, anticipating my intention, he pulled the chair out from under me — he moved. He slid his body to the side, and I lost my balance, backpedaling awkwardly toward the sideline. I must've looked like a cartoon character falling in slow motion. It felt like I was watching from outside my body as my legs attempted to catch up with my momentum. They didn't. I fell, sliding backward on my butt.

I don't know what Tom thought; I didn't ask. We'd played basketball for years; it must've been obvious that everything had changed. That was the last time I played, and it was enough to finally break me. I resigned myself to calling my doctor.

CHAPTER 2

ALL QUESTIONS, NO ANSWERS

It is important to realize that these exercises will not strengthen muscles that have been weakened by ALS. Once the supply of motor neurons that control a particular muscle has degenerated, it cannot be regenerated by exercise.

- From the Range of Motion Exercises section

of the ALS Association website

1.

After the basketball debacle, I flipped the switch in my mind: it was time to take action. It took me three days to get up the nerve. Unable to find the privacy I felt I needed anywhere in the office, I called from my car. I forced from my lips a combination of yet-to-be-labeled symptoms. My voice was shaking. I tried to describe what was happening, but I was sheepish, embarrassed. I didn't tell any stories; I left out my fears. "My hands are really cold a lot…and when they are, they don't work very well. My feet are always hot and sweaty… like right now, in my shoes, they're really uncomfortable. I just…I feel weak. My ankles seem weak, my legs seem weak…"

The gravity of the moment felt heavy in my chest as I hung up the phone. *Relax. Breathe.* I opened the car door and stood in the cold winter air. *Inhale…exhale…inhale…exhale.* I gazed at the sky and the building, unsure of how to continue my day. One phone call had started a journey. There was no turning back; I had to face it, whatever it was.

My appointment finally arrived on May 3. Like it was any other visit, the nurse took my vitals, and the doctor came in and began to ask questions. A big guy with a beard and a smile, he couldn't have been much more than forty. Discussing what he must've known could be very serious, we chatted casually as if we were friends. He looked closely at my hands, pointing out some atrophy along the side of my palm, at the base of my pinkie. We went into the hall, and he watched as I followed instructions.

"Walk to the end, turn and come back…a little faster, side-to-side, OK, stop."

I narrated every action, upbeat in tone. I thought he'd agree that my walking was fine. He didn't say much; I left knowing only that there was more work to do.

I didn't know at the time, but the summary from that first visit listed three things:

- Weakness of both lower extremities
- Upper extremity weakness
- Gait instability

My next visit wouldn't come for more than a month. In the meantime, I moved into a new place in Stowe. I now had three roommates from whom to hide my ever-increasing anxiety.

I met with a neurologist and it was more of the same: a little poking and prodding, a few questions, no information forthcoming, and another referral. I was scheduled for an MRI the next day.

I arrived in the evening — eight or nine — to a near-empty Fletcher Allen Hospital (now the main campus of UVM Medical Center). The technician struck me with an off-the-cuff comment. He looked at me in my hospital gown and said, "Well, you're young for an MRI."

I still didn't know what to think, and I didn't try to find out. I didn't spend my nights obsessively Googling; I tried to avoid it instead. With each step, I was hoping to get closer to an answer, but that comment scared me. Up until then, I'd been dealing with a table full of poker players. An MRI tech — without thinking — showed me his hand. *Maybe it's time to start worrying.*

I lay in the machine, my mind racing in every direction. *What are they looking for? What if they find something? Should I want them to find something? If they find something, maybe we can do something about it. What if there's something wrong with my brain?*

As the machine powered down, I felt some relief — at least that part was over. I drove back to Stowe, having learned nothing. My mind raced on; I tried to stay hopeful. I wanted to hide; I needed to escape. *When will this nightmare be over?*

In August, they brought me in again. They took blood and gave me a large, plastic, collapsible bottle for urine. I was to pee in the bottle for twelve hours, or until it was full, keeping it in the refrigerator throughout. I wasn't about to tell my roommates that I was a science experiment. I left the plastic bottle in my trunk. I never filled it. No one ever asked.

***

I had already missed a bunch of work for appointments, so I felt I had to say something to my boss. I broke the news in one of our weekly one-on-one meetings in a tiny, windowless conference room. I downplayed my fears; I was embarrassed to have to tell him at all. I reiterated what I'd been telling myself: it's probably something fixable, curable — I hope.

My parents started getting mail in my name. I should've called the hospital and corrected my address, but due to my proclivity for procrastination and hatred of menial tasks — especially of the telephonic variety — I didn't. When the second or third round of appointment summaries, billing information, and "keep for your records" trash arrived at their door, I had to explain what was happening. Starting that day — when a mother had to pry information from her son — my parents were in the loop, involved and not going away.

I'm not sure exactly why I was so reluctant at every stage to share my experiences, even with those close to me. Part of it was embarrassment. I felt embarrassed from the beginning, and somehow, I still do. But I also knew that telling people would make it real. If I kept everything to myself, then it wouldn't be happening outside of my own head. Until there was something to tell, i.e., a diagnosis, and until I believed and accepted that diagnosis, I didn't want to face it.

***

About a week later, I had yet another appointment at the hospital. It was a long walk from the parking garage to the exam room; my feet were swollen, sweating, and throbbing by the time I arrived. Having already changed into a gown, I sat on a table and peeled off my socks.

"Are they always like this?" the woman asked, touching my feet. I was in my own head when she introduced herself. She may have been a nurse; she may have been a doctor.

"They're not always this bad. But yeah, they're always bothering me," I said. For reasons unknown, she put my feet in a bucket of cool water.

Two tests were conducted that day: one was quick and painless, the other was an EMG. Electromyography measures the response to a nerve's stimulation of a muscle. A needle electrode shoots a series of pulses into the muscle, and the results are recorded. It's a continuous insertion of needles into just about every muscle group in the body, accompanied by a minor electrical shock at each stop.

One by one, the doctor moved the needle around my body. My arms, legs, and torso were all thoroughly covered. Though I didn't particularly enjoy lying face down on a table while a guy shocked the muscles in my back and my body jerked involuntarily, it wasn't that bad. (It only felt faintly like torture; had I been holding information, I could have held out indefinitely.) When it was finished, the administering doctor looked me in the eye and, in an unmistakably somber, sentimental tone, told me it could be something very serious.

I didn't know what that meant, and I didn't ask. *What's an EMG used for?* I could have found out but chose not to. I knew I was getting close to an answer; I didn't think I'd want to know what it was. I didn't sleep that night; I couldn't erase the image of that look.

2.

Mom and I drove to Fletcher Allen the following Wednesday and met a neurologist in her office at nine. Wednesday was her day off. That was the first thing out of her mouth when we walked through the door.

We sat down, and she got right to the point. Completely unprepared, I watched the letters come out of her mouth: ALS. I don't remember what happened next. There's a blank space in my memory, like my mind skipped ahead. Mom says I burst into tears. I guess my brain didn't want to remember.

After months of anticipation, it's easy to see how any news at all would draw an outpouring of emotion. I imagine if the news were something positive — or really anything definitive at all — I may have reacted in much the same way. I wasn't sad. I didn't know enough to be sad. I was in shock.

What did I know about ALS? About the same as anyone else: very little. I knew it was bad; I didn't know it was hopeless. My brain didn't know what to do with those letters.

I sat in the chair, stone-faced and staring at nothing, my body drained of emotion. The doctor kept talking, and I listened. I heard her, but also, I didn't. My mind was off in a million directions at once.

In an attempt to convey some perspective, she spoke of a friend who'd been recently diagnosed. She told us a horror story. The disease went straight for the face, throat, and lungs. In a short time, her friend couldn't speak or swallow and was struggling to breathe. Mine was beginning at the periphery — in my hands and feet. In a way, I was lucky, she told us.

I didn't want to hear it. Instead of releasing my inner monologue — full of angry cursing — I nodded along silently. Soon, her focus circled back to me. She gave us the bullet points, repeating "it varies" and "on average" several times. She prescribed the only approved ALS treatment — it was shown to add a few months to the lifespan, "on average." She didn't communicate anything resembling hope. It was all meaningless anyway. After those three letters, what did it matter? As a final reminder of my dire situation — a parting gift and definitive part of the protocol — she also prescribed an antidepressant.

She told me to eat fatty foods — my body needed more calories. She told me to be a couch potato. She told me that my life would never be the same.

MY SUMMER WITH MOLLY

When I was eighteen, I met a girl named Molly. She was twenty-one — a friend of a friend — and had been recently diagnosed with Friedreich's ataxia, a genetic, degenerative neurological disease. My friend told me her news with no other purpose than to explain her hardly noticeable limp. I didn't know what that meant. I didn't look it up, and I didn't ask questions. He couldn't have answered them anyhow.

It was a few weeks after my brother had passed; I was back from college, working at Dave's and living at home. Everything in my life was in flux — my family, the college I attended, my friends. I may not have known it, but I needed something to grab onto. I found Molly.

I liked her right away. She was the kind of person that everyone liked right away. She was bright and sunny, warm, and easy to talk to. She seemed confident and outgoing, blonde, and beautiful. It wasn't meant to be a setup, but that seemed to change quickly. Before the day was out, my buddy and his girlfriend were playing middle-school matchmakers, and I was all for it. We were soon exchanging calls, making plans, and turning into an item.

We were together all the time. If I wasn't working, and she wasn't working, we were together. We talked constantly. I told her everything — every story and thought in my head. It didn't matter what we did, I just wanted to be with her.

My high school friends and I, all home after a freshman year apart, drank beers and smoked pot at her third-floor apartment on King Street in Burlington. We seemed to spend every night there — weekdays, weekends, it didn't matter. I climbed those stairs dozens of times (through the front door that opened into the apartment and the meandering wooden fire escape around back), and I saw Molly climb them. It was nothing more than a blip in my mind. I saw her deliberate pace — her hand always holding the rail — but I didn't think much of it. I didn't consider that she might be scared, that she could fall, or offer any help. As an eighteen-year-old, I was oblivious, and Molly wasn't about to ask for help.

Maybe she was still in denial and didn't want to talk about it. Maybe she was afraid I'd run if I knew the whole truth. Maybe she wanted to live one more summer like the girl she'd always been, doing everything she could to make sure we saw her that way. Maybe she'd thought it through and planned to take each day as it came and try to enjoy every moment.

I didn't think about what that diagnosis meant to her life — mentally, physically, and emotionally. I couldn't have begun to imagine what that would feel like at twenty-one. I didn't realize that her FA diagnosis would forever define her. I didn't try to put myself in her shoes; it never even occurred to me. In the all-too-common naiveté of my young life, I only saw the person right in front of me.

That summer was pure and simple and gloriously fun; I didn't think about the future. I'd found happiness in the saddest time in my life. Maybe she felt the same. I think we wanted to enjoy it. I think we needed to enjoy it.

***

Two or three years later — while waiting tables at the Sheraton on a Saturday night — I ran into Molly. She was at a wedding among her nursing school friends in a wheelchair. It was strange seeing her like that, and I didn't take the time to consider what should've been obvious.

In my navy-blue polyester uniform jacket with its plastic gold buttons, with some sad, uneven fuzz growing out of my chin, I pulled up a chair and said hello. The music was playing, and a mutual friend asked us together for a dance. Molly rose to the dance floor, and I held her for a song.

Once again, I didn't understand. I kept thinking, *If you can stand, why do you need the chair?* It didn't make sense. But then, I'd learn in the intervening years, I was an idiot.

3.

Mom and I drove in silence back to my parents' house in South Burlington. We didn't talk about what had just happened. What was there to say? When we got to the house, she made hot dogs for lunch.

We were sitting at the table when my dad walked in and asked how it went. He worked just a few miles away and usually came home for lunch. Mom and I looked at each other in silence. We didn't know how to tell him the news. I could see his mind racing; Mom let it out: "He has ALS."

He paced frantically around the living room, his mind and body not sure what to do.

"So, what do we do? What's the plan?"

"Nothing," she told him. "There's a drug they prescribed, but it doesn't sound like it does much."

More pacing.

After Dad went back to work (busy hands are happy hands in my family), Mom and I drove out to Hinesburg to see the site of their future house. The property was in the early stages: ground leveled, basement dug, dirt piles everywhere. As I had done on my first visit — like an eight-year-old — I climbed the biggest heap and surveyed my surroundings. For the first time, Mom watched with a new perspective. "Be careful, Nathan," she told me.

On the return trip, Mom had a question at the ready.

"When are you going to tell your friends?"

I'm not sure it occurred to her how difficult that would be. Instead of communicating my fears, I nodded along — as sons do. It didn't matter how hard it would be; I knew she was right. I had to.

How am I supposed to tell anyone? How am I supposed to tell my friends? I can't look Lenny or Tom in the eye and give them this news. I don't even know what it means. Am I telling them I'm dying? I don't know what's going to happen; I don't know how long I'll live. How can I even be thinking about this? I'm twenty-seven years old. I'm thinking about how I'm going to tell my friends that I'm dying?!

I sent Lenny a text and invited myself over that evening. That was the easy part — just another night at Lenny and Laura's. I invited Tom and Katie — he could make it, she couldn't. I thought I could get the four of them in a room and rip off the Band-Aid. *What about after that?*

Will I call people up, one by one, and tell them my news? Can I really do that? Maybe just for a few. Should I give them permission to spread the word? Should I ask them to do it? Should I put that on people? Shouldn't I do it myself? Why not post something on Facebook and be done with it?

I wasn't ready to tell the world. I wasn't ready to admit what had happened. I didn't believe it myself.

WORDS ON A PAGE

If you were to Google ALS, you could learn all sorts of things — statistics of every measure. You could read of the symptoms and the cause, of the treatments, ages of onset, life expectancies, and ultimate causes of death. You could study the history, frequency, and research; you might even try to understand what it feels like.

You would discover that 90-95 percent of cases — called sporadic ALS — *have* no known cause, while the remaining cases — familial ALS — are linked to a family history of the disease. That the average age of onset — for sporadic ALS — is about sixty, and the average sufferer survives two to four years after onset. You would see that only 10 percent live more than ten years.

You might also research Stephen Hawking — that slumped-over famous guy known more for the sound of his speech-generating device than his scientific achievements — and his 1963 diagnosis at the tender age of twenty-one. The doctors gave him two years. His fierce independence and unwillingness to acquiesce to any of the limitations before him might be inspiring. He was twice married, had three children, and finally lost out to the disease only recently, at the age of 76.

I've read many of these things — trying to learn what was to come — in brief moments of strength between long periods of avoidance. I'm not sure that any of it meant a thing. You might think that it would have prepared me, like a roadmap to my future, but they were just words on a page.

4.

I met Lenny and Laura in college; Lenny started working at Dave's in the summer of 2004. When, about a year later, neither of us had a half-reliable car to get us to the restaurant in Milton, we were both able to get walking-distance jobs at the Sheraton. We walked together in the dark, below-zero temperatures to arrive at five a.m. for the breakfast shift and brought sausage-and-bacon-filled Styrofoam containers home to our sad, empty fridges. I knew both sets of their parents and had spent time in each of their homes. Lenny and I had played in a band together — our rehearsal space, his parents' basement. I'd spent more time and eaten more meals at the apartments they'd shared (since moving in together in college) than anyplace but my own. They were, and are, family.

On Wednesday night — eight hours after receiving my ALS diagnosis — I had dinner with three of my closest friends. I thought it mattered what I said; I repeated the words in my mind. That was my first mistake. I tried to find the right moment. That was my second mistake. Whenever, however I opened my mouth, it would ruin the night. The good times would immediately disappear — replaced by tears, sadness, and disbelief.

We sampled beers, hung out in the kitchen and living room, ate whatever we ate, and — as was always the case — laughed a lot. It felt like all those nights we'd hung out since college, and the more time that passed, the less likely I'd ruin it. It felt warm and familiar, like the escape I desperately needed. With each drink, each laugh, each passing second, my will became weaker. I didn't want to do it, and I buckled: *I don't have to.*

My left headlight had been out a few days. I knew exactly which one to buy and how to install it, but I'd put it off. The headlight — and the forty-five-minute drive back to Stowe — should've been on my mind as I drank another beer and hit the (marijuana) pipe. It's not that I felt pressure to partake — I could've been responsible. I could've told them about the headlight if I needed an excuse. I told myself I didn't care about the consequences.

The failed attempt behind me, I got in my car around eleven. Ten minutes later, within view of the highway, I saw blue lights behind me. It felt like a badge of honor. *Fuck it! I don't give a shit! Let them throw me in jail! Drag me off in cuffs, I don't care!*

We'd been sampling beers — sharing a bunch of bottles between us — and I wasn't sure how much I'd actually had. Would I seem drunk or stoned? What would happen if I did? It was tricky to know what drunk or stoned felt like; I didn't know "normal" anymore. There was one thing I felt like I knew: if given a car-side sobriety test, I'd fail.

When the officer approached, I told him, "Yes, I know I have a headlight out."

Then, unprovoked, my voice shaking, I added, "I was diagnosed with ALS today."

"Today?"

"Yes, today." I reached out my left arm, locked my elbow, and stared at my trembling hand.

He went about the usual routine, like a robot. I couldn't tell if he believed me. *Who would make up such a thing? How do you prove you're not lying?*

As he sat in the cruiser — its lights flashing in my eyes in the mirror — my mind raced. Even as I felt the invincibility of knowing my day couldn't possibly get worse, my body shook with nervous energy — I couldn't begin to control it. I flip-flopped my feelings: going to jail would definitely make my day worse.

He came back to my window, told me to fix the headlight, and sent me on my way. He never asked if I'd been drinking, smoking — nothing.

I could feel my heart pumping as I put on my seatbelt, started the car, pushed down the blinker, checked the cruiser in my rearview, and pulled away from the curb. I turned onto the highway and though there was traffic in both directions, flipped on my fully functional high-beams. I obsessively watched the miles tick by until finally, I reached Exit 10: Waterbury/Stowe.

Driving up Route 100, I had to make a choice: drive through Stowe Village or take my chances on the lesser-traveled Moscow Road. I knew the Moscow Road was a common speed trap (I could picture the cop sitting in the church parking lot of the twenty-five-mile-per-hour zone), but I couldn't see driving right through the village. There were not *always* police on the Moscow Road; it was, in fact, the road less traveled. I can't say that I made the wrong decision (I may have been caught either way), but a few minutes later, while closely following an SUV at twenty-eight miles per hour, a cop pulled out from the very spot I'd imagined and glued itself to my bumper.

The car followed me around the corner and up the hill, undoubtedly watching for a slip-up. Wracked with anxiety, I drove as if an instructor sat at my side, compulsively checking my speedometer against the signposts. The lights came on just before Stowe High School. As I would later confirm, they'd followed me for two miles — five minutes of fear-building.

I pulled into the high school parking lot, rolled down the window, and awaited another pleasant conversation. An officer appeared at each window, flashlights engaged. Startled and unsure of my actions (*Should I roll the passenger window down? Who do I talk to? Where do I look?*), I already knew this time wouldn't go so smoothly.

"Do you know why we pulled you over?"

"Yeah. I have a headlight out. I was pulled over in Williston."

"Tonight?"

"Yeah. A half-hour ago."

They did their thing, took my papers — which were already out on the passenger seat — and walked back to their car. Nervous as before, I couldn't help but think: *This is such a nuisance.* Though I knew there was a bigger picture, my mind was rationalizing again. *I don't give a shit. Damn it, I just want to go home.*

I answered the usual questions when they returned (Where are you coming from? Where are you headed?) and, thinking it had done me some good the first time, told them of my diagnosis that morning. I'm not sure if they heard — or understood, or believed me — but it seemed to have no effect. I showed my shaky hand and tried to explain. They weren't listening. I wanted to scream. *Don't you understand what that means?! It means I'm dying, you fucking morons! Look at me! Are you even listening?!* It seemed they'd already moved on.

Things quickly escalated from there. They asked if I'd been drinking; I lied; I was told to get out of the vehicle. Standing in the parking lot around midnight, blue lights flashing in my face, I explained my diagnosis as I thought it pertained to the current situation. I would surely fail any sobriety tests, I told them. "I'm not normal; I can't walk a straight line." They didn't say a word; I was presented with a Breathalyzer. I'd done this once before — as a teenager at a busted-up party where I was the pot-head designated driver and knew I'd blow zeros — but this time, I wasn't so sure.

"Do I have to?" I asked sheepishly, unaware of my rights.

"You can come down to the station."

Fuck it.

I blew well below the legal limit, further proof that I could no longer accurately gauge my level of inebriation (and also that there is not an effective process for marijuana detection). I was also very fortunate. I'm sure they could have brought me in if they really wanted to see me in cuffs.

They immediately lost interest and allowed me back in my car. They sat and watched as I reapplied my seatbelt, started the engine, and flipped on the blinker to pull away from the nightmarish scene. My knee trembled wildly as I pushed in the clutch. I held it down and breathed deeply, trying to relax. *You're fine. Everything's fine. Calm down. Breathe.* I put the car in gear and shakily released the clutch, driving through the parking lot with one eye on the rearview. Expecting a tail that never came, I pulled onto the road.

I walked into a sleeping house that night. I didn't tell my roommates what had happened. I got up and went to work in the morning.

I've never told anyone the full truth of what was sadly one of the most eventful days of my life.

THE BIG QUESTION

Of course, I think about it — The Big Question. Why? Why did this happen? Was it my fault? Was there a cause, or was it inevitable? If not for one thing or one moment in my life, could things have been different?

A lot of people dream up reasons for the things that happen in their lives. I'm not one of those people. I don't think I know all the answers. I'm not going to tell you that it will all work out, that it was meant to be, or that everything happens for a reason. All of those people seem to have a profound misunderstanding of cause and effect. I don't need to subscribe to simplistic platitudes to get through my days. Nothing is as simple as that. I am, however, interested in the never-ending quest for the truth, the science, the reason.

Right from the start, you begin to ask why. The questions flow in and out of your head, gaining and losing importance as you shuffle them around. I could never share all of the thoughts in my mind; I haven't talked about it in years. It's a dauntingly dark, unending conversation that will never bear fruit. Whatever my thoughts, those of the experts, or anyone else, they ultimately don't matter — at least not to my life. If tomorrow I found out the origin of my pain, I wouldn't be cured.

Was it the concussion I suffered when I was twelve — when I dove headlong into a post in pursuit of a Wiffle ball? Or the fights I got into in middle school? The black eye in my sixth-grade portrait is tough to ignore. Was it the baseball I took to the forehead at five? Again, school picture, plain to see. Or the boxing we did in Matt's basement? It gave me a headache — that much I know.

Was it the stress of my job and getting up hours early to study? Did I get enough sleep — real, restful sleep, free of a racing mind? It all started during that time — trying to balance the Chartered Financial Analyst exams and pick up the slack to cover for a fully checked-out colleague. Was it too much? Was it the coffee? I never drank that much. Should I have had breakfast? Did my body need food before noon? Was I meant to sit at a desk all day, bent over paperwork? Did that mess with my spine? Was it too much time at the computer, staring at the screen through my glasses? Should I have taken them off? Should I have changed chairs, walked around, or switched to a standing desk? Why did it start when it did? I'm not even sure when that was.

Was it the running at lunch on an empty stomach? Or the cold showers after, dressing, and invariably sweating at my desk? Should I have worn shower shoes? Was there a fungus or something I caught?

Did I drink too much? Maybe I developed an allergy. Did I smoke too much pot? Maybe it fried my nerves. Was I unhappy? How could that matter? Should I have been more careful — with everything? Did I bring this on myself? Was it my fault?

Sometimes I think I know — I feel convinced of the answers — but then I take a step back. I remind myself of all of the other people who have done all of the things on my list. People with more concussions than they can count; addicts of every drug imaginable; people who starve themselves or live on caffeine, sugar, and fat; people who live their whole lives in a chair; those on multiple medications to deal with stress, get through the day, get a night's rest, or just stay alive.

It is both the most important and most useless of quandaries. It will forever go unanswered and never go away. No, there's nothing unique about me except ALS.

5.

I met Tom through Lenny in college. They were best friends in high school and roommates in the UVM dorms. Tom and I spent many nights in college drinking too much, hitting the bars, chasing girls, and waking up with stories to (hopefully) tell. We played basketball, hiked, skied, and golfed. He was the singer in our band. I knew his parents and three sisters and had spent time at their house. He'd twice been my roommate. I'd known Katie almost as long; we'd met on trips to visit friends at Keene State. When she and Tom started dating long distance, she'd half-lived with us at

6 Patrick. I'd spent a ton of time at the Winooski apartment they shared. They were, and are, family.

Two days later, on a Friday night at Tom and Katie's, I was determined to get it right. I'd wanted Laura and Katie to be there, but it was just the three of us guys. I should have made myself do it as soon as I walked through the door. I didn't; I foolishly let it weigh on my mind.

I was sitting on the couch with a bottle of beer in my hand when the turntable stopped — my turn to pick a new record. It was an obvious break in the action; I saw my opportunity. Instead of getting up off the couch, I froze, stared at the floor, and tried again to find the impossible words.

"I have to tell you guys something. I've known something was wrong with me for a long time, and I've had a lot of doctor's appointments lately, and I finally found out what it is. I have ALS."

I didn't look at either of them as I spoke. I just tried to get the words out. Through tears and sniffles, I could barely do that.

With the cat out of the bag — Lenny tearing up and Tom beside me on the couch, his arm on my back — I started to let go. The words poured from my mouth; I told them everything I could think of. I told them how difficult this was, how I'd tried to tell them two days before. I told them about the last months and longer, but nothing about the future. I didn't know what my future held; I wasn't able to think about it. With my thoughts and emotions out on the table, I could finally look my friends in the eye.

I got through it. We got through it. I released all of my emotion and felt relief. My burden was lifted; the truth was on the table. I didn't have to hide anymore.

Tom and I drank another beer and Lenny went home for the night. He called me a few minutes later. Could he and Laura come back? She wanted to see me.

I stood up from the couch as they came through the door. We locked eyes as she hurried toward me. Like a long-awaited reunion in a movie, we came together with force, and our bodies fell onto the couch.

6.

On the day of my diagnosis, I was prescribed a number of vitamins and supplements as well as two prescription drugs: one for ALS, one for depression. As soon as they were available, I started taking both. I didn't seem to feel any different at first, but after a few weeks or a month, I noticed the changes. What now seems obvious didn't occur to me: my ALS hadn't changed overnight; it was also the drugs. They seemed to amplify my symptoms and cause all sorts of new ones.

The stiffness in my joints went through the roof. Every time I stood up from my desk, I had to stretch out my legs and hips like I'd been on a five-hour drive. I felt like the tin man before he got his hands on an oil can, like a clenched fist that wouldn't let go.

My body wouldn't relax when I'd lay down at night. All sorts of muscles — large and small, all over my body — fired uncontrollably. It was as if there was a battle being waged, a tug-of-war between muscle movement and the forceful resistance of such movement. Laying still on my back, I'd feel a spasm building until I practically kicked off the sheets. There was a dull pain deep in my legs, reminiscent of the growing pains that had kept me awake as a child.

I began to experience muscle cramping — mostly at night — with which I continue to suffer to this day. I'd stretch my legs and point my toes, and one of my calves would lock up in pain, keeping my foot pointing involuntarily. The muscle was unnaturally, forcefully flexed; I'd struggle to pull back my foot with the other and release it.

The bottle of whatever antidepressant it was — I think I tried two — advised against driving "until you know how xyz drug affects you." That's hardly realistic for anyone. It gave me a head-in-the-clouds effect, for sure. On one afternoon, I was driving from Waterbury to Burlington, and I felt particularly disconnected.

Driving has always made my mind wander — I don't know why. *What if I just cranked the wheel doing eighty on the highway? Would*

I skid? Would I roll? What would happen? In high school, driving my Saab on the highway to Dave's, sometimes I'd play a little game with myself. I'd close my eyes for as long as I could take. A few seconds would pass and I'd open them back up, almost disappointed when things looked the same. It was a stupid teenage boy thing to do, but that *what if* premise has never completely gone away.

Those thoughts felt more powerful than ever that day. There was a fight in my brain to determine what was, in fact, real. *Isn't it weird that I could turn the wheel this much and potentially cause a huge accident? Maybe even kill someone? What if my car just went right through the oncoming traffic? Like a ghost. Could I do that?* Fortunately, these ideas never won out — sanity beat them back — but this new prescription seemed to hand them a lot more ammunition.

I reported some of my new symptoms — specifically leg-spasm-induced insomnia — and my neurologist prescribed baclofen, a muscle relaxer.

"It should help you sleep, but it also helps with the stiffness," he told me. "It could also cause drowsiness, and don't drink too much. If you're going to have more than a drink or two, don't take your evening dose."

"What happens if I drink too much?"

"You don't wake up," he said casually — as if he didn't mean that I could die.

I added the baclofen to my growing regimen. It seemed to function as advertised, or at least it did better than nothing. I didn't feel anywhere near normal — or even as normal as I'd felt before any of the drugs — but they were supposed to keep me alive; I didn't consider taking them a choice.

The baclofen did wonders relaxing my digestive tract — it all but put it to sleep. Adding to my newfound drug-induced sluggishness, I now felt uncomfortably bloated, gassy, and constipated. With another new drug, I was another step further removed from the person I'd been.

I tried to find a solution. I cut down on dairy, which had never been a great friend and — in reading about people's various digestive challenges — decided to try cutting out gluten. No more cereal and milk; no more pizza and grilled cheese sandwiches; and, most seriously, no more beer. Perhaps taking my web-based health article reading and dietary experimentation a few steps too far, I cut out caffeine and sugar as well. I just had to do something, anything.

My team at the ALS clinic had no answers. They wanted me to eat as much as possible — this wouldn't help. I asked about ALS and a gluten-free diet, ALS and sugar, ALS and caffeine, ALS and alcohol. They didn't have answers; instead, I was told the same thing: you need to keep your calorie intake high. I call it the Ice Cream Directive. Every discussion I've had with my nutritionist has included ice cream; it seems to be the ultimate fat-maker. In response to my outside-the-box questions, I was directed to a collection of studies that functioned as a fact-checking website called ALS Untangled. Allow me to save you the trouble and summarize their findings: nothing encouraging; nothing conclusive; nothing helps.

I allowed myself a bit of sugar and alcohol after a couple of months — though in reality or inside my head, I felt a bit better on my ultraclean diet. I stayed off caffeine for longer — as much as six months — marking the first of many flip-flops in the coming years. (My brain loves caffeine, my body doesn't. It makes me shaky, sweaty, and dehydrated. Sometimes it's worth it.) I lived without gluten much longer and restored a good portion of digestive regularity. I bought all those substitute products you see in the store and learned most are not worth buying. I drank wine and whiskey, bought the occasional gluten-free beer, and tried (and failed) to find a lunchtime substitute for the sandwich. When people asked me how I did it: How do you not eat pizza and pasta and bread? Oh, glorious bread? I'd tell them it's simple: it's better than the alternative.

DELUSIONS

I drifted somewhere between denial and acceptance for much longer than any reasonable person would believe. I'd feel optimistic and think I'd learned something, then my hopes would deflate and I'd fall back into depression. I kept finding reasons — different items to latch onto, some bigger than others — to think my diagnosis could have been a mistake.

There was nothing to point at to prove anything. There wasn't a tumor, genetic deficiency, virus, or infection to name as the cause. All anyone had was my symptoms; it was impossible to believe there could be only one answer.

At first, it was my feet. They were causing such problems, it had to be them. While I still retained almost all of my physical abilities, before anything else, there were my feet. They were hot and swollen, sweaty and tingling, alive and temperamental. The most minor of physical activities would throw the nerves in my feet into high-level panic, flashing needless, energy-sucking signals. From the very beginning, I talked about them, trying to point the way to the obvious and visible source of my problems.

The feet are a common-sense indicator of the body. That's what they told me. They were not the cause of my myriad of problems. Instead, they were merely a symptom — of ALS as well as a lot of other unrelated maladies.

I couldn't believe that; I treated the symptom. I saw a podiatrist and showed him the evidence. I expected him, as a foot doctor, to understand my symptoms. He didn't. I had a stubborn case of athlete's foot; that was all. I wanted to throw a brick through his window.

I tried the antifungals he prescribed, but nothing was effective in the least. Every time I put my shoes on, my symptoms came roaring back. I tried to find a solution on my own: foot balms, tea tree oil, Vick's, footbaths of every variety. Alone in my apartment above the garage, I put my feet in sloshing Ziploc bags of hydrogen peroxide. Nothing had any lasting effect. Staying off of my feet — keeping them cool, dry, and comfortable — was the best thing to do to feel normal.

I felt so much better after eating; I was stronger the more meals I had in me. I felt strikingly different from one time of day to the next. Sometimes I'd be tired and lethargic; sometimes I'd be shivering and shaking. I always felt my best — and had the most energy — after dinner.

I didn't know if any of it was normal (consistent with my diagnosis), so I asked. I repeatedly tried to explain my ever-changing symptoms, waiting for something to ring a bell. I was searching for an alternative explanation, but my satisfying answer never came. Each patient's experience is different, they'd respond. I felt like they were giving me an automated response. They weren't even listening to my questions.

Any change that I made, where I saw an improvement, had to mean something major was afoot. Chiropractic adjustments were the greatest example. Each time I got on the table, I released some part of the overwhelming tension I was holding. Sometimes my body would physically jump. I felt more at ease, more relaxed. Some of the stiffness — the "tone" that defined my diagnosis — had seemingly lifted.

My balance felt better; my confidence grew. I found myself standing with casual, bent knees instead of the perpetual knee-lock I'd come to trust. Some function came back to my hands and fingers; I could grab things again much more easily.

Though my improvements may have been minor — indistinguishable to all but the closest observer — they meant a whole lot to me in my day-to-day life. And they meant a whole lot to my mental well-being. Though ALS's downward trajectory inevitably continued, I felt like I was building momentum. I was waiting for all the small changes to add up to something meaningful. Instead — though unquestionably significant in my mind — they seemed to plateau, and my hope for something greater slowly faded.

7.

I rarely went to the doctor as a child; my mom treated most every-thing at home. I never went for a cold, or the flu, or strep throat. There were times when that pink earache medicine could be found in our fridge, but everything else — save broken bones and con-cussions; I had one of each — had a simple remedy. I used the electric bush trimmers for the first time when I was twelve — I almost cut off two fingers. Mom washed the wound in the kitch-en sink while the neighborhood kids — playing Wiffle ball in my backyard, as always — were treated to a gruesome demonstration of screams. I didn't go immediately for stitches.

I wasn't accustomed to the waiting rooms and fluorescent lights, the cold temperatures and demeanors. After months of one-off tests and visits, I was about to enter a world of never-ending checkups. My first taste of this new, scheduled misery came on September 15, 2011.

Mom and I arrived at Fanny Allen Hospital before nine-thirty and were directed down the hall to an elevator to the basement. We checked in at another desk, filled out the usual paperwork, and sat in the waiting area. We watched as a middle-aged man was wheeled out, motionless and silent. I noticed the Lou Gehrig plaque on the wall, but didn't so much as approach it.

Before long, a nurse came to get us — an older woman with a ready smile. She introduced herself in a way that went far beyond a cursory greeting. She knew she'd be seeing us again; she was wel-coming us to the family. Before anything else, closely focused on my every move, she walked me to a scale. I stepped onto the wide, wheelchair-bearing, loading-dock-style platform, and the nurse said out loud, "one-forty-four." One of the few finite numbers used to show my progress, my weight was a big deal.

We turned the corner and walked into a large open space with a number of stations for a variety of physical therapy activities. I wondered what each person was doing — some walking awkwardly, some lying on mats, others using all sorts of machines. I didn't ask who they were or what they were doing; I never thought they might be like me.

I didn't think much of anything; I shut down my brain and followed directions. If I'd allowed myself to consider all that was happening, I'd have lost it. It was all too much to take in. For pride or embarrassment, I didn't want to spend the day in tears. I just wanted to get through it. I went through the day like an animal, entrenched in each moment without judgment.

Off the main room, we entered a small, windowless cell. It had office-building fluorescent lights covered with a colorful, wispy-clouded blue-sky piece of plastic. It was just like any other examination room except that instead of the counter-high exam table, it was equipped with a foot-pedal-operated, bench-level padded table. A ten-by-ten room with two chairs and a bench — that would be our home for the day.

There was a piece of paper taped to the wall outside the door. At the top was my name; listed beneath was my list of visitors. I didn't know how my day would unfold but had I seen the list, I wouldn't have liked it.

The list was long. In my first clinic visit, Mom and I saw a nurse, an occupational therapist, a physical therapist, a social worker, a representative from the Muscular Dystrophy Association, a speech therapist, a respiratory therapist, a palliative care specialist, a nutritionist, a nun in charge of my spiritual guidance, and a neurologist. The neurologist was a man, the other ten were women. One after another — separated by dead time to stare at the wall — they came and went.

Each introduced herself with a smile, chatted pleasantly, ran tests, and asked questions. With my permission — which I breezily granted — some brought understudies, students, or interns to follow along. I quickly learned how this would go: they were here to measure my progress, to watch and listen while I performed little tasks, to advise on the present and what the future would inevitably bring.

Though each of them asked if I needed anything — and obviously, whole-heartedly cared — most had no useful advice to provide.

The nurse checked my vitals and painstakingly covered every inch of a questionnaire. It asked about everything from eating and sleeping to bathing and toileting (the correct clinical term). In the visits to come, I would learn that she also — with help from the questionnaire and our conversations — organized the rest of my day.

The occupational therapist played with my hands and arms and gave me little tests, saying the results aloud as she recorded them. *Wrist up, wrist down, closed palm, open palm. Can you touch your thumb and pinkie? Lift your arms high. I'm going to provide some resistance — push as hard as you can. Three, three, five, four, one.*

The physical therapist focused on my legs in much the same way. She put me through a series of strength tests, then brought me into the big room and watched me walk. *Walk slowly to that spot, turn around and come back. Now, let's do it faster. Can you walk backward at all? OK, try that slowly. Now walk as fast as you can, safely. Let's go down the hall and try some stairs.* She followed nervously beside me, arms in ready position, waiting for me to fall. Fortunately, I never did — I think both of us would've been hurt.

The speech therapist watched and listened intently, describing the experiences of other sufferers. She talked about food and drink, chewing and swallowing, mucus and saliva. We spoke about foods that might give me trouble — popcorn was high on the list. Her focus was not only on speech but on safety and choking — anything involving the mouth, tongue, and throat.

The respiratory therapist was there for one reason — my lungs. She asked questions and administered a couple of lung strength and capacity tests. *How many pillows do you sleep with? How do you sleep? On your side? On your back? Do you sleep through the night? Do you wake up rested? Do you wake up with a headache?*

Only the nutritionist offered anything real: she told me to eat. *How's your appetite? Are you hungry at mealtimes? What do you eat? For breakfast? For lunch? For dinner? For dessert? You should always eat dessert. Ice cream. Fruits, vegetables, bread, pasta, meat, snacks, dairy. Have a glass of milk with a meal. Do you drink beer? Have a beer before dinner, it might increase your appetite.*

She would always start in the same place: *How's your weight?* Inevitably, it was always a little less, and she would tell me again: *Eat!* It wasn't that she was scolding me; she was encouraging. It wasn't long before I found it annoying.

The neurologist felt like the dentist who comes in at the end to check everyone's work. He often brought an understudy, another set of eyes to examine the human embodiment of what was in books. I never had a problem with the students and interns. They were always kind, quiet, and polite — you'd hardly know they were in the room. But I knew they were brought in for a reason. I didn't feel like just another ALS case, and I wasn't. I was barely twenty-seven. My journey was only beginning. I wasn't the same as these old guys in power chairs. I felt like a must-see attraction.

He asked questions, performed a few cursory tests — measuring the strength and spasticity of a muscle — and spoke of the science, the research, and the like. As with the rest of them, he ended with a request for questions. His answers were never at all satisfying. Had he been honest and comically inclined, he'd have said something like, *Yeah, it's a motherfucker.*

We were finally released around five. We'd been sent to the cafeteria for lunch, adding time to our day. We learned to bring our own snacks, to eat in the downtimes, and power through to the finish.

The big room was deserted by the time we were ready to go. We drove back to my parents', where Dad awaited answers, encouragement, anything. We'd spent all day with a team of doctors; surely, we had learned something. They must be able to do something — steroids, stem cells, HGH, something! Mom and I looked at each other: *Not really.*

They wanted me back every three months. At first, I didn't consider it a choice; I complied. Despite my adopted stoicism, I couldn't always hide my dwindling patience. The team began to eliminate a few of my visitors to knock an hour or two off my day.

The nun was the first one to go. I don't even remember what she was there for — preparing for death, that sort of thing. I guess it was our fault. She asked about religion, Mom said Catholic, and she had her direction.

She leaned in — speaking quietly in those somber, holy tones — while Mom nodded along, and I tried not to look physically ill. It was a lot of that "we know what God has in store for us" garbage. Had she taken it further — had she gone down the "everything happens for a reason" road — I may not have been able to take it.

Having been largely removed from the Catholic (or any other) Church for so long, I found the whole thing to be condescending bullshit. *I don't need this utterly ridiculous, positive spin. I don't need to be told what to think. I'm not a child.* Had I thought of things differently, I'd have known that it was all for my benefit. I could've spoken my mind: *You don't know anything more than I do.*

PAIN

People ask if I'm in pain. "Not really," is my go-to response. It's a very broad question; I've thought about it often. If I wished to elaborate, here's what I'd say.

I'm probably not in the type of pain you might imagine or would be familiar to regular people. I'm not sick to my stomach; I don't often have a headache or fever; I don't have coughing attacks; I don't have chronic soreness or muscle aches.

I feel fatigued. All of the time. Every little action — from chewing and swallowing and especially talking to standing in place and holding my head up — is tiresome. My muscles have been steadily shrinking — some more than others — for years. I've long recognized that "tired" and "weak" are one and the same.

Weakness itself causes all sorts of problems and can manifest as pain. My muscles aren't strong enough to hold my body together as they should. Posture has become very important to try to appease an increasingly fussy spine. The human body was designed to walk upright, not sit in a chair for eternity. I'm constantly readjusting — pulling my butt back and arching my spine — to keep the dull pain that accompanies slouching from festering in my lower back. A bone at the bottom of my spine pops out of its holding place several times a day, no matter the precautions. My neck is the worst: its weakness means it is always in need of rest. It pops and cracks wildly when I lean all the way back. A dizzying rush to my brain accompanies the more severe adjustments.

Sometimes, when I sneeze, one or several of my ab muscles lock up. It can be incredibly painful. It's hard to believe they still have the power to malfunction with such superhuman ferocity. It's as if a few little muscles have been unleashed to Incredible Hulk levels — of cramping pain rather than purpose. I have to move quickly to release them. I arch my back in a ridiculous, exaggerated manner, gritting my teeth until my abs pulse like a flickering light before finally releasing entirely.

It happens all over — in my feet and calves, hips and groin, and my jaw, neck, and throat. I don't open my mouth to the fullest extent for fear of the deep seething pain at the back of my jaw. I'm incredibly inflexible, and when I occasionally test my limits — to reach down to pick something off the floor (even from a seated position), for example — muscles I'd forgotten existed come screaming to unpleasant life. If my task has yet to be completed — like when my hip flexors grab while I try to reach my feet to put socks on — I'm in for a repeat performance.

Muscle and fat shield vulnerable nerves from the everyday dangers of the world. Losing those layers of protection has made me more sensitive to everything: cold air and water, hot sun, and the pressure of hard surfaces against my body.

I never used to understand seat cushions. As a middle schooler — and regular — at Vermont Expos games (a minor league baseball team affiliated with the Montréal Expos), I'd see all the people carrying their cushions to the concrete grandstands and wonder why they bothered. I was well under five feet and must've weighed all of eighty pounds; I couldn't fathom my butt cushion not being enough.

I was sitting on the wooden bench on the deck last week, reading in the unseasonably warm sunshine of the first days of spring. I found myself having to slump back to get more meat between the bench and the bottom of my pelvis. Along with the running, hiking, and biking, my muscular butt once served a much simpler function as a comfortable seat.

At a certain age, our mom's favorite punishment was to make my brother and me kneel in the corner. We fought all the time, and when the weather was bad, we'd be stuck in the house. Nick would routinely — and calmly, given the circumstances — go to Mom and ask, "Can I kill Nate?" I was an instigator.

When her saintly patience ran out, we'd end up kneeling on the hardwood in the corners of separate rooms, directed to stare at the wall. It was meant to be painful, and maybe it was, but our knees were young. Mostly, it was boring. I can no longer kneel on a hardwood floor without razor-sharp, debilitating screams of pain from raw, exposed nerves.

My feet have been a problem from the beginning. I wake up every morning, and they're on fire, red-hot and tingling under the covers. They were much more of a problem when I spent more time on them. For years, even in sandals or my long-time go-to green Crocs, merely walking caused them to sweat and swell. Upon arriving home from work at my Waterbury apartment, the first thing I did — a relief far beyond ridding oneself of a tight-fitting tie, or even, I imagine, a bra — was to kick off my shoes and peel off my socks.

I have the usual aches and everyday pains of life. My left kneecap hurts to the touch; the ball of my right foot is tender as I rise to stand. They're not injuries, nor do I expect them to improve. Every pain, weakness, and loss of function are not problems to be solved over time. They're permanent additions, in my mind.

Whether they actually are — and let's face it, usually they are — I always think they're forever.

When I get sick or injure myself in some way, it's hard for me to believe I'll get better. My neurologist has told me that if I were to break a bone or get an infection, there's a good chance it might never heal. I know it was meant as a warning — I need to be careful, especially with falls — but the years have taught me to believe my own experience over the textbooks. I know I've gotten over those sorts of things before, but when I'm in those moments — further incapacitated by headache, never-ending snot, or a sore ankle — I group them with my other irreversible deteriorations. While it seems like my body can heal the same as anyone's, there's always doubt creeping in. I don't expect things to get better.

8.

The day I was diagnosed, I was prescribed an antidepressant and scheduled to see a psychiatrist. Like everything else, I didn't consider these choices. I started taking the pills and showed up for the appointments.

I drove forty-five minutes for the first of my hour-long sessions. After a long, circuitous walk from the farthest parking spot in the depths of the Fletcher Allen garage, I entered what seemed a typical intellectual's office, complete with a graying, bespectacled, sweater-clad psychiatrist. The hour passed like I imagine every first session does, with answers to the broad get-to-know-you questions. And though I do remember breaking down more than once, like most young men, I didn't go all-in. I couldn't open up.

I only went the one time. I was a no-show at my second scheduled appointment. *I should be depressed. Why wouldn't I be? It'd be abnormal if I wasn't depressed. Why should I see a psychiatrist? It's not going to change anything. How is talking about it going to help?*

I could've looked at things differently: seeing a psychiatrist could be beneficial regardless of my diagnosis. He might help me find direction in my new life; he might help me with the impossible task of moving on. My world was so dominated by a singular, immovable fact, I was blind to everything else.

I think he could've helped immensely had it gone a different way. More than anything, I needed someone to make me understand: the time is now. I needed my brain to comprehend the impossible: though you think it's bad now, it will only get worse.

9.

In December, I drove to Boston with Dad for a second opinion. Such a trip is not ventured without hope. *They must have experts, better equipment, more advanced techniques. Why else would they recommend such a thing? There must be something to be gained.*

There was an understanding silence, a difficult tension on the drive. I brought a couple of CDs I thought he might like — no small task. They played to a silent audience. I'd hoped some music might change the mood — like the classic road-trip scene from a movie — but it couldn't break through. We both knew the purpose of our trip.

We were staying at The Liberty, a former prison-turned ultra-swank Beacon Hill hotel. Through its association with Mass General, we received some kind of discount. It seemed like an easy choice, regardless of the only slightly less-extravagant price.

We pulled up to the building, and a valet came running. I don't think he saw a lot of pickups, especially with oversized mud tires. Having no doubt driven luxury cars from all over the world, this kid was pumped to climb into a stick-shift Tacoma.

With a backpack-full of luggage for our one-night stay, we entered the lobby. I approached the escalator with apprehension — it had been a while; I'd changed. I paused to determine my best course of action. *OK, here we are. Put your left hand on the railing. But it's moving! Put both hands on the railings, and be quick. Get both arms up and ready, take a step forward, and hold on with both hands. OK, go!* I stepped on in my calculated manner, rode to the top, and shuffled off as best I could. *Going down will be different.*

Dad and I didn't take trips together. In the six years since I'd stopped working at the family restaurant, we'd grown further apart. I'm not sure he could handle my diagnosis. He couldn't take that there was nothing he could do. Mom had stood by my side every step of the way; she'd have done more if I'd let her. She'd always been a rock, undertaking the most difficult tasks and dragging us along. She was the mom; she was responsible. But sometimes, it broke her. Migraines were her price to pay.

Dad and I were not about to sit in our room and focus on the potentially life-altering task the next day. We seemed to be pretending we were just another father and son out on the town. We were on a quest for distraction, making a memory while we could.

We set down our things and left to walk the streets. Dad went to college in Boston and — though his intentions went mostly unspoken — was no doubt looking forward to retracing some steps. Primarily, he wanted to take me to Cheers.

I've heard it a hundred times: the supposed site of Cheers, from the exterior shots in the long-running sitcom, was actually the Bull & Finch, the only bar he drank at in college. (He attended Graham Junior College in Kenmore Square. In the mid-'70s, the legal drinking age was eighteen.) It was only about a half-mile away — a pleasant stroll of posh shops, bay windows, and brick facade called Charles Street. Across the street from the Boston Common, we glimpsed the iconic sign and staircase to the basement bar.

The current establishment is a nostalgia-soaked tourist trap, as I imagine any television-show-themed restaurant would have to be. The menu lists items like the Giant Norm Burger and Ma Clavin's Soups. It was nearly empty in the late afternoon as we sat down for a beer.

"So, what brings you to Boston?" the waiter asked.

"I have an appointment at Mass General for a second opinion."

"Nothing too serious, I hope."

"It is," I said, eyes on the floor.

It didn't take long for my (former pizza shop owner and food-obsessed) dad to start asking about pizza. He told them he knew all the usual spots and was looking for something new. After a brief description of mob movies and David Ortiz (he told us the Red Sox star was a regular there), we were in a cab to East Boston.

"Where ya headed?"

"Santarpio's in East Boston."

The cabbie started on his route and asked the routine questions: Where are you from? What are you doing in Boston? We asked him about his medallion, the taxicab license that cost big money, and in the days before rideshare, meant big money. Then he got right to the point.

"So why ya wanna go to Santarpio's? Place is a dump. Why not go someplace nice?"

"I asked about pizza, and the kid at Cheers told us about it. I've been to Regina, some of the other famous places — I wanted something different."

He continued to bash our destination, which only piqued our interest in the "hole-in-the-wall."

We came to a stop on a corner across from a highway overpass. A man sat smoking a cigarette on the stoop, using a #10 can of Stanislaus 7/11 — Ground Tomatoes for the ash. I'd opened many just like it in the back room of Dave's. The building certainly looked like the seedy establishment we'd been described. Dad pulled open the glass door, and we grabbed two seats at the long bar to the right.

The place was dark, dingy, and nearly empty. It looked unchanged from about the '70s. This was the kind of place the guys from *Goodfellas* might meet because no one would ask questions. (I could see Ray Liotta and Joe Pesci at a booth in the back, talking quietly, then one of them exploding with rage.) There was a brick oven at the front of the building behind the bar and an open door to the back kitchen at the far end of the room.

There was no beer on tap and only a few bottles. We asked for a couple of Buds. Through the open door at the back, there was a guy with a knife and a huge piece of meat. He wore a white apron, covered in blood, and was hacking pieces from what looked like a whole leg of lamb.

We ordered a couple of pizzas, and though they didn't seem to be on the menu, some of the meat skewers we saw cooking on the fire. The old guy behind the bar, without so much as a word, walked over to attend to the grilling meat. He put two on a plate for us to share. We each took a piece in our fingers, and with a bite, immediately nodded our approval.

The pizza was great, really. I'm not going to pretend I'm a food critic — after three or four beers, nearly anything would've hit the spot — but it was most excellent. We polished off two of the smallish, one-size-only pies, paid the bill, and generously voiced our appreciation.

After a full-bellied, slightly nauseous cab ride, Dad wanted to stop at the lobby bar. I approached the escalator — drowsy and afraid of a fall — repeated my self-made instructions and stepped on. The step off at the top nearly threw me, but after a few uneven steps, I regained my balance.

As I sipped from a glass of Knob Creek at a perfectly crafted, overtly pretentious bar, I thought of our night. *We must be the only people in the world to go from Santarpio's, with their domestic beer and $3 table wine, to this, a bar with a list of rare spirits and a dozen brands of champagne.* (In 2020, their menu lists 1 ½ ounces of Remy Martin Louis VIII for $360.)

We had an early breakfast at the hotel in the morning and walked to Mass General to see the doctor. He met us in his office and talked from behind an oversized wooden desk.

"So, you came down from Vermont? How's the snow?"

He told us he liked to ski at Stowe — cross-country, he corrected me.

There were no tests, no questions, nothing. Dad asked a few questions, and we were given the standard, hopeless answers. I had but one thought: *Why are we here?*

He talked to us the same way I'd been hearing for months. He repeated all of the things I knew but didn't want to. He could've done the same with a phone call. *I don't know why you came down here* is the most honest thing he could have said. He spoke as if we'd accepted my fate, like we'd made the trip without any hope at all.

Deflated and numb, we drove home in silence.

UNQUESTIONABLE

No one I've seen in more than ten years has ever questioned my diagnosis. It always seems like the thought has never crossed anyone's mind. There is no cause to point to, just a series of effects. I've never quite been able to wrap my head around that particularly thorny reality.

With each visit, I ask questions and bring up ideas, trying at least to evoke a response. They stare at me with blank faces, seemingly unwilling to weigh in. I ask about a symptom I've experienced, looking for insight or reassurance, and they return nothing. It's almost like they're not listening, like I could say anything, and they'd hold up a sign: You Have ALS.

Everything after the diagnosis — every visit to the clinic, every conversation, every measurement and appraisal — seems like a monumental and tragic waste of time. I can't find any possible use for a neurologist. Other than diagnosing people, I don't even know what they do.

I'm just so tired of the official, know-nothing response. I wish someone would suggest something — even to try, even if it didn't work — to give me something to do, if not to evoke the slimmest of hopes. Tell me to cut out alcohol, or gulp down green tea, load up on potassium, or only eat steak. Tell me to hang upside-down, sit in an ice bath, try acupuncture or massage. Tell me to eat a big bowl of dog shit at mealtimes. Tell me it would help, and I'd do it. Please just tell me something. I leave every appointment with the same set of thoughts: *I know more about me.*

10.

I was a no-show at my appointment in May; I didn't return until the following February. I attended three clinic days in 2013, three in 2014, and two in 2015. Every new visit was more of the same.

They started asking about my driving; they wanted to set up some kind of test. They told me they could help make driving easier for me. I couldn't begin to believe that; I knew what this was about. *You want to take away my license, so you're not liable if I cause an accident.* I told them what I believed to be the truth: my driving was fine. "I'm probably not the best driver on the road, but I'm far from the worst." Mom, who drove with me often, confirmed.

We talked about the car I drove; they were stunned when I told them it had a manual transmission. Wasn't there something else I could drive? That's my car, I told them. Some of the staff kidded me. "I heard you're still driving a stick," and "I can't even drive a manual," they said. Some of them told me they'd rather not know.

Though clearly feeling a responsibility to keep other drivers and me safe, they never forced the issue. I wasn't about to voluntarily spend more time at the hospital, even if it was in the parking lot. Any chance of losing my license kept me from giving in.

After several years of successfully avoiding the issue, I learned that to get a handicapped placard, I had to take a driver's test. I was afraid I'd make a mistake, or the instructor would see through my fraudulent workarounds. *What if my legs start shaking on the pedals?*

I was nervous I'd trip and fall on the way to the car. I was afraid I'd take too long to grab my seatbelt, or he'd see me prop my hand on my knee to align the key with the ignition. I was fearful that although I could handle the wheel, he'd see the weakness in my shoulders and deem me unfit.

He put me through a typical license test. We did a hill-start, a three-point turn, and I parallel parked. I remembered my first road test when I was sixteen. The instructor was stern and seemed to look for reasons to fail me. This guy, who barely fit in the front seat of my Subaru, was pleasant and casual, chatting with me as I drove.

I felt comfortable behind the wheel. For a long time, I'd been more confident in the driver's seat than anywhere on foot. When we'd come to a stop, the instructor had but one comment: during the hill-start, with the parking brake engaged, I hadn't let my foot off the brake. Yes, I thought, that was by design. I wasn't sure I'd pulled the brake hard enough; I didn't want to start rolling backward. Had I pulled harder, I might not have had the strength to release it.

I passed with flying carpets (an ode to the Canadian mock-umentary series, *Trailer Park Boys*). The instructor didn't see any reason why I shouldn't be driving. I don't know if he knew of my diagnosis, but he told us, in his opinion, I shouldn't have had to come in.

11.

I never embraced the ALS community. I never attended any support groups or met a lot of fellow sufferers. I didn't see myself as one of them because I wasn't. More than two years after my diagnosis, I walked the 5K ALS Walk. How could I possibly identify with an unmoving old man in a wheelchair?

I didn't spend a lot of time comparing my findings to others. You hear cancer patients talk about their numbers — the size and number of their tumors — like scientists, like experts. There's a community among them; they share experiences, support, and learn from one another. They quickly become students of their disease and strive to use their knowledge to improve outcomes around them. I never felt that way about ALS. My long list of observations never seemed to raise a critical eyebrow. There simply isn't the knowledge to derive any meaningful purpose from even the ideal information. There are very few objectives to latch onto.

In the waiting room at one of those early clinics, I met someone who could've given me a glimpse into the future, but I didn't see it. He was in his mid-thirties, married, with a couple of kids, and worked for a local beverage distributor. He'd been diagnosed after me.

I watched as he stepped through the hallway to the desk, carefully planting each foot before moving the next one. Standing still to greet me, he looked awkward, uncomfortable, like he was propped up in position. He spoke with some difficulty, through a heavy slur — sometimes I couldn't understand.

The staff was concerned about some falls he'd taken. He'd smacked his head more than once, his face visibly damaged. It was clear to anyone who'd put eyes on him more than a few seconds: he shouldn't be walking. It seemed that for at least a little while longer, he was determined to keep his feet under him.

His wife was standing there next to him, spewing negativity. She was almost belligerent, stomping around with her face scrunched up like a three-year-old's. Seeing all that her husband was going through, it seemed she grew angry at the world. With every word out of her mouth, I scowled in disgust from the waiting room. Still, despite her insufferable attitude, I couldn't help but think: *At least he's married; at least he has kids.*

I saw him again a few months later. While I still drove to these appointments, he sat slumped in a motorized wheelchair. This time, he was accompanied by an aide, his wife nowhere to be found. We said hello, and he spoke, but his aide had to interpret; we couldn't understand him at all.

After a short interaction, we went our separate ways, and even sitting in my cell in the ALS clinic, I put him out of my mind. I was strong and independent; I could never be like him.

CHAPTER 3

PRETENDING ALL DAY

I have a closet full of shirts and ties.
I used to get to wear them.

1.

During my senior year, I went to a meet and greet with National Life Group on the UVM campus. When it was time for the event to begin, I sat alone with three suits and a humorously large stack of pizzas. "So, you want a job?" they joked.

Part of me thought they were serious, like they'd hire me on the spot or set up an interview. But that didn't happen, and a month or so later, I saw them at a job fair at the Sheraton. (Had I not *worked* at the Sheraton, I'd never have been there.) This time, I was to be sure: *Tell them you want a job; get an interview; don't leave without something in place.*

I hung around their booth, making small talk like a high-schooler waiting for an invite to the big party. *If they're here to hire someone, then why are they giggling and tiptoeing around?* Eventually, I outlasted the tension — they took my information and promised to contact me for an interview.

In my third-floor bedroom of our three-bedroom, town-house-style downtown apartment, in view of the spinning Nectar's sign two blocks north, I dressed in a new shirt, tie, suit, and shoes my parents had recently bought for this purpose. Past the dust bunnies in the hallway and coffee table of empty Busch Light cans, across the porch to the back lot, I made my way to the car. I drove to Montpelier in my seventeen-year-old Audi, which I'd recently found the money to bring back to life.

I'd never worked in an office. I felt intimidated by my surroundings: the building itself, its marble and granite lobby, the unnatural quiet, and the unknown "professional" people. Sitting in a chair in the corner wearing my brand-new suit, waiting for my interviewer to arrive, I felt out of place.

I was living the college life in almost every way: getting shamelessly stoned in the living room and stumbling home from the bars at three in the morning. But also studying, going to class, and working part-time to buy food and pay the rent. It all seemed pretty far from a stuffy nine to five.

I spent high school and college working in restaurants. In the ultracasual, fast-paced, youthful environment, I fit. Those jobs were always temporary and replaceable, and in that way, stress-free. I never felt like I wasn't good enough.

This felt like the opposite. I didn't know this world or its older, seemingly more serious people. I was afraid of learning a new language. And besides, clean-shaven and twenty-two, I didn't look much more than sixteen. But this wasn't the prom.

And that's how my interview went. Despite everything I knew about myself in both workplace and academic environments, I didn't have a single ounce of confidence in that setting. They hired me anyway. I guess they needed a warm body.

A short time later, I found myself working two days a week, scheduled to go full-time after graduation. A little over three years later, I'd had two promotions and was interviewing for my fourth position at the company. At the same time, midway through 2010, I was beginning to confront a new — unknown and unnamed — reality that was picking up ground in my head.

As part of my interview for the Compliance Associate position, I had to give a presentation. Before two of my would-be bosses, a would-be coworker, and an HR rep, I taught a PowerPoint lesson. I stood before them full of caffeine-enhanced nervous energy, but it was more than that. Though I'm sure no one noticed, my body was shivering and shaking. I felt confident in my head, but my body seemed terrified beyond reason. I did my best to ignore it, but I was covered in sweat by the end. Despite the extra obstacles my body had created, I got the job.

2.

One of the responsibilities of my new job in Compliance was to travel to the company's branches in every corner of the country. With my first doctor's visit rapidly approaching, I departed on my first solo audit trip. I'd called the offices, booked the flights and hotels, and done all my prep work. It was April of 2011; I was thoroughly convinced that something was wrong, but in silence, I plowed on ahead. Nothing else even occurred to me.

I flew to Harrisburg, Pennsylvania, via Philadelphia in seat 1A of a tiny commuter plane, rented a car, and checked into my hotel. On Monday morning, I ate the continental breakfast, got into my "midsize" Chevy Malibu, and plugged the office address into the TomTom (a pre-smartphone touchscreen GPS device) Mom had lent me for the trip. Full of nervous energy and hotel room coffee, I parked the car alongside a curb and retrieved my laptop bag from the back seat. I paused by the car for a minute, feeling the heavy bag on my shoulder, stretching my legs and collecting my confidence. With cold hands and sweaty feet — an unintended hitch in my step — I walked deliberately to the front door of what could've been a dental office.

I approached the receptionist and introduced myself. She looked at me, stunned; she had no idea I was coming. Though I'd made plans with the regional office, no one had told her or anyone here. And besides her, no one, in fact, *was* here.

She got on the phone with one of the sales reps, set me up in the conference room, and began to pull the paperwork I requested. I sat at the table with my suit jacket on, shivering. With uncooperative, freezing-cold hands that felt like bricks at the ends of my arms, I fumbled my way through the files. I couldn't thumb through the pages; I kept licking my fingers to try to get a grip. *This is so much more difficult than it should be.* I wondered whether the room was actually cold; the receptionist was wearing short sleeves. *I never used to be cold.*

I drove to Ocean City, Maryland, in the afternoon, arrived with the sun going down, and aimed straight for the hotel restaurant to find a much-needed meal. I'd had a long day, to be sure — a restless night of sleep, a tense, uneasy day in the office, and more than four hours in the car — but I was unusually worn out. In my twenty-six years, I'm not sure I'd felt so exhausted.

I sat at the bar, took ten seconds to look over the menu, and ordered the pizza. They were out. In fact, the barman informed me, they were out of a number of items. Like a runaway twelve-year-old, I ate chicken fingers and French fries and washed it all down in a gloriously satisfying manner with a couple of Budweiser bottles.

I was on the road south the next afternoon, crossing the venerable Chesapeake Bay Bridge-Tunnel on my way to Virginia Beach. I checked into a room with a sliding glass door and balcony right on the beach. I changed into my jeans and went out to explore.

I walked a long way, past countless identical hotels, casually looking for dinner. Every step in the sand felt unnatural and wrong. There was no fluidity in my gait; every move forward felt forced. *I can't even enjoy a walk on the beach; I can't even pretend to be fine. It's real — I can feel it.* I pushed down my fears and tried to refocus. *There's nothing you can do; go find some dinner.*

I visited one of the company's oldest sales reps (he was eighty-seven, if memory serves) at his three-story beach house in the morning. The sun was already blazing as my host greeted me in the driveway. "Take that jacket off," he assured me as he invited me in.

His office was on the first level, a dark room just inside the door. As noontime approached, he told me his wife would make lunch and laid out a few options to choose from. Knowing you're on the road alone, a lot of folks (not everyone, certainly not everyone) offer arrangements for lunch. Being a guest in his house, feeding me lunch was just part of the deal — in his mind. After an elevator ride to the third floor, we ate chicken salad sandwiches with ice-filled glasses of ginger ale and chips at the dining room table.

My last stop for the week was a small town somewhere up the James River. It was one of those places where everything seemed stuck in a time warp. Gas was cheap, and everyone still smoked — it was Mayberry.

My computer bag dug uncomfortably into my shoulder as I accompanied a thin, kindly gentleman in his fifties through the hall to his office. "Look out, everyone! The cops are here!" he joked. I was the cop.

I felt so out of place, not only because I was literally a stranger to these people, but I felt something more. I felt even further removed, like we weren't even the same species. I felt like I was only pretending to be the person they saw. I was becoming a stranger to myself.

Late in the afternoon, I dropped off my rental car and went through security at a nearly empty Newport News International. I changed out of my suit in the bathroom. After the obligatory stop in Newark, I arrived in Burlington and walked home to 6 Patrick.

I'd made it through all the handshakes and small talk, successfully disregarded all of my festering problems and completed my work. I was paid to fly on planes, eat in restaurants, and sleep in hotels. If only I could've enjoyed it.

3.

The Link (the glass-encased link between National Life's main building, built in the '50s, and its smaller sibling, built in the '70s), home to the licensing and compliance departments, was a weird place. Operations — where I'd worked for more than three years — was a big, low-cubicle, open space full of noise. There were always so many conversations and extraneous noises filling the room that it was rare to pick up one voice. Everything seemed to combine to form a lively white noise, like working inside a beehive.

The Link was dead by comparison. In a small space with less than ten desks, it was impossible to block out your neighbor's phone call. The pace was more deliberate, the atmosphere more serene. Calls weren't constantly pouring in; there was no assembly line in effect; movement was minimal.

I spent my first days learning from Hank. He'd been hired about two years before, in the same role that I'd be stepping into. Hank's was a legal mind (quite literally, he had a law degree) with wide-ranging interests. He was a kind and steady teacher; confident and calming, he was a rock. He didn't show me — wasn't interested in — only the what, but the why. I liked him right away.

We spent a great deal of time talking to each other's reflections in the window between our desks. We always seemed to be discussing something — from a mundane procedure to a broad legal topic to opinions on anything that popped into our heads — in the midst of our work. We bounced ideas back and forth between our cubicles, listening as much as we talked.

I never felt the need to filter my thoughts with Hank. He was never critical but always looking to guide and support me like a brother. He always seemed sincere — both of us did — like anything less wouldn't be worth the words.

I was sitting in the cafeteria by myself on a Thursday, killing a few minutes with a book after I'd eaten. Hank came through for an afternoon coffee, wandered over, and joined me. It was the only time he ever stopped by, and on the day after my diagnosis, I was done keeping secrets.

I didn't *decide* to do it, but in the empty cafeteria a few minutes before two, it just happened. I'd been keeping my ever-growing symptoms and numerous doctors' visits from everyone besides my boss. I hadn't been able to tell anyone; only my parents knew the truth.

I broke down at the table, sobbing and sniffling and sweating uncontrollably. Like I might've expected, his demeanor remained steady as he listened. I must've looked like the patient and he the psychiatrist. Thinking I might want some privacy, he asked if I wanted to take our conversation to one of the tables outside. I was in my own world; I didn't care about the eyeballs he sensed. When the surge of emotion had subsided, I wiped the tears from my face, the snot from my nose, and together — like it was any other day — we walked to our desks on the fourth floor.

BUSY HANDS ARE HAPPY HANDS

People say busy hands are happy hands; we always seem to be on a quest for distraction. There are so many things I never gave any thought because I didn't have to; I kept myself distracted. So many of the big thoughts — on my life and the broader world — went not only unanswered but unconsidered.

Maybe it's part of getting older to see inward and outward and past your own nose. Maybe it means I've gotten stronger. Maybe I should count myself lucky.

But escaping's more difficult these days. I spend time in thought — examining the world from all sorts of new angles — because I've lost so many forms of distraction. My body can't help me in the way that it used to.

I can't help but wonder how much of my time, how much of my *life* was spent in distraction. I'm not sure I needed to escape; maybe I just wanted to escape. Maybe I was taking the easy way out, ignoring my problems when I should've been facing them. Maybe all those distractions, masquerading as life's simple joys, were only a mask for my weaknesses.

I know what I've lost, but I also see what I've gained. I never saw the world so clearly. I don't have the distractions, and yet I feel stronger. I've learned to live honestly and not be afraid. It's easy to see that all of my fears were so trivial. In some sort of oxymoronic, astonishing manner, my self-esteem seems to have improved over the years. In more ways than ever, I finally feel like a confident man. If only I could live the life I'm no longer afraid of.

4.

In the spring of 2009, when I was playing evening rounds of golf accompanied only by my iPod, my buddies were home studying. They'd been talking for months about the Chartered Financial Analyst ("CFA") exams. I'd mostly ignored them. In my first eighteen months at the broker/dealer, I studied for and passed the Series 7, 24, and 53 licensing exams. In my first months out of college, while my roommates drank beer at the beach after work, I sat at the kitchen table and attempted to stare into a three-ring binder of unparalleled boredom. For the time being, I was done taking tests.

But I felt like I'd be left behind. I signed myself up for the Level 1 test in December. I paid the fee, ordered the books, and in whatever free time I could find, sat alone in my kitchen and stared down at a series of books.

The CFA designation is achieved, besides factors like industry experience, by passing a series of three successive exams. The first is given two days per year, in December and June, while the second and third are offered on a single day in June.

Each test runs from 9-noon, and 2-5, for a total of six sitting hours. The pass rates vary from year to year but usually fall between 40 and 50 percent. In 2010, for example, the Level 1 was passed by 42 percent of participants; the Level 2 by 39 percent, all of whom had passed the Level 1; and the Level 3 by 46 percent, all of whom had passed the first two exams. Some portion of each group is on their second (or third, or more) attempt. They're not easy exams.

I passed the Level 1 in December to catch up with my friends, and by February was right back to work. My job at the time (in Operations, before I moved on to The Link) mostly consisted of reviewing paperwork. It was almost impossible to sit down and study at the end of my day. Instead, I tried to get it done before I left for the office.

I'd set my alarm for around four and, with every ounce of willpower I could muster, get myself out of bed. For an unknowable number of hours, with head down and coffee in hand, I sat at the kitchen booth at 6 Patrick. By the time June arrived, I was thoroughly burned out. I was begging for the finish line with little regard for the result.

We took the Friday before the Saturday test off from work, ostensibly to study, but spent the day on the golf course — some much-needed leisure for overworked minds. Two of the three of us failed the Level 2 in June 2010. I wasn't the lucky one.

Everything started back up the next winter, with a twist. Despite my best efforts, my focus was gradually getting diverted. The signs were getting stronger; this (unnamed) thing wasn't going away.

Thanks to a mind well-versed in avoidance, I put my problems aside and once again tried to focus on another finish line in June. A month after my first doctor's visit, I sat for the Level 2 a second time in June 2011. I held tight to the railing as I climbed the uncommonly steep stairs in the main building of the aptly named College of Fine Arts (CFA) in Montpelier. I sat at the desk with my near-empty coffee mug, both sweating and shivering. Simply filling the answer sheet bubbles took patience and skill; the muscle memory in my fingers had all but disappeared. While all of my focus should have been on the question at hand, I was constantly fighting distraction.

I couldn't enjoy the cocktail afterward. It should've felt like a coronation, a collective relief with my CFA comrades, but it didn't. The three of us sat at a table in the old-school, carpeted, dimly lit J. Morgan's Steakhouse. In place of the Pabst Blue Ribbon "tall boys" we usually sucked down, we ordered martinis and Manhattans. In a different age, we would've been smoking cigars.

We'd golfed and skied and drank and carpooled to work since our college days ended. But I felt alone at the table. I was afraid of my drink and what it would do to me, afraid of my friends and what they might think, and afraid that I'd trip on the walk to the door. I could no longer just be myself; I felt like I couldn't enjoy anything. I held up my glass and laughed with my friends, but I only wanted to go home and hide.

In August, I found out I had passed. I received my three-letter label before the end of the month. I didn't have to decide what to do; I couldn't sit for the Level 3 until June.

I was still working full-time when the time came to study again. I hadn't told my news to the world or my CFA buddies. I wasn't ready to give up; I tried to plow ahead.

I filled notebooks with ink at the desk in my new Waterbury apartment. Unlike the bubbles of the first two, the Level 3 was half essay. My will to study, to work, and to do anything was waning a bit more with each passing day. More questions (excuses) weighed on my mind: *Could I even write well enough for the test? Couldn't I ask for help? They must offer help. Why am I even doing this? Do I even care?* At some point, as the test day became closer, I began to give up. I couldn't concentrate my efforts like I needed. I took a practice test or two and realized I wasn't nearly ready. A thought came into my head: *I don't have to do this.* I was more than prepared to let myself off the hook.

I didn't make it to Montpelier that first Saturday in June. I didn't have it in me. I just couldn't make myself care.

MONEY AND JEALOUSY

I used to carpool to work. Three of the four of us had sat in the same classrooms, completed the same major, and been hired by different departments of the same company. Though not on the same path exactly, we were in the same ballpark.

In those early years out of college, I felt like I was miles ahead. While many of my friends were still figuring it out, I wasn't stuck in college or somewhere in between. I had started a real career. I could actually afford to buy a few things, like a new TV and a car. I didn't have to count up the dollars at the grocery store. It was a whole new world.

I can't help but feel jealous when I see them all now. My carpool buddies have master's degrees, on top of the CFA after their names. Nearly everyone around me has found success in new or continued careers, purchased new cars, traveled the world, and bought first — and in some cases second — houses. I still think of us in basement apartments, living with roommates, just trying to find life's direction. It's heart-wrenching to admit that they've grown up without me.

Sometimes I wonder if I could've done it — finished the CFA program after my diagnosis made everything feel hopeless and impossible. I would've liked to have realized that accomplishment, to see the end of three years of toil. But I'm not sure I could've enjoyed it. Nothing could ever seem so important as it used to.

I'm not really jealous of the money. I've known for a long time that money doesn't matter. I'd gladly give it away, work a dead-end job, lose the security and struggle every day, all for a chance to be normal. But I can't help but look at all of the possibilities and know it could've been me.

When I stopped working, a few people joked (I hope they were joking) that they were jealous. Like an early retirement, they saw an end to the unwavering drudgery that dominated their lives. They may have been jokes, but the implication struck me: I was lucky.

I *am* lucky in one sense: at the time of my diagnosis, I was covered by an employer-sponsored disability policy. Had I worked in a kitchen or waiting tables someplace, I would've been out a sizable chunk of income each month. Nevertheless, I was thoroughly bitter at the thoughtlessly ignorant notion that I was in any way fortunate.

I have three sources of income: Social Security Disability, private disability insurance, and part-time work. There are limits on working while receiving disability, and my private disability payments are decreased by a portion of my earned income. But together with my penny-pinching lifestyle, my income has been enough for me to get by on my own.

But I don't want to simply get by. My career and the financial rewards it could've delivered have been yet another casualty of the war. It's impossible to know where I'd be in any aspect of life, but if I had confidence in anything, it'd be in my career. I truly can't picture myself with any of the things I may already have obtained: a fat 401(k) and bank account, posh living quarters, foreign travels, and a glorious but understated ride. If only I'd been allowed to grow up.

5.

A stark line was drawn in the sand on that morning at the hospital. Somehow, both everything and nothing changed in an instant. My life before and after would forever be separate, but I couldn't help thinking that nothing had changed. My physical body didn't change overnight; all that was new was my knowledge. There was no new problem; they'd just named it. But while that was certainly true, it was the knowledge that made all the difference.

Making myself go to work became more of a chore with each passing day. Though my new commute from Waterbury was a breezy fifteen minutes, I was showing up later than ever. I never seemed to have any energy; every morning routine felt like a slog through the mud. Just arriving at my desk felt like an accomplishment.

Hank's long-anticipated departure left the neighboring desk empty. I was feeling empty as well. I plopped down each morning like a pouty child who'd been dragged to Sunday morning Mass. I sat at my desk, finishing my coffee, open all my programs, read my email, and listen to my voice mail — anything to avoid human contact for as long as I could.

The girls at the next desk began to notice a slur in my speech early in the morning; even my tongue couldn't wake up. My feet were on fire in my shoes; I started taking them off under the desk. I'd hide in my cubicle in my socks, drinking hot coffee in a cold sweat. I couldn't imagine *not* drinking coffee. It was part of my routine from the day I was hired, but I started to begrudgingly admit that caffeine only made everything worse.

Every so often, I'd have to sign something on letterhead with fresh ink. I'd print the letter, walk to the printer, bring it back to my desk, sit down, and attempt to make a satisfactory signature. I used to sign dozens of documents each day (all without effort and on the first try!), but now I struggled to form a passable mark. I'd print the same letter multiple times, wear a path to the printer, and try to get it right.

My typing deficiencies were starting to show. I'd be working on something with a colleague and feel myself under the microscope, fumbling around on the keyboard. It wasn't enough to hinder my work in any meaningful way, but I couldn't help but feel fearful and embarrassed. I was always afraid that someone would ask why.

Seemingly overnight, a bunch of my symptoms grew stronger. Each time I got up from my desk, I found myself meandering down the aisle like a drunk. My every move needed constant attention only to avoid bumping into the cubicles. Simply walking to the bathroom became an adventure.

Every time someone approached from behind, I jumped three feet in the air. I'd be making a copy, and someone would throw me a chipper "Hey Nate" as they entered the room. I'd react like they'd snuck up and grabbed me, like they'd jumped out of the wall with a knife. It happened all the time; I couldn't help it.

It took me a long time to realize it wasn't just the ALS. I was on medication for the first time in my life. It was hard to know where my ALS symptoms ended, and the drugs began; it all became muddled in my mind. I was another step removed from my old self.

LAUGHING AND CRYING

Do you laugh or cry inappropriately? Do you have trouble controlling your emotions? Do you find yourself prone to excessive outbursts of laughter in social situations? I was asked all of these questions early on.

From the beginning, the answers were obvious: yes, I do.

I get choked up more easily than most, but the impact is minimal. We don't normally engage in sob-inducing conversations on a regular basis. My avoidance of tears only makes me appear normal.

I've always liked to laugh, and I think, laughed pretty easily. So many of my memories, from growing up in the neighborhood through college and beyond, still bring a chuckle to my mind. A lot of the people I chose to spend time with were, at their core, goofballs. Time spent among friends — whether in the backyard, at baseball practice, in college, at social gatherings, or even at work — always brought out an endless array of effortless comedy.

I knew this was something different altogether. As with everything else, I don't remember when it started; it was gradual, imperceptible at first. My friends might remember — one day, I was laughing a little harder.

It's mostly an exaggeration of what's already there. There's always something that tickles me, from the outside world or deep in my mind, and I get fixated on the most minor of notions. Sometimes, I rather enjoy it.

Countless times since my symptoms began, I've been sitting around a table with friends, barely able to sneak a gulp from my beer, continually incapacitated by laughter. On one occasion, freshly stoned and watching a Red Sox game on TV, my laughter at my roommate's nicknames for the players (only Carl Crawdad comes to mind, for Boston outfielder Carl Crawford) was so maniacally uncontrollable, it started to hurt. We were high and it was funny, but I must've seemed insane.

I hear of comedians finding humor in all the wrong places. They laugh to themselves — at the dark, or the distasteful, the insignificant thoughts that continually run through their heads. They see the humor in everything. That's how I feel. That's how I've always felt. Only now, any control, any filter I possessed, has all but disappeared.

There was one time at work (there was more than one time, but this comes to mind) that my laughter got the best of me. In front of a room full of people, I was having a discussion with a longtime colleague. Or should I say she was having a discussion with me? She was describing and reiterating the written procedure for whatever it was that had her a-frazzle. Unable to muster anything but nonchalance, I flatly told her that it wasn't happening. She was always a very letter-of-the-law type; I'm more of a spirit-of-the-rule guy. I see the world in shades of gray and use logic as my guide. That is to say, I am smarter/better/more sophisticated — choose your adjective. Had we interacted more, our differences would've been a problem.

I, and seemingly everyone around me, could see her blood pressure rising as her volume led the way. Though she wasn't my boss, and in fact, worked in a different department, it looked like she was dressing me down in front of the group. I don't know if it was her predictable overreaction to what I considered the most insignificant of details, but I was tickled. Standing three feet in front of her, I reacted to her red-faced anger with an unimpeachable smile and muted giggles. I wonder what would've happened had I let loose entirely — laughed in her face and walked away.

6.

Though it was becoming more deliberate by the day, I was still taking the stairs on my daily trips to the cafeteria. I always hated the small talk and awkward silence machine — the elevator. I stopped carrying my wallet and brought only my debit card; I'd grown tired of fumbling around at the register. I always held my plate with two hands — my thumb and wrist were too weak to confidently support it with one.

One day, a few minutes after one, I was walking through the lobby. I moved purposefully through a near-empty room — after most of the building had finished lunch and before the time for afternoon coffee. I was approaching the cafeteria's entryway, its heavy glass doors pulled open against each wall. Passing by the security desk to my left, the trays and silverware in sight, my foot caught the floor, flinging me forward. *Oh, shit!* I tumbled to the floor and my right shoulder slammed against the mammoth door. It rang like a gong.

Shocked and embarrassed, I scrambled to my feet. Feeling the eyes from my left, I stared straight ahead as if nothing had happened. *You're fine. You're back up, and you're fine. Nobody's coming over to help; just keep moving.* I grabbed a tray off the stack and kept moving. No one in the cafeteria would have to know.

I wondered whether that security guard, in his decades behind the desk, had ever seen anything like that. And if anyone else had seen what had happened. I'd tripped like that before, on sidewalks and living room carpets, but mostly alone. I arrived back at my desk with sandwich in hand. It was just another secret to add to my brain.

7.

In the summer and fall of 2011 — with little regard for the life-changing news in between — I continued to go out on the road. At the same time that I was visiting doctors, answering questions, and undergoing tests, I was also flying to new cities, meeting new people, conducting audits, and giving presentations. It was part of the job I still had.

I flew to Cincinnati and drove a yellow Ford Fiesta to Indianapolis. I bought a ticket to see the Yankees play the Reds, but the game was canceled for a thunderstorm that never came. I went to Cleveland and Kansas City without a license. I'd put off its renewal until the day before I left. The Department of Motor Vehicles wasn't open on Bennington Battle Day. I drove to Albany and Syracuse and Rochester, booked a flight back to Burlington but was stranded in Newark. I rented a car around midnight and finally arrived home around seven a.m.

I flew to the West Coast in March of 2012, more than six months after that Wednesday morning at the hospital. My enthusiasm — truly my ability to function and keep going at all — had already faded beyond anything I could've imagined just five years into my career. I hadn't yet allowed myself to consider quitting; I didn't know what else I'd do. I spent most of my time on autopilot.

I shook hands with the head of the agency in Bothell (suburban Seattle) and tried to pretend it was normal. My index finger wouldn't straighten; it was curled up as I extended my arm. It made for a horrible handshake, like I was trying to tickle his palm with my finger. I was embarrassed to consider what he was thinking as we parted. I had scheduled two days in the office, but after a short day in a newly opened branch — where I was stuck in the corner and ignored — I was on the road to Portland the next morning.

I pulled into the tiny lot of the two-story motel-style Jupiter Hotel in the early afternoon. By the time I worked through my ever-growing malaise, it was about all I could book at the last minute. Hipster-modern might be an apt description — Portland all the way, for sure. The mattress was two feet off the floor on a wooden platform that stuck out a foot too far in every direction — just asking to bloody your shins. Over a desk on the wall was a small flat-screen that seemed like an afterthought. On a bedside table, in a dish like they were complimentary chocolates, were two condoms — one yellow, one blue.

Portland is (and was) a great beer city, and thanks to my fortuitous day off, I was going to see for myself. I spent a few minutes on my laptop, jotted down four locations on a scrap of paper, and because I didn't have a GPS-capable phone, grabbed my TomTom from the car. In jeans and a hoodie on an overcast afternoon, I walked out of my room with nothing and everything on my mind.

I walked all over the city that day, visited four breweries, stopped into Powell's City of Books, and ate three (smallish) meals. Having all but given up shaving over the winter, I was sporting a gnarly beard. As I would discover, in Portland, Oregon, home of the beard-ed white twentysomethings, I couldn't have looked more like a local.

The highlight was a visit to the Deschutes Brewery's Portland Public House. I sat at the bar and, seeing the long line of taps, asked about a sampler. Without so much as a word, the bartender produced an order sheet and pencil. Carefully examining the list of more than twenty-five beers, I began to mark the eight I'd try.

The NCAA Men's Basketball Tournament was underway, and as I sat down, I glimpsed the TV behind the bar. Two announcers were talking during a break in the action. When next I looked up from my homework, the game was back on. It was Vermont!

Having been one of the last teams to qualify — that is, they barely got in — UVM was in one of the First Four (a play-in game to get into the sixty-four-team tournament) games in Dayton, Ohio. As I started on my tasting schedule at this, my second bar of the afternoon, I couldn't believe my luck. The game against Lamar University was still in the first half.

I had two rounds of samples, a flatbread pizza, and at least one pint glass of water while mostly staring up at the game. By the time it had finished, every once-empty seat in the place had been filled. Feeling bloated and tipsy after drinking a few ounces of nearly every beer in the building, happy to have witnessed a UVM win, I walked out in search of my next destination.

Wandering the streets in the dark, I headed back to the bridge, repeatedly stopping to turn and gaze at the neon sign hanging high over the river. I'd found a (temporary) escape in those moments. I stood there in simplicity, staring mesmerized like a child at a fireworks show. The White Stag sign, for forty years a banner for White Stag Sportswear, was first illuminated in 1940. It was acquired by the city, and the lettering changed to the now-iconic "Portland, Oregon" in 2010.

It started raining, the light misting rain of the Pacific Northwest. Lifting my cotton hood onto my head, I found my way to my last stop. Still early in the night, I pulled open the door to Burnside Brewing, two blocks from the Jupiter Hotel.

I sat at a booth in a dark restaurant and ordered some sort of romaine wedge and another ill-advised sampler of beers. The waiter brought me what appeared to be a head of romaine straight from the bag, topped with bacon bits (the real kind; only the best!) and a wooden, circular tower displaying eight small glasses on different levels. It looked like a lazy Susan of beer.

I felt no need to use the bathroom as I stood up to leave. A few steps out the door, sloshing down the block, that had changed. I really had to pee. I scanned the streets and sidewalk; there was nowhere to go. It wasn't two a.m. on some random block in Burlington; it was ten p.m. on a main road in Portland. *It's only two blocks; you'll be fine.* I stepped quickly and awkwardly, like a race-walker in slow motion, one thing dominating my mind.

In sight of the building, a little pee came out, but I stopped it. Nervously, I swiveled my head. *No one around.* A few steps later, it happened again, and this time — in my compromised state — I didn't have the strength or the will to prevent it. *Shit, here it comes. I guess this is happening. Fuck.* On a sidewalk under some trees, the dam broke, and I stood dead-still in the darkness as what felt like gallons of warm liquid poured down my legs.

I put my head down, scurried past the diner-turned-nightclub, through the parking lot, and up the stairs to my door — afraid to be seen, or smelled, along the way. I went straight to the bathroom and stripped naked from the waist down. I stood there bottomless, filling the sink with hot water and soap. I cursed myself out; I had to get them clean. Besides a single pair of suit pants, my jeans were all I had with me.

I washed my socks, underwear, and pants, emptied the sink, and washed them again. I rinsed them in the tub, wrung them out as best I could, threw them over the shower rod, and wondered what the maid might think. I had to hope they would dry. Finally, I drank some water, showered, and, with a crowd beginning to gather outside the nightclub next door, got into bed.

After a restless night of sleep I was all too familiar with on the road, I drove across town to the office. In my suit and tie, I talked to the reps and reviewed the necessary paperwork as if I hadn't drunkenly pissed myself the night before. I drove back to the hotel at the end of the day, but pulling into the lot, I found nowhere to park. Rather than asking at the front desk, I drove off in search of a spot on the street.

With one eye on the uninterrupted line of parked cars, in the right lane at an intersection, I took a right. Immediately, I realized my mistake: I was heading right into traffic; it was a one-way. *Shit! Shit; what do I do? Damn it.* Amid a chorus of shouting and honking, I hugged the curb and drove slowly up the block. Luckily there were multiple lanes, plenty of room for traffic to pass by.

I took another right and got back into parking-spot mode. Suddenly, I spotted a break in the cars; it called to me as if lighted from above. Only a few blocks away despite the adventure, I schlepped back to the hotel with my laptop bag over my shoulder.

Back in the room, I checked on my pants. They were *sort of* dry — dry enough to wear. Walking down the street a few minutes later, my phone rang. I should've answered the 503-area code, and when I listened to the voice mail, I understood why. My car was in a loading zone; it'd be towed if I didn't come quickly. I got over there immediately and was met with anger and name-calling.

"What are you, an idiot?! Can't you see this is a driveway?!"

I apologized over and over.

"You're lucky I saw that hotel sign; this car should be gone! Another ten minutes, and it would be gone!"

I thought about offering some cash as a thank you, but I didn't have any on me. There was still some pizza from the other night — *I can't offer him leftovers.* As the business owner explained to me, I was very fortunate he spotted the Jupiter Hotel placard on the dash.

With an evening flight and an entire day ahead of me, as well as the memory of trying to change a flight over the phone, I decided to go to the airport early and try my luck at the counter. I didn't fully think my plan through: when I couldn't book an earlier flight, I was stuck without a car, bound to spend eight hours at Portland International Airport ("PDX"). I browsed books at Powell's at PDX, ate two meals and over an Alaska-brewed beer, watched the University of North Carolina best UVM in the 1-16 matchup. I spent most of the day drawing stares as I failed to contain boisterous laughter while reading Bill Bryson's *I'm a Stranger Here Myself.*

Like the second-opinion visit to Boston a few months before, I was seeking distraction in the Pacific Northwest. I completed my work, but the business purpose of my journey felt like a mere inconvenience. I was excited to spend a few days in Seattle and Portland; I tried to enjoy the opportunity to escape.

NEWFOUND VULNERABILITY

I spent much of my life convinced of my own invincibility. All of the things that were meant to scare me — physical things, tough-guy things — were only hurdles. In the backyard among the older kids, on the school bus with the bullies, jumping the cliffs, skiing the mountain, and getting in fights, I learned to be, had to be, fearless. It never seemed like a choice; I was always proving myself. Don't question my toughness.

On what would be the last of my audit trips in the spring of 2012, I was walking back to the hotel after dinner. Besides the raucous Tuesday night crowd at Empire Brewing — where I'd enjoyed a burger and, ignored by the bartender, a single pint of nitro stout — the streets were empty in that particular corner of Syracuse.

Afraid to miss a turn in the dark, I was looking toward a street sign when someone yelled at my back.

"Hey! Can I use your phone?" boomed the voice.

Startled, I looked over my shoulder and saw a man across the street walking toward me. I ignored him and kept moving, my eyes straight ahead.

"Hey!! I need to make a call! You got any money?"

I looked back again: *I'm all right; he isn't gaining.* As if it wasn't already (and always) on my mind, I felt very aware of my limitations. I may have looked normal, like anyone else, but I felt much more vulnerable. *If this guy wants to rob me, beat me up, or whatever, he will. I can't run; I can't fight; my fate's in his hands. There's nothing I can do.*

Annoyed and cursing me out, he gave up and turned away.

Calm down. Nothing happened. You could've given him your phone. Don't be so paranoid.

I probably did the right thing, and if I were fully healthy — capable of running, for one — I may have acted the same. But I would never have felt that debilitating loss of control.

It used to be such a big part of my being — the independence, the I-don't-need-anyone attitude. I learned it young, and I learned it well: be a man; don't show weakness. I took it for granted.

I mourned another loss that night in Syracuse; another piece of my identity was gone. I wasn't invincible, strong, and independent. I was fearful, vulnerable, and weak.

8.

One of my tasks on the road at the agencies was to conduct the annual compliance meeting. In most of the offices, we'd sit around a table, pausing for questions while I made my way through the material. An informal presentation with a handful of attendees — that's what I was used to.

In the spring of 2012, I presided over my largest group yet. All of the Vermont reps, some of their office managers and personnel, as well as a smattering of home office folks, were in Montpelier to fulfill the annual requirement. With the PowerPoint queued, in a stadium-seating lecture hall of about fifty, a closeted ALS patient stood ready to begin.

I wore a sweater over my shirt and tie that day, but I was still shivering underneath. There was nothing to be worried about: I knew the material inside and out, even without the PowerPoint. But I couldn't shut my caffeine-heightened nerves off. *Maybe I shouldn't have had the coffee. How could I do this without coffee?* As I started to speak, attempting to command the attention of the group, I heard my voice. It was shaking. I never considered asking for mercy. Though we'd been moving forward like nothing had changed, my boss knew what I was going through. I didn't have to be there; someone else could've done it. But I was still wholly consumed by the fantasy image of myself. I had to be the same person that everyone knew. I couldn't show weakness; it wasn't me.

I stood like a statue with locked knees, my brain trying to get my body to relax. I'd felt it before, my feet glued to the floor, knees knocking in terror. I'd have liked to sit down, taken the weight off my legs and my mind.

I plowed through the presentation like a robot. My mind began to wander as I heard myself echoing the same words I'd spoken ten times before. I was muttering a mantra in my head. *Relax. You're OK. This is easy. You've done this before. Just get through it. You'll be fine.*

The limited amount of casual charisma I'd seemingly possessed at previous meetings was nowhere to be found in that room. I felt like a prisoner up there, like a stand-up comedian before a silent audience. I wanted to run; if only I could.

Without stopping for questions, I completed my task in record time. What might've taken an hour to thoroughly complete, I raced through in thirty-five minutes. The majority of the audience was undoubtedly thrilled.

My feet were still stuck in place as I came to the end. My legs had been noticeably shaking since I'd taken my place at the front of the room. Beads of sweat covered my body, pooling and dripping down my legs. My feet were on fire and throbbing. My face must've been noticeably flushed.

Though I knew there were questions to be answered, I was all too eager to get off the stage. I was afraid if I moved, I might fall. *If I fell on my face, the charade would be over; everyone might get to know the truth.* I didn't have the strength to go through that. I couldn't take the embarrassment. Concentrating hard on each step, I moved deliberately to my right. I must've looked like Forrest Gump running out of his leg braces — my legs loosened more with each step.

Somewhere among the recitation of meaningless words, I wondered again why it had to be so difficult. I felt like a fraud, hiding in plain sight. Each additional eyeball brought with it more pressure. At some point, surely, I'd snap.

9.

I continued to drift and, with each passing day, my will to continue to work grew weaker. *Am I really going to keep working? How can I possibly care about this job?* By keeping my life moving forward, I didn't have to face all that had changed. I didn't know what else to do. I continued on the same path; it was easier.

With Hank long departed, and the position still open, my workload was piling up all the time. Most of it had no real deadline, and I was usually left alone to manage my time. The longer I spent in that chair, the more I was willing to skew my priorities. Big project that I should be doing? Tedious phone calls that I need to make? I'll work on whatever I find easiest. I'd lost any feeling of purpose. Why should I care? It started to feel like I was just killing time. It felt like a battle to keep going, and I wasn't ready to let myself lose. I didn't know what my next step should be. I didn't know how to handle it, and I didn't ask for advice.

On a Monday morning in May of 2012, while getting ready for work at my Waterbury apartment, I finally broke. It wasn't my plan; it just happened. I let myself off the hook: I didn't go in; I didn't call.

My boss was out of the office — on the road on an audit trip — and my absence fell through the cracks. Tuesday came, and I didn't go in. Still, no one called. On Wednesday morning, I called George, the big boss, and thankfully (and expectedly), he didn't pick up. In a teary message, I raised the white flag. "I can't do it anymore..." I confessed.

I holed up in my apartment and watched my phone go to voice mail. I'd quit my job. I told only my parents.

CHAPTER 4

LOSING MYSELF

Whatever your relationship with exercise, it is better than mine. We used to have such a great time together. You helped me meet people and make friends. I used you when I felt lonely or bored or trapped or stressed or sad or angry. You were always there, like a brother when I lost mine. You gave me a sense of accomplishment, pride, and confidence. You drove me to compete, to give it everything and more. I spent so much of my time with you. How will I ever expect to get along alone?

1.

Rob and I had sat in the same classrooms in college, graduating in the same year with the same major. We'd partied during senior week, carpooled to work, spent days golfing and skiing, and nights drinking. He'd moved with friends to what had been a seasonal rental — half ski chalet, half rustic log cabin — on the Mountain Road in Stowe. One Saturday afternoon in the winter of '10-'11 — which Rob and his roommates had spent skiing while I sat on my ass at 6 Patrick — I drove up to their place.

We were drinking beers the moment I walked through the door, preparing for a night at the bars. Theirs was a bit like a frat house, and I had to join in. Playing quarters (each player attempts to bounce a quarter into a shot glass, passing it along when successful) at the kitchen table, it was immediately obvious that I couldn't keep up.

I'd lost some dexterity and feeling in my fingers. I didn't consider telling anyone; what would I say? I didn't have an explanation. I had trouble picking a flat quarter up off the table and struggled to move it in my palm. I looked at my friends and their effortless movements; I couldn't understand how they did it. I felt like I had a new set of hands; I couldn't control them like I used to.

Quarters is a game of speed as much as skill. Every additional second between shots is more time for your opponents to catch you. It wasn't just a problem of ineptitude and subsequent embarrassment, I had to drink more. I kept losing and was constantly trying to finish a beer, making things worse. I should've gotten up from the table, walked away from the problem, but that wasn't me — not the person I knew.

I knew we'd head out to the bar, and I couldn't handle it. I couldn't drink like I used to; a few beers and my balance and coordination were shit. I couldn't binge drink Pabst Blue Ribbon ("PBR") and try to fit in. I'd surely embarrass myself: subtly, playing quarters or cards, or in a major way, like falling down the stairs. There was no pleasure in drinking like that, but what could I tell them? I wanted to curl up in a ball in the corner and escape.

I didn't know what to do, so I tried to find a way out. I snuck away down the stairs and saw the coat-covered couch. *Maybe I could just pass out here, and they'd leave me behind. Maybe I could just leave, get in my car and drive home.*

It certainly wasn't the first time I'd had a bad idea. They call it the Irish goodbye. I'd done it before — too drunk and unable (or unwilling) to tell anyone I had to surrender. But never by car, and never before the night had even started.

Standing in the relative calm of the dark room, away from the drunken noise upstairs, I made my move. A few feet from the escape I desperately needed, I grabbed my coat, put on my boots, and snuck out the door. I got in my car and turned the key. I was drunk, I knew that, but I had to get out of there. That was more important.

The driveway was wide near the top but narrow toward the road. There was a snow-filled ditch running alongside the street — a culvert under the driveway. Drunk in the dark — but reasonably clear-headed — I didn't want to back out onto the Mountain Road with its fifty-mile-per-hour speed limit and risk a high-speed collision. Thinking I'd turn the car around — trying to navigate a packed driveway — I backed my Subaru toward the ditch. Before I knew what was happening, the rear wheels lost traction. I couldn't pull forward. *Oh, shit.*

With the rear wheels still spinning, I pulled the emergency brake as hard as I could. Hoping the loss of 140 pounds from the front seat wouldn't cause the car to lurch backward, I swung the door open and stepped out. There it was, front wheels still firmly planted on the pavement, rears somewhere back there suspended above the snow. Typical of my inebriated state, the severity of the problem didn't really register. *Damn. Hope it stays.*

Forced to abandon my escape, I reentered the house with the tale of the runaway car. "I was getting something out of my car, and it must've popped into neutral," I told everyone. The laughs poured out. My drunken buffoonery was exhaustively ridiculed, but I think they believed me.

I tried to remove myself from the drinking. I didn't know how to say that I'd had enough. That's not how it works when you're "one of the guys." I escaped to the kitchen, filling and gulping a pint glass at the sink. Before much time had passed, a cab pulled into the driveway.

People go to the bar for a sense of community. With a drink in your hand, and a few more in your liver, everyday anxieties (temporarily) melt away. A medicated brain and a functioning body together create an alternative perception. Like everyone else in the place — all of whom seem to belong — you can just *be*. The alcohol and atmosphere combine to create a place where people can simply exist.

I no longer felt any of those things. The old me was gone; the new me a stranger. While others were coasting through the night, their minds free from worry, I stood in a state of hyperawareness. It's almost as if I was there but not there. I was physically trying to maintain the most basic of human functions. The beer in my hand and the people around me were only causing more stress to build in my mind.

When a group of guys goes out, they buy rounds. That's the code. In this way, it's difficult to try *not* to drink. As much as the voice was screaming in my head — *Don't drink any more; you need water, not beer* — it wouldn't be me to try to opt out.

I was handed a pint glass, gulped some down, and placed it on the bar table beside me. My days of standing and holding sixteen ounces of liquid — chest-high with bent elbow, casually awaiting the next sip — were behind me. My biceps and wrist didn't have the strength to maintain that position for long. It was as if I were lifting weights on a balance beam; the simple act of holding a beer required more concentration than any drunkard has the ability to provide.

The guys came and went, mixing in with the crowd as I kept to my spot on the sidelines by my table. They gave me a number of gentle reminders: it was my round. I walked a few steps to the end of the bar and ordered four PBRs. Before the bartender finished pouring, I grabbed two brimming glasses and carried them back to the table. I walked very slowly, one calculated step at a time, my eyes on the beer all the way. Still, I spilled some. My roommates grabbed the other two beers from the end of the bar. "Thanks, Natty." *Thank you (for getting them yourselves and sparing me the embarrassment),* I thought.

My roommates — scattering in every direction, mingling with all sorts of familiar faces — had left me alone on the sidelines. I felt like I was biding my time, waiting for the night to be over.

I checked my phone for the time. I'd have had more fun in the Department of Motor Vehicles line.

Seeing my full-bellied (and not hungry for brains) zombie impersonation, Rob pulled me onto the dance floor. Without so much as a word, he grabbed a girl nearby and awkwardly shoved us together. He thought I just needed a push, but I had no interest in getting close to anyone.

I couldn't dance with a girl; it was all I could do to avoid falling on my face. I hadn't so much as looked at the girls in the bar. I was trying my best to keep everyone in my life at arm's length. I didn't recognize myself, and I was embarrassed that someone might see what I saw.

I've never been so uncomfortable. I barely bothered to look at her; I certainly didn't try to talk. I couldn't describe a single thing about her physical appearance. I stood there moving my feet for what felt like forever. I don't know why she didn't walk away.

I had to get out of there. Soon, without notice, I did. I walked out the door and into the cold. The air felt refreshing; I tried to breathe deep its sobriety.

Outside the venerable Rimrock's Mountain Tavern — the bar of choice on that particular evening — a group of girls stood on an outdoor patio, one smoking a cigarette, the others keeping her company. Having nowhere to go, I joined them and struck up a conversation. Or, more likely, I sidled up in dumb silence until one of them talked to me.

Within minutes, a few guys came outside and joined the girls. These were the boyfriends. One of them got angry with me almost immediately. I should say that he got angry *at* me because I'm sure I didn't do anything but exist in the vicinity of his property (girl-friend). Encouraged by a head full of drunken brain cells and a preexisting inferiority complex, he got in my face and pushed me, like Elaine on *Seinfeld* — two hands in the chest. I didn't take a step back and try to regain my balance; I didn't try to put my hands out to catch myself; I didn't move my feet. I went to the ground like a felled tree, only faster. One of the girls couldn't control her laughter. It must've been an act. I was a stuntman working hard to make it look real. The others looked on in stunned silence. It was unnatural. They'd never seen someone fall like that.

I offered nothing as an explanation as I got to my feet. Embarrassed once again, I made my escape. Unsure what else to do, I walked back to the door. Perhaps a witness to my fall, the bouncer wouldn't let me in. I was too drunk.

I'd never been too drunk to get into a bar. The only time I was refused at the door was during (UVM) senior week, when a bouncer was witness to four of us chicken fighting in the street. (That's the thing you see kids doing in the pool, with one on the other's shoulders. Our arteries pulsing with alcohol in the weeks before graduation, I was perched on Tom's shoulders, grappling with Rob and his partner on the side of Saint Paul Street. Each of us fell to the street at least once as we waited to get into What Ales You?) Don't get me wrong, there'd been many times that I'd been too drunk to need to get into a bar to be served more alcohol, but no one ever stopped me from doing so. In my experience, the gatekeepers seemed to go by the mantra: If you can stand, you can drink. For the first time in my life, I couldn't hurdle that incredibly low bar — I could barely stand.

Slowly and aimlessly, I walked out to the parking lot at the Baggy Knees Shopping Center. I paced around looking at the cars — one had a wide-open door. *Should I call a cab? Maybe I could walk.*

Seeing my drunken wandering, someone offered me a ride. I joined a big group piling into an old Volvo. Suddenly, I found myself sitting backward in the station wagon's trunk, back to the rear seat, peering through the heavily frosted glass.

One of them asked where I lived and told me their destination — a motel up the street from the house. I gave them the meaningless number (3062) and tried to explain its location. But drunk, unfamiliar with the area — especially at night — facing the wrong direction and looking through an icy window, I failed to identify the house. Awaiting a signal that never came, the driver took us all the way to The Matterhorn (après ski mainstay; last stop before Stowe Mountain Resort) before suggesting we must've gone too far. Starting to feel like a burden as we made our way slowly back down the hill, I repeatedly assured them it was close to their motel, and I could walk from there.

I thanked them repeatedly as we pulled into the motel. I found my bearings on foot — my stubborn intuition was right; it wasn't far. I walked alongside the dark, winding, shoulderless road as a few unsuspecting drivers passed dangerously close. I soon came to the house, pulled open the (predictably) unlocked door, climbed the stairs, and fell onto the couch.

I heard everyone get home sometime later. As drunk as I was, I couldn't seem to pass out like I used to. My body wouldn't calm; alcohol only made it worse. I was still drifting in and out of sleep when the first of them discovered me on the couch. They'd called me repeatedly. I'd ignored them.

I stood staring out the oversized picture window the next morning. Instead of gazing up at the snow-covered eastern slopes of Mount Mansfield — for which the window was intended — I looked down at my car in the driveway. Had I not needed help getting it back onto the pavement, I'd have left before anyone awoke. Instead, I drank a lot of water, lay back on the couch, and shut my eyes.

When everyone was up, I told them what happened: I was drunk, went outside for some air, and they wouldn't let me back in, so I found a ride home. No one thought anything of it.

It took a bit of pleading, but reluctantly, a group of groggy hangovers stepped into the cold to try to dislodge my Subaru. Three guys climbed onto the snowbank in the ditch behind the car as I got into the driver's seat. With everyone yelling instructions, I started the car and slowly, fearfully, released the parking brake. Incredibly, it held its position, and the guys began to push. I took my foot off the brake, moved the gear shift into first, and carefully, fearfully gave it some gas. Had the car started to roll backward, nothing could've been done; the guys would've scattered to avoid being crushed. Somehow, it held its ground, and the worst they got was a pummeling of snow from the spinning rear tires. Quickly and rather impressively — or with profound luck — we had the car safely in the driveway. Impossibly relieved, I thanked them, rolled up my window, and was on my way home to 6 Patrick.

I spent the following days trying not to think about my night. It was another giant brick in the wall between my present and my past. Whatever the indisputable facts, I couldn't admit that I wasn't the same person anymore. I kept making excuses, holding onto delusions. I might have chosen to be blind, but the wall was growing higher all the time.

THE FOREGONE CONCLUSION

I've spent a lot of time being lonely — in my life altogether, but certainly since my symptoms began. When I started to notice changes, I didn't know what was happening. I was afraid to share it with anyone; I was afraid someone would find out. When finally, I received my diagnosis, my instinct was to protect myself further. I wanted to crawl inside of myself, engage my armor, and keep everyone out.

I never wanted to tell anyone, in part because I couldn't accept it myself, but also because I was embarrassed. I'm still somehow embarrassed. I was always afraid of my faults, afraid that the world would see faults in me, whether they actually existed or not. When this new fault arrived, I became all the more guarded. I pushed them away.

I've spent my life protecting myself. I was always the little kid, and I was picked on and outright bullied by older "friends" in the neighborhood and assholes on the middle school bus. I learned to stand up for myself, fight, and make jokes. It forged my identity. Nothing bothered me; I was strong, tough.

But I also think it made me closed off and unable to display that dreaded but all-too-important quality: vulnerability. I don't know why anyone is surprised that men grow up unable to show emotion or ask questions but rather feign confidence all of the time. That's what we were taught. *That's what men are*, or so we were told.

When my symptoms began, if I'd had a girlfriend, eventually I would've told her, or she would've noticed. Or maybe I'd have pulled away and gotten out. Instead, any romantic interests I had, I kept at arm's length — until this goes away, or I know what it is, I told myself. I kept going over it in my mind: *What if she notices something? What will I say? How could I tell her the truth?* I didn't even know what it was.

After I knew, the burden became greater. How could I tell someone I wanted to like me, someone I just met, something so terrible? I could never do that.

And so, I was alone. I couldn't see any other possibility.

2.

Over the winter of '10-'11, I bought a membership for the following season at Country Club of Vermont ("CCV"). Despite what should have been overwhelmingly obvious, in February, I committed to another year of golf.

On a drizzly March day in the 40s, long before CCV or any other respectable course opened for the season, four of us played nine holes at Lang Farm in Essex. It didn't go well for me. I was miserably cold; I couldn't grip my clubs.

I'd never before paid any attention to my grip strength. Gripping a baseball bat, tennis racquet, or golf club isn't something to focus on. It's muscle memory — an afterthought.

But that fundamental task was almost too much. With every swing, it felt like the club would fly from my hands. Failing that first step took away any chance of success at all of the other things that make up hitting a golf ball. I tried to blame the weather, but none of my friends seemed to have the same trouble.

A few weeks later, Rob and I went to a driving range, and I found — though my grip felt better in the warmer weather — that wasn't it. I was used to shaking the rust off each spring, but this was much more than that. I could say that it felt like I'd never swung a club before, but that wasn't it. It felt worse. It felt like I was a different person.

When the CCV driving range — with its beautiful natural-grass tee boxes and flawlessly stacked golf ball pyramids — finally opened after an unusually wet spring, I drove up alone, and things became a little clearer. I choked up and hit an easy wedge toward the green about ninety yards out. It came up short. I took a full swing, and again it fell short. I swung harder. I tried again and again. Same result. I was making good contact, but there wasn't the same force; the ball just wasn't flying like it used to.

I grabbed my 7-iron and aimed for another green, around 150. Somehow it was worse. I turned and aimed for the pitching wedge green. I made it. Beginning to feel embarrassed that I was hitting a 100-yard 7-iron, I looked up and down the row of tee boxes. *Everyone must be looking; they're laughing at you!* Everyone was hitting golf balls. No one had noticed me at all.

After a few swings with a 5-iron, I gave up. I didn't make solid contact even once. After half an hour at the best driving range I'd ever visited, I grabbed my bag and walked to my car, completely and utterly defeated.

I should've been defeated, should've called it quits altogether, but I was too stubborn. I'd visited my doctor, explained my symptoms, and was painfully awaiting a solution. As I answered questions and underwent tests, I continued to attempt to play golf. The course was less than twenty minutes from work, and unlike Burlington and Williston — where I'd spent the last two summers — it was invitingly empty in the evenings. I couldn't help but think of how lucky we were. All across the country, people were getting off work, sitting in traffic, or on public transit for another mind-numbing commute. A half an hour after leaving the office, we were walking down the first fairway, with idyllic views of Camel's Hump and Mount Mansfield, the private course seemingly to ourselves. It was glorious.

Or it could have been. But with a golf bag on my back, every step on that fairway made me uneasy; each footfall felt awkward and uneven. *I can't even walk without focus; what am I doing on a golf course?* I was focused on all the wrong things. I kept trying to enjoy it but couldn't.

***

In previous years, I'd changed in the parking lot — stripped off my shirt, pants, shoes, and socks by the backdoor of my car. Now I'd arrive in the locker room after work, sit on the bench, remove my unbearably hot shoes, and strip my sweat-soaked socks from my swollen feet. I'm not sure I could've done it standing up; I was struggling just to pull on clean socks. I was always lagging behind, my friends impatiently waiting at the tee box.

Despite all of it, I continued to show up at the course. On a Tuesday night, Rob and I subbed into the club's men's league, and I had the opportunity to embarrass myself to a new audience. I thought back to those times when I felt confident playing with strangers. It was never so much to impress anyone, just to hold my own — to belong.

It was beginning to feel like I didn't belong anywhere, certainly not on a golf course. To gain control over my driver, I had to choke up. I couldn't swing big like I used to; I must've looked like I was eighty years old. I couldn't hit my long irons, and I stopped trying. My arms, wrists, and shoulders simply didn't have the strength anymore. My former self, who'd finally learned to escape the sand trap without fear, had been replaced by a common hacker, just hoping to get the ball airborne. Bending over to place a tee in the ground — the most routine act of all — had become mentally taxing. I started going to one knee so I didn't tip over. Constantly coming up short on my approach shots, from fifty yards and in, I was a pro. My putting never felt better, but that may too have been a mirage — merely a bright spot in the dark.

I stopped keeping my own score almost immediately. For my ego's sake and to maintain some shred of denial, I couldn't. On every tee box, I'd hang back, knowing I'd be hitting last. I was constantly lost in an unending round of frustration, head-hanging, and indifference.

Gradually, I stopped going. I didn't tell my friends; I don't know what they thought. I left a jacket and some socks in my locker, unable to make myself retrieve them. By midsummer, I'd played my last round of golf. For months, as if I'd forgotten, my clubs remained hidden in my trunk.

3.

I'd been living at 6 Patrick for three years. As part of its long-running plan to purchase the surrounding real estate — purportedly to create a sound buffer for the long-running F-16s and incoming F-35s — the airport was about to take the property off our hands. In June of 2011, I moved into a room in the house on the Mountain Road. It was an easy thing to do. I didn't have to find a new place. This one fell in my lap.

Moving into the smallest room in the house, with no idea where everything would go, I borrowed my dad's pickup and started making trips to Stowe. I was still holding onto the old me; I wouldn't dream of asking for help. I loaded and uploaded most of the furniture myself, except for the hardwood-trimmed, spring-loaded, futon-style (legendary) blue couch. (The [legendary] blue couch had belonged to my mémère and pépère. It had been a fixture in their house since the '50s. It had a maple frame held together by heavy steel hinges; it was an innerspring mattress that folded in half. I held it in special regard. I slept on the [legendary] blue couch the night my brother died.) Moving that gargantuan object required — as Dad liked to say — two men and a small boy.

The room was the smallest I'd ever lived in — smaller than my childhood bedroom, smaller than a dorm room. There was a single mattress on a rickety metal frame and a set of drawers built into the wall. Almost all of my stuff was headed for the garage.

After living alone or with one roommate, I moved into a four-bedroom house with three other guys. I'd recently seen my doctor and was scheduled for a follow-up to try to understand what was happening. For more than a year, I'd been keeping an increasing number of things to myself.

One day, I dragged that tiny bed to the garage, hauled my queen-sized mattress and box spring up the stairs, and dropped them in place. My new bed took up most of the room. A tiny room with a latching door was my hiding place for the summer.

I GREW UP IN THE BACKYARD

I grew up in the backyard, on the sidewalks, streets, and driveways, and in the half-dozen parcels of woods that made up the neighborhood. My brother and I, and the handful of kids close by, grew up under each other's supervision, mostly outside. We rode bikes and built tree forts (three that I can think of); we played basketball in the driveway and roller hockey in the street; we spent winters walking with sleds to hills in the woods known only to kids. We made up and adapted games, from "poor golf" to "tree ball" and "0-2" to playing ping-pong with cardboard cake-round paddles on an unhinged door in the basement. We built an ice rink with full-size plywood boards and made our own goals, many of us learning to skate in the process. We spent every spare moment — throughout the spring, summer, and fall, during the day and under the lights, in the heat and in the cold — playing game after game of Wiffle ball at "Dumont Diamond" in my backyard.

I never thought of any of it as exercise. When other kids would say they liked to "hang out with friends" on the weekends, I was confused, unsure what that meant. *But what did you do?* I'd think to myself. The kids in the neighborhood, from across the street and a few blocks away, were always in motion.

It's what we did and became who we were. As I made my way through high school and college, and the neighborhood's activities and characters were gradually left behind, I found new interests among new friends. In my brother's footsteps, I took up cross-country skiing; we went running and hiked mountains, always with speed and ease, like we'd done it before. In college, I started downhill skiing, going on canoe and camping trips, playing pickup basketball, and walking, biking, and rollerblading all over town. Early in my post-college career, I added more golf and spent my winter weekends at the mountain.

Almost all of the people I spent time with, throughout each of the phases of my life, I met through sports. I never thought to ask what we had in common; I never had to. Though my life was always full of more questions than answers, I never needed to wonder who I was or what I liked in the world of athletics and competition.

Through the difficult times in my life — whether sad, or lonely, or stressed — physical activity was always there. When I needed to clear my head or feel the satisfying, familiar sense of accomplishment, I instinctively knew where to turn. When I began to lose that pillar of my life, I did the only thing I could: I fought to keep it.

4.

Still maintaining a stubborn (or perhaps stupid) resolve, I tried a couple of times to get out for a run. It had been a little over a year since the Corporate Cup 5K. I already knew how much I had changed; I could never forget the countless examples.

I slunk down the stairs and out the front door before any-one could offer to join me. I crossed the Mountain Road to the bike path and began to jog slowly. In no time at all, I wanted to stop. It didn't feel right or even OK. Everything felt heartbreak-ingly slow. My legs simply couldn't move like they used to; they couldn't keep up with my brain.

Sweating, exhausted, and indescribably uncomfortable after less than ten minutes, I tried harder. I looked up and down the path, searching for the eyeballs I'd imagined. No one was around. I tried to sprint. I pushed as hard as I could, gave it everything I had. It was unbelievable how slowly I was moving, worse than I could've imagined. My hamstrings were tight and inflexible; my calves had no strength; my hips couldn't make me go faster. I felt like I didn't have ankles, like my feet were welded on at a right an-gle. I couldn't push off; I felt like I was running flat-footed. In less than ten seconds — convinced of my ineptitude, consumed by the fear of tripping and falling — I gave up and slowed to a walk.

I was so thoroughly embarrassed, I could've sat down and cried for an hour. Had I known the finality built into those mo-ments, the pain would've been indescribable. But I was still a couple months shy of learning my possibility-crushing fate. In hardly any time at all, my will had been defeated. I'd never again attempt to go out for a run.

5.

I wasn't nearly ready to give up on exercise entirely, so I switched to another solitary activity: biking. I treated my new hobby in much the same way — going out on my own, welcoming no guests. Just getting on the bike was a danger. I could've used a fa-ther figure to hold me steady as I hopped onto the seat and tried to gain momentum down the driveway.

I always took the same basic route, never crossing the Mountain Road. I'd hug the shoulder to Edson Hill Road and turn up the big hill. I don't know what I hoped to accomplish, but I switched the bike into a low gear and attacked the hill. If for no other reason, I wanted to feel the pain; I wanted to remember what it felt like.

With numb legs and tired lungs, I explored the dirt roads high up on the hill — the postcard views of Mount Mansfield and the incredible properties all around. A rush of independence took over my brain. Alone on my bike, high in the hills above the Stowe Valley — despite continuous reminders from my body — I felt alive.

I thought about the bike I was riding. My Audi had been parked behind my college apartment, awaiting some costly repairs, and I showed up at my parents' one Sunday afternoon on a heavy-as-shit ten-speed straight out of the '80s. The tires were bald, the gearshift finicky and unpredictable, and the brakes worn low and ineffective. My parents bought me the new Trek shortly after. It was kind of a mountain bike for the city: no active suspension, wide tires with minimal tread, and disc brakes.

On the flat sections, I tried to release the handlebars. It used to be so easy on those wide tires. I loosened my grip and lifted my hands; control slipped away in an instant. I'd barely let go at all; my heart raced a little faster as I grabbed back on tightly to safety.

I thought of the times back in college, riding the rickety old ten-speed around town. I would stand tall on the pedals, arms resting at my sides with my backpack on, and blast down the steepest hills in Burlington. In the middle of the road. I didn't even own a helmet. An ill-placed pebble or unseen car could've sent me to the hospital or worse. Those were the days without fear; I still try to imagine the feeling.

The downhills were scary. The disc brakes had plenty of stopping power, but I felt like I had to ride them to avoid losing control. I'd have loved to let myself fly down the hill, but I knew the smallest bump or a skidding tire was all it would take to throw my precarious balance. Like a ninety-year-old riding a single-speed bike with a basket full of groceries, I rode slow (and boring).

Each time I arrived back in the driveway, I fought to navigate the turn, avoid the parked cars, and slow to a stop without falling. One of my roommates always seemed to be around to watch. With two feet on the ground — full of relief at another successful driveway reentry — I walked my bike into the garage, never thinking that this could've been the last time.

6.

One morning I was getting ready for work in a rush — as was becoming the norm. Everything was taking a bit longer: showering, shaving, dressing. Suddenly, coffee alone wasn't enough; I had to eat breakfast. I'd sit in the kitchen in a dark and quiet house and eat granola with whole milk. I wasn't hungry at seven, but I was beginning to learn an important lesson: my body needed the calories to function.

Though our schedules didn't quite match up, and he was always running late, Rob and I were trying to carpool to work. One cool summer morning, we rushed out the door at our usual pace. With a tie in my hand, I jumped in the passenger seat of Rob's Volvo. As he sped down the road on the way to the highway, I finished buttoning my shirt and tied my tie. I couldn't seem to get the button-down collar to latch. Midway through the half-hour drive, I was still fiddling with it. Frustrated and blaming the existence of such impossibly small buttons, I gave up several times before resuming.

In a rare show of honesty, I even voiced my feelings aloud. "Goddamn button," I believe I said. Had I thought he'd draw any conclusions from my inability to push a small piece of plastic through a fabric slot, I'd never have said anything. But as with all of my other "successful" hiding, he may have thought something, but said nothing.

Finally, by some small miracle, I got the button through. I could go back to pretending I was normal.

7.

As the summer went on and my health took up more of my mind, I kept to myself all the more. When asked to play golf or tennis or to go for a hike, I began to decline, whether or not I had plans. I felt like I had no other choice — my body wouldn't let me participate. Hiding in plain sight, I sat on the deck and read in the sun. Attempting to avoid the weekend scene and its many obstacles, I drove up to Burlington or Winooski and resurfaced on Sunday. One day, an old friend got in touch, and we made plans to get together in Waterbury.

Dan was one of my best friends in high school, but I hadn't seen him in five years. On a Saturday night in August, we had drinks and ate dinner at The Alchemist. One thought dominated my mind as we sat and talked at the bar: *Don't fall off the stool.*

After a few beers and a pair of massive burritos, we made it across the street to a newly opened, pint-sized watering hole with an unfinished bar and a handful of stools: The Blackback. It felt like a secret, like a friend's basement with a killer tap list. We sat there for a couple of beers — some Hill Farmstead for sure — and shot the shit with the fortyish former lawyer, Yankees-cap-wearing owner.

As the bar began to close down, Dan asked me if I wanted to crash on his girlfriend's couch. She lived a block down the street. I was in no condition to make the twenty-minute drive back to Stowe. I'd been trying only to enjoy the moment; as was obvious to Dan, I had no other plan. The last two of a Saturday night crowd that might've topped out at five, we paid our bill, thanked the owner with a handshake, and walked up the street to a dark second-floor apartment above a garage. I found the couch as Dan quietly entered one of the bedrooms.

I met the girls who lived there in the morning — two sisters with plans to start a year as traveling nurses in the fall. Having already started an apartment search with Rob, I complimented the place, and the girls immediately texted their landlord on my behalf. They scrambled to clean up a bit (threw stuff in closets) as the landlord, who lived in the main house, came upstairs to meet her potential new tenant.

I received my diagnosis three days later. I didn't know what to do with any aspect of my life, never mind the apartment. *Can I keep living on my own? Do I have to move in with my parents?* My brain was coasting on autopilot, completely overwhelmed and incapable of critical thought.

I owed a confirmation email to my new landlord but put it off. I was at my desk at work on Friday morning, swinging back and forth between attempted distraction and fearful reality, when I decided on the only option in front of me. I typed up an email, told her about my diagnosis and resulting indecision, and went ahead with the apartment.

On a rainy Sunday morning, I drove back to Waterbury to sign a lease. After spending the summer in what I had always considered temporary housing in a frat house in Stowe, I was excited it was time to move on. I met with the landlord in her living room and joined Dan upstairs for a celebratory bowl and some rainy-day couch time.

I drove back to Stowe in the continuing rain, ran into Rob at the door, and told him about my new place. I invited him to join me in Waterbury, but I knew he'd decline. He'd been looking in Stowe, near the mountain and the bars — he was a Stowe-Bro (I've coined a new term) through and through.

I drove to work Monday morning past torn-off chunks of the Mountain Road. It looked like someone had taken bites from the shoulder over the Little River. Hurricane Irene caused the worst flooding in a century. The Winooski River had overflown its banks; downtown Waterbury was under six feet of water. Though my new apartment, at the crest of a small hill, was left untouched, much of the town would never be the same.

With the news of my impending departure and building anxiety from my newly labeled secret, I drew in even further in the month of September. In a house with three single, mid-twenties roommates, I'd stopped trying to be part of the group. I didn't have it in me. I was more than ready to escape.

CHAPTER 5

PERFECTING SECLUSION

A lot of people never go a single day
without talking to another person.
I've gone many days on many occasions.

1.

In October of 2011, I moved from a small room in a four-bed-room frat house on the fifty-mile-per-hour highway to Stowe Mountain Resort, to a two-bedroom apartment above a garage on Main Street in Waterbury Village. The fresh recipient of an ALS diagnosis, unable to summon much focus for anything, I made a halfhearted effort at finding a roommate. I asked two people, rationalized that I could afford the rent on my own, and resigned myself to living alone. I saw myself walking to the restaurants, bars, post office, drug and grocery stores in the village. It'd been years since I lived in a walkable town. I missed it.

I lived in two off-campus apartments while attending UVM. About halfway through my first year off campus — with rent, food, and Busch Light (among many) thirty-packs eating through my part-time income — I had to give up my car. It didn't help that, against my parents' wishes, I'd bought a predictably troublesome old Audi the year before. With my $500 credit card limit stretched to the max by repairs, I had to quit working for my parents at Dave's and get something local.

I spent the better part of two years on my feet or two wheels. I applied to wait tables at a dozen downtown restaurants before being hired as a banquet server up the hill at the Sheraton. (I'd worked in kitchens since I was fifteen, I knew who made the money.)

Maybe it was the college life that I liked, but walking was part of it. It wasn't always fun or easy — walking home from a shift in the rain, riding the bus to my parents' with a duffel bag full of laundry, and layering up in the winter — but almost everything was nearby; I liked that. There was tremendous freedom in being able to walk almost everywhere I needed to go. I just strolled out the door — to class, to work, to friends', to the store, to a bar or a restaurant; it was all so easy.

It was always so peaceful — that's what I remember. Walking down College and Church Streets after my singular eight o'clock class, everything seemed quiet and simple — the many restaurants taking deliveries, preparing for the day. Walking home across town late at night — on Willard or Union — past comforting landmarks on dark, empty sidewalks. In those moments alone, I seemed to take solace, refreshed by the simplicity of walking.

When I moved to Waterbury Village, I tried to recapture those feelings. I walked out the door with a smile in my mind. I walked to the bank and the post office; I walked to the park and the library; I walked to the drugstore, bagel shop, and diner; I walked to the restaurants and bars.

I went to Village Market, bought a hand-cart of groceries and a six-pack, and stubbornly strolled the half-mile home. I wanted the experience to match my memories, but things had changed. I had changed. Carrying two or three grocery bags and a sixer a half-mile, while carefree and nostalgic in my mind, was, in reality, a pain in the ass. The bags, like the weight of cinder blocks straightening my elbows, nearly dragged on the sidewalk. They bumped against my legs with every step; my shoulders weren't strong enough to hold them the requisite few inches from my body. My wrist couldn't hold the beer parallel to my body; it turned inward and knocked against my thigh with each step.

I gave up on those trips to the market, but tried to hold on to my image of walking. I wanted to like it — I knew I should like it — but each awkward step wore at my resolve. It was no longer carefree; my mind had to focus to avoid falling. I couldn't feel the freedom of walking; the joy was gone. It just wasn't the same.

2.

When I moved in, I didn't immediately get the Internet hooked up — for whatever reason (overwhelming depression). My laptop picked up an unprotected signal that, as long as I kept it in one of a few spots, worked OK — most of the time. It was a one-bar signal that was constantly disconnecting, attempting to, and then yes, reconnecting.

At night, I drank beers and listened to the (baseball) playoffs on the old Bose Wave Radio I inherited from Dave's. The divisional playoffs, Yankees/Tigers; the championship series, Rangers/Tigers; and the World Series, Rangers/Cardinals. Sometimes I'd sit in the dark. I didn't really care about the outcome. Maybe I relished the peaceful nothingness of sitting alone in the dark. Maybe I wanted to prove to myself I was strong: I could handle whatever external or self-made depravity I might face. I'd been trying to prove it my entire life, and in my most vulnerable state, unconsciously, my M.O. didn't change: I don't need anything (or anyone).

Twenty-seven years old, newly diagnosed with a terminal disease, I sat up alone in my apartment. I didn't think, *This is the time to do something;* I didn't think anything at all. I was tired and broken and hiding. That was all I had in me to do.

THE STUFF IN THE CLOSET

At the top of the stairs was a closet; I filled it with memories the day I moved in. Hiking boots and running shoes; basketball and tennis racquet; Rollerblades and baseball glove; hockey stick, skates, pads, and helmet; skis, poles, and boots; golf clubs and Frisbees; backpacks and duffle bags — all piled in a dark corner just outside my door.

I bought the baseball glove in high school; I'd hardly used it since college. I'd played catch by the dorms and long-tossed with it in the park. It followed me to every apartment. It seemed like a lifetime ago that — over a friend's offer to steal it after his shift — I'd piled up the cash on the counter. I knew that I'd use it forever; I thought that forever would be longer.

I used to play Frisbee a lot. At Villanova and UVM, Smalley Park and Leddy Beach, we always played barefoot in the sun. In lazy hours on campus, frolfing (Frisbee golfing) with Lenny, and after too many beers late at night at the park. It was always so easy to spend time outdoors among friends; all we needed was a Frisbee.

My brother and I learned to skate at the neighbor's — Foley Forum we called it. I was in the sixth grade when the older kids — fifteen or sixteen at most — built an ice rink in a tiny backyard. Like the tree forts before — with handsaws, hammers, and leftover wood scoured from garages — they constructed a place to have fun. There were full-height, reinforced, checkable (that is to say, they were diagonally braced with two-by-fours and wouldn't crumble when run into) boards, two benches with cutouts, goals built from two-by-fours, and an ice-covered staircase coming out the back door.

It was truly a glorious achievement — and undoubtedly all-consuming with the watering and shoveling alone. It was the wintertime version of our three-season Wiffle ball obsession. We played under repurposed Wiffle ball lights well into the night and skated alone when we wanted. (They were the kind of light towers you see on the side of the highway at night. I don't know where we got them; I was the little guy — I never asked.)

I'd played here and there off and on since. I bought and borrowed some ratty old gear. The skates in the closet were hand-me-downs; they'd one time belonged to my brother.

The Rollerblades got a lot of use. A lace-up, hockey-style pair of Bauers, they'd also belonged to my brother. Besides the street hockey games for which they were intended, I used them in college a lot.

In bare feet and cargo shorts — with or without a shirt — I'd walk up the hill from my apartment on the corner of Church Street and Maple. Sometimes with Lenny, often stoned, I carried my Rollerblades over my shoulder — laces tied together, gym socks inside. I'd plug into my iPod if I was alone.

I'd sit on the curb at the top of the hill, wipe the pebbles from my feet, pull on my socks, and lace-up my skates. From Redstone and Athletic over to Main Campus and the Green, I'd shoot off to the north, come back across town, and slalom the Hill Section back home. I'd skate the paths around campus, avoiding the people, take to the roads and their cars, jumping onto the sidewalks when needed. I'd use turns to slow down like a skier.

I didn't own a helmet or kneepads; I took the worn brakes off the skates. I only ever fell twice: once because an unavoidable patch of pavement had been torn up on a downhill, once because I jumped a curb onto sand and came to an immediate halt. Both times resulted only in scrapes.

There it sat: a dirty, sweaty mountain of crap. It was only nostalgia; any real purpose was left squarely in the past. All I had left were the memories of the times we'd spent together.

3.

At a company function on a Saturday in the summer of 2011, I met a girl. My buddy and work neighbor Hank asked me to join him for the (company-sponsored, breast cancer charity) dragon boat races on the Burlington waterfront. In our group were a couple of girls I didn't recognize. A month before my diagnosis, with some gentle encouragement from Hank, I tried to play it cool with someone new.

She wore baggy black shorts and a T-shirt, her athletic body mostly hidden from view. She stood separate from the group with a friend, her dark curly hair down despite the wind off the lake. I'd never seen her in the building; surely, I'd remember her if I had. Attractive women a few years out of college didn't exactly dominate the hallways of National Life.

She disappeared for a time and reappeared wearing tights. Hank and I silently acknowledged the improvement. The egocentric man that I am, I thought, *Did she do that for me?*

I've never been particularly adept in the pursuit of the opposite sex. By that I mean, I didn't pursue; sometimes, they fell in my lap. When unnamed, unexplained things started happening to my body, I put up the fences; I closed myself off even further. The girl I met at the bar, we'd talked on the phone, but I had a new series of excuses for not taking things further. The old fling that came back into my life, I didn't think she'd recognize the person I was becoming. I was afraid they would see what I saw. I had a whole new barrier between me and the world, an unavoidable reason for inaction and fear.

After my diagnosis, I tried to feel a new motivation. I didn't know what the future would bring; it was time to stop allowing excuses to keep me suspended in loneliness. I had to do something; I at least had to try.

One day at work, I sent out an email and asked her to dinner. I might've asked her in person, but I still never saw her in the building. She said yes, and my anxiety moved on to the next step.

I met her at The Daily Planet — my choice. I thought that seemed hip, fun. I got there a few minutes early, scanned the room, and grabbed a seat at the bar for a beer. I tried to remember my old ways and feel comfortable with a drink in my hand. I ordered a Wolaver's Oatmeal Stout and kept one eye on the door at my back.

The restaurant was slow on a Wednesday; we were shown to a table once she arrived.

I grabbed my mostly full pint glass, and we walked through the bar to our table. From my current perspective, smoothly carrying a glass full of liquid is truly a marvel. Witnessing a waitress navigate a set of stairs with a tray of martinis rivals the Cirque du Soleil in my world. I robotically traversed the room, staring intently at the sloshing liquid in my glass. Every synapse in my mind was focused entirely on the physical act of crossing the room with my beer.

I was hiding right off the bat. I never even considered telling her my news. I didn't even believe it myself; how could I tell a near-stranger?

Somehow, I made it to the table, and our first date began. I'd never really had a first date — that is, a restaurant meal with a stranger. Despite a few awkward silences (for which I illogically felt responsible), I felt comfortable sitting across from her. I was (relatively) confident in conversation; I wasn't being distracted by my body.

I offered to walk her home after dinner; she lived just down the hill from my Church Street apartment. Standing outside the restaurant's door, she told me she'd driven. I was dumbstruck. When I lived downtown, I never drove anywhere. I thought, *Is she one of those people who won't walk across a parking lot?!* and was judgmentally bummed. I should have thought nothing. "Young woman would rather not walk across town alone at night," is hardly a story. I had a little aww-shucks moment to myself, walked her the twenty feet to her car, and said goodnight.

I didn't try to kiss her; I couldn't seem to find the right time. I didn't care in the least. I'd made it through the night without embarrassment. That was enough.

We met for a drink after work a week later. Down the street from my place, and conveniently on her way home to Burlington, The Reservoir was an easy choice. We got beers, sat at the bar for a few minutes, and she asked if I wanted to play pool. I loved to play pool; I loved that she'd *asked* to play pool. Maybe she was only trying to fill the silence with an activity, but I thought she was fun and independent. I instantly liked her a little more.

I thought back to all those times at The Monkey — Lenny and I spent so much time at the table. Shooting game after game in an empty bar after work and competing with strangers on a jammed Saturday night, I'd become perfectly at home in that world. But those nights were only a memory.

If I were being true to myself, I never would have picked up a cue. I'd tested my skills at The Matterhorn the winter before. More than six months of medical tests and further deterioration later, I knew it would go badly. But it wouldn't be me to decline.

Somewhere along the way, lost in the myriad of newfound physical oddities, my palms became permanently clammy. I couldn't slide my hand gracefully down a handrail; the cue would stick to the underside of my finger. Forgetting the unease I felt merely standing and bending my body over the table, my hands, arms, and shoulders had taken the brunt of the ALS-induced atrophy. My most noticeable symptom was what the medical community called the "tone" in my muscles. Despite every effort, I couldn't move any part of my body with any fluidity. Muscles seemed to work well in one direction but unpredictably and sporadically grabbed upon release. The difficulty I had with every action — from walking or descending a staircase to striking a small white ball with the half-inch end of a long stick — was due to my inability to predict what my muscles would do.

I set up the table and offered her the break. That would've been my biggest giveaway. The larger and more forceful the movement, the less predictable its outcome. I could see myself winding up and missing the cue ball entirely or grazing it into a corner.

Together we could've made one passable pool player. She could physically hit the ball but didn't really know what she was doing; I knew what I wanted to do but couldn't physically perform the tasks in my mind. Somehow, excruciatingly slowly, I made it through a game of 8-ball. Much like what had happened to my golf game, I excelled at the short touch shots and struggled mightily at anything that required more strength. Oftentimes, I was fortunate merely to make contact.

I was so utterly embarrassed the entire time. I tried to maintain a light and flirty conversation while my soul was being crushed again and again. She was wearing a black skirt and removed a sweater to reveal a sleeveless top that was practically see-through. She was stunning, but I was too preoccupied to pay much attention.

It killed me not to excel at those casual little athletic activities — the sorts of things where everyone participates. Things like bowling or horseshoes or kickball or ping-pong or volleyball, or anything. I'd recently won a ridiculous cantaloupe-sized rubber-band-ball trophy in the Law and Compliance Department miniature golf tournament. On several occasions, I almost fell over picking the ball out of the hole; I had to go down on one knee. Using my personal putter — a women's model I'd shamelessly bought at Dick's Sporting Goods because it was shorter (and because I was stoned) — I won by four strokes. Weak competition.

When, finally, the 8-ball fell into the pocket, I was granted relief from the charade. We put down the cues and stepped away from the table. Maybe she sensed my need for mercy; maybe she didn't want to watch my awkward movements anymore.

With a breezy goodnight, she was on her way home. A quick drink after work didn't turn into anything more. Except for more plans — dinner at my place.

Dinner at my place. Oh, man, what should I make? What does she like? I don't know. I make a mean mac & cheese; I know she'd like that.

This is where my shortsighted, self-destructive tendencies took over. I could've bought the groceries the day before; I could've bought them at lunch and delivered them to my apartment; I could've made up an excuse and left work early. But instead, I waited until the last minute. Though I emailed her a heads-up, I still made her wait in her car in my driveway. Smooth.

I grabbed the bags from the backseat and tried to feign nonchalance as the weight of the milk, cheese, and wine pulled down on my arms. I took them in one hand as I pulled open the door and led her up the stairs to my apartment; I needed my left hand for the railing. I'd always been one of those people who ran up and down stairs, but I'd altered my form. I used a railing-assisted two-stair approach. Instead of greeting my date, I was focused on the physical machinations of getting myself and the groceries up the stairs.

I put the bags on the counter, welcomed her to my apartment, excused myself, and changed out of my work clothes. I wasn't one to immediately shed my shirt and tie for jeans and a hoodie; I actually enjoyed wearing my work clothes out in the world. But these days, I always came home uncomfortably sweaty. I applied a fresh coat of deodorant and changed my shirt, pants, socks, and underwear. Yes, I even changed my underwear.

I reappeared in a baggy old pair of jeans and a zip-up sweatshirt because I was both cold and sweaty. There she was in her sexy accountant outfit (trust me), and suddenly her date was dressed for a night alone on the couch. I must've looked like I'd given up; I could've been wearing a Snuggie. I was only trying to conceal my discomfort; my appearance barely registered in my mind.

As I started to get things together for dinner, I asked her to open the bottle of wine. Quickly and expertly, she had the cork out, and two glasses poured. I didn't ask her because I was busy with dinner, I asked because I was afraid. I wasn't a big wine drinker; I couldn't remember the last time I'd used a corkscrew. I didn't want her to watch me try to figure out if I still had the skill.

I got the mac & cheese going; it always took longer than I thought. She stood by the counter, eating a hunk of bread and sipping her wine, while I stood at the stove whisking my milk-and-roux mixture. When I'd finally finished preparing the meal — bereft of a dining room table — we ate on the (legendary) blue couch.

Before I knew it, we were into a post-meal couch conversation. One thing I didn't do — at that time or any other since we had met — was compliment her. I never uttered so much as, "You look nice." I sat on the couch, completely absorbed in my all-engrossing secret, just trying to muddle my way through. My eyes looked at her, my voice talked to her, but my mind was entirely elsewhere. I was terrified she'd see the real me. I'd never felt like such a fraud. But even with the pressure building in my mind, I never considered telling her the truth.

I sat beside this beautiful woman who'd agreed to have dinner at my apartment, like a lump. It wasn't that I couldn't make myself do what I wanted. I was buried under lies; I only wanted to escape. She moved the conversation to tattoos, giving the chance to show hers. It was a couple of small symbols or a group of Greek letters I'd seen on a chalkboard. I actually called it dorky; I couldn't help myself. I couldn't let go of my fears. Had she a hammer in her pocket, she could've stood up, bashed me on the head, and yelled, "That's not the point, you thick-headed moron!"

And it wasn't. The tattoo was on the side of her ribcage, under her bra strap. She'd showed me her bra, and still I sat paralyzed, my brain still dying to escape. She was done trying to get my attention, gave up, made an excuse, and ran out of there. I half expected a kiss at the door. What an idiot.

I never saw her again, at least not for more than a second in the hallway at work. I never had the chance to explain: *No, I am not repulsed by you; I couldn't let you in.*

4.

I got home from work one day in November and didn't want to go straight to the couch. I felt good, positive, full of possibilities. I took off my tie and decided to get in a little workout on the stairs — fifteen wooden steps and a cement landing.

I wasn't ready to let go of the idea of exercise — not altogether anyhow. Everyone told me it wouldn't do any good; my muscles could never be strengthened. I knew it was true. I knew there was no going back. But I couldn't help trying to hold on a little longer.

As a kid, I delivered newspapers on Rollerblades, jumping up and down front stoops at warp speed. I jumped out the neighbor's back door and skated down icy stairs to the rink in his backyard. I lived on the third floor in a dorm and two different apartments in college, and no amount of alcohol ever caused me to fall. I never gave it a second thought. I never once worried about whether a place was upstairs, downstairs, or otherwise. Over the years, I forgot what that felt like. I began to see a flight of stairs and look for the handrail.

Stairs were among the first signs of trouble. At the frat house in Stowe, every time I left the house and ambled down the stairs, I felt it: something was wrong with my ankles, or my legs, or my balance — I didn't know. I had to be careful, pay attention where I hadn't; each trip down the stairs felt all the weirder.

Still wearing my neatly creased brown pants, light green button-down, and brown leather shoes, I made my way up and down (actually down and up) the stairs a couple of times. It's not that I lacked strength, I had much more difficulty descending than ascending. My calves and Achilles tendons were tight, more like springboards than shock absorbers.

I began one final descent, my right hand merely grazing the rail as before. Only a few steps in, I began to lose control. I felt like a skier in the woods, barreling toward a tree with no way out. In haphazard, rapid succession, my feet hit three or four steps, each one sending more energy into my legs through rubber-band ankles.

If you think there's any possibility of falling down a flight of stairs, don't lean out over your legs. Lean back. If you fall, fall on your butt. Don't keep your hand *near* the handrail; keep it *on* the handrail. These are the things that I've learned.

With five or six steps still below me, my body launched into an out-of-control somersault. Almost before I knew what was happening, I found myself sprawled out on the cold cement landing, head jammed against the wall. My right hip hit the floor and everything stopped. Had anyone been there to inquire, "Are you OK?" I couldn't have answered. I don't know if there's a term for it, other than shock. It's like getting the wind knocked out of you, but in the body. In that instant, I felt paralyzed. *Can I move?*

I lay still on the concrete, only trying to breathe. I let out a groan, shifted my body, and unwedged my neck from the wall. Assessing the level of damage, I turned myself over, got onto a knee, and stood up at the base of the stairs. I grabbed onto the handrail, and with only my ears to hear, moaned and mumbled in pain as I slowly climbed one step at a time.

I was never again so casual about using the handrail. I began to see stairs for more of the hazard they were. Without pausing for sorrow, I'd left another piece of myself in the past.

5.

I sat at the front of the classroom-style conference room for the usual Friday morning meeting. Sipping from my travel mug of caffeine, I expected to endure a few words of instruction before escaping to my desk. Often, in my recent mental state, I neglected even to show up for these meetings. No one seemed to miss me; I had the ultimate excuse.

The last item on the agenda was a surprise. Just as I expected things to wrap up, I was called to the front of the room. My boss stood with a plaque and a smile as he announced I'd been with the company for five years. Begrudgingly (and slowly, and carefully), I placed my coffee on the floor, stood up, and displayed a smile to the room. My nerves were immediately on edge. I was becoming accustomed to the feeling — it was paralyzing. My whole body was shivering from the inside, like I was too cold to move.

My former boss, Chelsea, sitting to my left, gave me a friendly push on the shoulder. She'd taken my deliberate movement as reluctant embarrassment. For a brief moment, I saw myself falling face down on the carpet.

I made it the few steps to the front, said my obligatory thank yous, and joined the exiting crowd. I had an inkling as I stood at the front of the room: I could use this opportunity to out myself. It would only take a few words; I could rip off the Band-Aid and be done with it. *Wouldn't that make everything easier? I wouldn't have to feel like I was hiding all the time.*

I couldn't do it; I didn't even come close. I couldn't unload my crushing knowledge on the group. I shielded them like children. I couldn't turn that Friday into a funeral.

***

A few weeks or a month later, I made a phone call and began a new life filled with nothing. I'd never experienced anything like it. I felt like I'd quit on life. I couldn't bring myself to care about — or even to consider — what lay ahead. I'd never spent my days alone — going nowhere, talking to no one. At first, it felt like nothing more than a break. Like I was playing hooky; like I was getting away with something.

Other than the two weeks I took for a cross-country road trip right at the start; I hadn't so much as taken a full week off in my five years with the company. It didn't feel real; it didn't seem permanent. As I watched the days pass, holed up in my apartment, reinforced in my mind was something I had learned when my brother had passed: the world doesn't stop.

I spent loads of time alone; I mostly enjoyed it. I didn't leave the apartment for days. I had a friend in high school who would half-jokingly call me "hermit" because of my occasional propensity to disappear for long periods for no obvious reason. I guess I've always been a bit of a depressive.

I had no schedule to keep, no one dropping by; I could relax with an unlimited amount of *me* time. Compared to the claustrophobic dorm life and the frat house in Stowe, I could get used to being alone. That's what I told myself — and it was mostly true — but once the night came, I felt differently. Loneliness set in when the sun went down.

For hours at a time, I drank coffee and read David McCullough books on the (legendary) blue couch. I plowed through *John Adams* (752 pages), *The Brooklyn Bridge* (636 pages), and *Truman* (1,120 pages) in long sessions in the apartment. I'd stand up after hours of unprecedented focus and stretch out, feeling a stiffness in my joints and muscles that would become more familiar with time.

It was a lonely existence in Waterbury; I didn't know what to do with myself. I didn't want to move forward, and I didn't know how. I'd never been (and never felt) so different than the people around me. In all the hours in my head, I never had any great epiphany. I spent my time in paralysis, unable to find a new way.

I'd still see friends on the weekends — often drinking and crashing on couches — and we'd act like nothing had changed. I didn't tell them I'd spent my week in seclusion; we didn't talk about me. I couldn't face the reality that had taken over my life.

THE GIFT OF TIME

A strange thought came over me as I contemplated life without work: I'd been given the gift of time. As delusional as I knew it was to think that being diagnosed with a terminal illness was in any sense a gift, the thought still remained. Never in my adult life had I had this kind of free time, and I couldn't help but dream about what I'd like to do with it.

Every dream I imagined fell flat in the face of reality. I'd walk to the window — completely deflated — look out and wonder, *What can I do with my days?* People would tell me to live life to the fullest; I wanted to laugh in their faces. *I could've done anything just a few years ago. How can I live life to the fullest? I can't seem to do any of the things that I want.*

I wanted to do big things. I wanted to hike the (273-mile) Long Trail in its entirety, set out on a multistate bike ride, or spend every day at the golf course like I had retired. I wanted to set out on a road trip and drink myself silly at the bar. I wanted to go on adventures.

I couldn't stop longing for the old me — the person I'd known and accepted for so long. I was entirely focused on all of the things I could no longer do. I couldn't see the future and the tough times to come. I knew only the past from my memories. How could I appreciate all that I had and not focus on what I had lost? I couldn't help each day to think, *This is the worst day of my life.*

I hadn't accepted the person I'd inevitably become. I'd seen the motorized wheelchairs, limp necks, and silenced voices. How could I appreciate those images of the future? I'd barely grown up enough to be comfortable in my own skin — in full health — in my mid-twenties. How could I expect to start over?

6.

After an undetermined number of days, a coworker called me a couple of times and left messages. I saw the calls, knew the number, and listened sadly to the voicemails. He was concerned, didn't know where I was. He wanted to know if I was OK.

I don't know how much of my story he knew; I hadn't considered telling anyone to spread the news. I couldn't make myself care. There's no way I was calling him back.

On a hot, sunny, midweek afternoon, I was smoking a (relatively rare, midday) bowl on the (legendary) blue couch when my silence was interrupted by a purposeful knock on the door at the bottom of the stairs. The smoke floated in beams of sunlight as I stepped to the window to look down. I had no desire to see anyone; I could pretend not to be home and silently wait for my visitor to give up and leave. Looking up toward my window, pacing around my driveway, was a cop.

"Nathan Methot, are you there?" *Damn it. I'd better go downstairs.*

I unlocked the door, jammed my feet into the waiting pair of shoes on the landing, and slowly and nervously descended the stairs. I pulled open the door and stepped into the sunshine with a heavy squint.

"We got a call. You haven't been to work. Some people are concerned."

"Yeah, I'm fine. I told my boss. I guess he didn't tell anyone else. I'll call them."

The exchange only lasted a few minutes, but it felt like much longer. I kept waiting for the next line of questions. "Wow, you reek of pot," would've made sense. My knees were shaking uncontrollably; my legs locked in place. I was afraid I'd fall on my face if I attempted to move in the slightest. He had to see the physical evidence of my anxiety; it was staring him right in the face.

"Alright, have a good day."

He turned to leave, and I escaped back into the stairway. I stood at the base of the stairs — free from his stare — trying to breathe and wait out the shakes before grabbing the handrail. *I can't believe he didn't say anything about the pot. I can't believe he didn't ask more questions.*

7.

A week later, feeling suffocated in my second-floor apartment on a beautiful day, I drove the half-hour to Beverage Warehouse to peruse the beer aisles in the afternoon. I ran into a teacher friend, off for the summer.

I wanted to dive behind some shelving, anything to avoid a conversation. He didn't know of my diagnosis, let alone my newfound retirement. I wasn't about to share either one.

"Natty! What's going on? You take the day off?"

It was a Wednesday.

"Yeah, what are you up to?" I asked, turning the attention away from myself as quickly as possible.

Meanwhile, my mind was on repeat: *I quit my job. I have ALS. I'm dying.*

Our exchange ended quickly, and I felt some relief. Lying was far easier than the alternative.

A YEAR IN THE LIFE

When, overnight, my older brother (my only brother) was gone, I could only see the action, the shock of his death. I wouldn't for a long time see its consequences. I'd spend the rest of my life alone in a way I'd never known.

He died of cardiac arrhythmia; his heart simply stopped beating. They'd performed an autopsy, tested and dissected his twenty-one-year-old body. That's what they tell you when there's no other cause.

I went to work the next day. Dad and I drove in together; a twelve-hour shift was our Saturday regular. Ten feet from him at the mixer, I started my day at the slicer a few minutes after eight. We stood there like zombies, our brains and bodies disconnected, the silence broken only by machines.

The day mostly unfolded like any other — we were lost in the restaurant grind before long. I barely talked to anyone beyond the necessary chatter of a kitchen. I'll never forget the faces as my co-workers greeted me.

I surrounded myself with friends that summer, or rather, they made sure to gather around me. I threw myself into a new and exciting relationship with Molly, put in long days at the restaurant, and seemed to spend most every evening among friends. I didn't wallow; I didn't let it sink in. I kept myself busy, my mind on other things.

Maybe that's what I needed, but it couldn't last forever. With the arrival of classes in the fall, my blissful existence deteriorated.

New to UVM, living off-campus with Molly, I felt more alone than any time before.

All of the challenges before me — a new campus where I felt wholly invisible, a challenging engineering school workload, and a relationship past its gleeful beginning — would require effort to overcome. I didn't have it in me. I was drifting: on autopilot in public, broken in private.

It all fell apart as fall turned to winter. Grades had always come easy: I paid attention, did my homework, and took the tests. I didn't stick to any schedule; I didn't need to be overly disciplined; I never felt lost or overwhelmed. But suddenly, that was changing. I was taking classes like Calculus III and Intro to Electromagnetism. I didn't do the work and quickly fell behind. I couldn't bring myself to make a real effort. I didn't seek out help; I didn't know how. Failure overcame me, and I gave up. I stopped going to class altogether.

I couldn't seem to make any friends. I didn't join any clubs or intramural sports; I didn't reach out to the few kids I knew from high school. I needed the safety of old friends; I couldn't face the vulnerability of meeting new ones.

I took my sorrows out on Molly every night. She tried to help with practical advice, but I was in no place to hear her. Starting her senior year in nursing school, recently diagnosed with a lifelong (and hopeless) muscular disease, she listened to my troubles — my able-bodied problems — without complaint.

I tried not to notice as she slowly pulled away. One day she told me it wasn't working. She was the kindest of souls, and she was right. I found myself back at my parents', alone in the basement.

With the house to myself in the day and the semester coming to a close, I began to wallow in earnest. One night in my room, I scribbled a letter in a frenzy on some scrap paper. I was shouting from the rooftops, questioning everything. *What's the point of school? How do people do this? What's the point of life?*

A semester of failing grades was accompanied by a letter from the dean. I was in violation of the school's academic policy, teetering on the edge of expulsion. It scared me, to be sure, but it also validated the rebellion burning inside. It let me off the hook; I was free. *Good! Fuck 'em! I don't need 'em!*

With some time to reflect on being kicked out of school and both of my parents unwilling to allow my bullshit any daylight, I made a half-hearted effort to my judge and jury. Though my status as a college student hung by a thread, I couldn't see the significance and show up for a meeting as requested. I made my appeal in a letter.

I was summoned to a meeting upon receipt. I sat before my three deciders, and they asked about my letter. They pushed a copy across the table.

I read aloud my words about my brother and the difficulties I'd faced the previous semester. I dripped tears on the page as I spoke and kept my head down until reaching the end.

***

I moved into a dorm to start the spring semester. We all agreed it might help me feel more connected. I met my roommate, and he asked if I was a partier. Having never been to a UVM party, with a (compulsory) renewed focus on academics, I played the cool guy to the stranger in the room. I told him, "Sort of," and I shrugged.

He moved to the third floor with a friend. He was on academic probation, he told me. I couldn't bring myself to tell him, *So am I.*

To anyone who has experienced life in a dormitory — most importantly, me, who spent the first months of college in a forced triple — a room to yourself sounds like heaven, only less realistic. No one would even dream of the possibility. I didn't see it as such a gift at the time.

I barely ate in the dining hall; I didn't have the confidence to sit alone. I'd stop in the on-campus store — in the very same building — and order a sandwich to-go. Back in my safe space, with the television noise drowning out the life beyond my door, I ate dinner.

I spent far too much time alone in that room. I went to class, drove to work, and completed my homework each night. I passed strangers in the hall and listened painfully to the bustling, joyful life all around me. I sat on the sidelines by myself.

I wanted people around me, to be accepted by my classmates. But I felt like a fraud. I couldn't be myself and meet new people; I wasn't able to be happy. None of these people knew what I'd been through; surely, no one could know how I felt. I'd have to put on a face and pretend. I didn't want to be someone new.

I'd go home for Sunday dinner and take beers from the fridge in the basement. I started with only a couple but increased the count when no one seemed to notice. I loaded them into my backpack, carried them into my room, and lined them up on the ledge outside my window in the cold. I drank every last one alone.

I listened to the same songs on repeat. I'd post my favorite lyrics as AOL Instant Messenger away messages. Things like, "Have you seen me lately?" and "I want to have a good time, just like everybody," both from Counting Crows songs. I'd never felt so strongly about song lyrics; I'd never needed to feel like maybe someone understood.

I tried to find things to do alone. I bought an acoustic guitar and sat at my desk learning to play. I obsessed over a car I found online: an enthusiast favorite rare Audi Coupe Quattro. Against my parents' advice (and common sense), I flew to North Carolina and drove it back. A temporary distraction, it did little to fill the hole in my life.

Friday and Saturday nights were the worst. I'd get back from work at around nine and try to find something to do. Sometimes I'd call up old friends from the neighborhood; sometimes, I couldn't even do that. The dorm would be empty — it seemed everyone was out having fun — I couldn't sit alone in my room.

I went out for a run a few times; I'd be out and alone altogether. One time it was raining as I stood at the corner of Main and South Prospect. It was ten-thirty on a Friday, and some girls from my high school were stopped at the light. One rolled down her window and yelled to me, inviting me to a party she knew of. I was embarrassed to have been seen; what possible reason could I be running in a cold winter rain on a Friday night? I had no intention of going to a party.

On another Sunday night in my room, I was having some beers and getting stoned by myself. I opened the deadbolt to prop the door open and walked to the bathroom down the hall. I didn't want to bring my key and never learned (and never asked) how to put the door in the unlocked position. As I came out to the bathroom, a UVM cop stood waiting at my door.

For a moment, I thought I'd ignore him and walk out the front door like it wasn't my room. He locked in on me as I approached, correctly assuming the pot smell was mine. We went into my room and talked for a while. He asked about the half-dozen beer cans and incorrectly presumed they were left from the weekend.

He started writing some kind of ticket and giving me the bad news. I'd kept my thoughts to myself to that point, but I lost my nerve and started to panic. "I can't get in trouble," I repeated as I broke down and opened the floodgates of information. I told him about my last semester and my brother. I told him how well I'd been doing — and I had, academically anyhow. I told him the truth and waited to see if he was human.

He watched as I flushed the tiny bit of pot I had left (I never had much anyway) and gave me his best fatherly advice. I didn't receive any punishment, and to my knowledge, no record was kept of the incident. I thanked him for his kindness and vowed (to myself) to be more careful in the future.

Gradually, I came out of the dark and found a new way. A friend from my high school baseball team, nicknamed "Perch," invited me to hang at his downtown apartment. I started spending some time with friends from work. I slowly became comfortable with new people around me — people who never knew the person I remembered. One day at a time, I became a new version of myself.

8.

I'd lose track of the days; my weeks flew by alone. On weekends — while my friends were out doing things, glorious, physical things — I'd sit home and wait for the evening. It became a routine to leave the apartment for the first time around five — Fridays and Saturdays to friends', Sundays for dinner at my parents'.

I pulled into the driveway on the evening of July 4th to find my landlords hosting a barbeque on the back lawn. Happy-go-lucky as always — a handful of revelers, coolers, and lawn games — they asked me to join in the fun. *There's no way I'm going to make chipper small-talk with strangers.* I told them I had plans for the fireworks and disappeared up the stairs.

I drank a beer in still silence and felt bad for myself. When it got dark, my landlord's son began to pound on the door at the bottom of the stairs, alerting me of the impending excitement. I didn't move. *Even if he comes upstairs and bangs on my door, I'm not here.* He never did.

I didn't watch TV, read, or surf the web. I sat drinking on the (legendary) blue couch, listening to the booming fireworks and joyful sounds of life beneath my open windows. I sat alone and felt sorry for myself, gentle tears falling from my eyes.

9.

I skipped my ten-year high school reunion. I got the Facebook invite but didn't respond. My former self would've been there, but I hadn't accepted my new reality; I absolutely wasn't ready to share.

It seemed like a casual affair, organized by the usual suspects: the class presidents, members of the Key Club (whatever that is), and the like. It'd be held at a bar — Red Square in Burlington — an apparent attempt at the polar opposite of the name-tag, banquet-hall reunions cliché to the Hollywood movie. I knew I'd be welcome there; it'd be nice to see people, but I couldn't make myself go.

I'd lost touch with nearly all of my high school friends by the time I'd finished college. It wasn't deliberate; I think I'd just changed and moved on. I felt like a different person — I'd found a new world with new friends after Nick died — and my worlds didn't mesh in my mind.

But I would've gone, had some drinks and some laughs, and gone home afterward. Nothing would've come of it — no great epiphanies, major embarrassments, and few stories to tell. It would've been a few hours with old friends, nothing more.

But my physical deterioration was beyond hiding. I couldn't drink at a bar, talk, laugh, and pretend. A year earlier, I could have — and probably would have — but not anymore.

I hadn't yet outed myself to the world. I'd kept my circle of trust and support very small. To the rest of the world, I didn't exist; the old me was still what they pictured.

It would've been easy to tell them — in the Facebook group or a message to the organizers — but that would've made the whole thing about me. I'd be the headliner before I walked through the door. I'd have to see the look in their eyes, the sullen disbelief that'd been burned in my mind.

Even before my diagnosis — before I had to tell anyone the news — I knew that look. I could see it in the faces as I gazed out on the room as my brother lay still in a casket. Some of my classmates had been there — a roomful of kids utterly unprepared for the moment.

Shock, disbelief, and overwhelming sadness. No, I couldn't see those faces once again. I'd have to stay home.

SOMETIMES I FEEL LIKE I'M ALREADY GONE

If it's not already obvious, the old me could be aptly described as adventurous. I'm told that at ten months, I decided I needed to walk, and after a great number of falls, I finally succeeded. Not satisfied with my tricycle, I stood on the stoop to climb onto Nick's

training-wheel-enabled big-kid bike. My first time on ice skates —
sometime around ten — I went as fast as I could, lost control, flew
up, and landed hard on my back. On a school day around noon,
my driver's license but a few months old, I got a ticket for going
ninety-five on the highway. We were doing 110 down a hill in my
Saab. I was both pumped and terrified to jump out of a plane at
seventeen, but I didn't get the chance. They found out I was only
seventeen.

Along with my trademark sarcastic wit and love of laughter,
inability to give or receive a compliment (that might make me vulnerable), and book smarts but not street smarts intelligence, it was
always the willingness to go for it that defined my not-fully-grown-
up self. That was the old me, the person my friends knew. He's still
somewhere inside, continually searching for a way to get out.

Other than the obvious, the physical deterioration of my body,
perhaps my greatest challenge has been with my identity. I think
about it a lot, still, as I sit here today more than ten years after this
story began. Sometimes I look back through rosy frames like I had
all the answers before. At best, I had partially completed the puzzle
before it all fell apart.

I look at my friends and former colleagues, who they've become, and what they've accomplished. I've attended their weddings, seen them move through their careers, share pictures from
far-off locales, and start families. I used to think we were the same.

We went through high school and college, worked the same
part-time jobs, played sports and made music together. We joked
and laughed and hung out together. We went camping and skiing,
took road trips, and became roommates.

A lot of times, I still think they're the same people I remember.
I see my friends as I prefer to see myself, before I was lost. I see
twentysomethings in crappy apartments. I see all the things we did
together — all of the reasons we were friends.

They've all moved forward together — their lives are different from those days, but they have each other. I see them share

in their experiences, give advice, and receive support. They're in a new place, navigating a host of new problems, but they're in the game together. I'm off on the bench, only watching.

I don't think they know how to talk to me anymore. I ask questions, and we talk about their lives; I share memories, and they compare them with the present. They tell stories about the old me; we laugh about the immature, obnoxious things we all did. It feels like I no longer exist.

I can't help thinking, indeed knowing, that I'm not the same person that was a friend to those people. I think of all of the reasons I was friends with anyone throughout my life, and almost all of it has vanished. I don't even know what my interests are. I know that I can't be who I was, but I need to be someone.

I'm not alone in missing those times, but it's more than that. I miss the experiences, sure, but really, I miss myself. I mourn the loss of the person I used to be. I can't be the only one. When my friends look at me, who do they see? Sometimes I feel like I'm already gone.

10.

I sank into my routine, always looking for something to break the monotony. I went grocery shopping in the middle of the day and took aimless, meandering drives. I tried to ride my bike, and I went out for walks.

Driving was, in some ways, the perfect activity: not physically demanding and out of the house. I'd take back roads, sans GPS, and try to get lost. Sometimes I'd drive somewhere, get out and go for a walk. The drive back always felt like a slog. I'd arrive home bored and tired — more than ready for my outing to be over — and think, *What was the point?*

I took out my bike for the last few times that summer in Waterbury. I'd climb awkwardly on and gain momentum down the driveway. As I came to Main Street, I knew if I stopped, I'd immediately end up on the sidewalk. Light midday traffic and wishful thinking combined to safely propel me across. Had I considered the possibility of getting hit by a car, I'd never have made it out of the driveway.

If you've seen the episode of *Frasier* where Niles and Frasier learn to ride bikes — that's what I looked like. Arms not quite steady, gripping the handlebars tight and frantically shifting gears; legs pushing the spinning pedals, trying to find a balance; butt firmly planted on the seat, because anything else would be suicide. All of it merely a desperate attempt to hold on to the past.

I rode down Winooski Street and over the bridge to a peaceful place without traffic. I followed the pavement until it came to an end and continued on the soft, sandy surface. Coming the other way was a mother out biking with her two children, one on training wheels. She smiled, and I nodded, maintaining my death grip on the handlebars all the while. The children were laughing — joyously, breezily laughing — as I gritted my teeth and made every effort to remain upright. I was running up a mountain, and they just hopped off the ski lift.

Already tired after what must've been only a mile, it was time to turn around. But the road was sandy and narrow. I couldn't simply stop and turn the bike; my legs couldn't be trusted to transition from pedal to ground. I could have really used training wheels. *How do I keep my momentum while turning a circle?* It didn't seem possible.

I started out wide to the right and cut across both lanes while throwing up dust. At the top of the turn, I started to tip and tried to get a foot on the ground. My feeble attempt was no match for gravity, and as if the bike had no rider, we went down. Embarrassed, with no one around — covered in dust — I scrambled to my feet and got myself out of the road. *I really don't want to have to walk my bike all the way home.* Like so many things I'd been through each day, this was my first time in this moment. My physical abilities diminished every day: I never really knew where I stood. I wasn't sure I could get back on the bike. Somehow, despite my tired, shaking body, I climbed on and started pedaling toward home.

I faced the same dilemma at Main Street again: if I slowed too much, I'd surely fall; if I didn't, I'd risk getting hit by a car. My head and eyes darted back and forth, assessing the traffic. Using my predetermined preference more than my eyesight — *I really don't wanna fall again* — I rode on through. Because I wasn't hit, nor was I honked at, I marked it as a success. I approached the garage doors, slowed near a stop, and unceremoniously fell to the ground. I got up, looked around for witnesses, and walked my bike into the garage.

***

The walks began as a bike replacement — a reason to get out, to break up the time between meals. I walked all over town: up Stowe Street and under the highway, down Winooski Street and across the bridge, up and down Main Street and the recently flooded sections of town. I brought a book down to the river's edge, stuck in my feet, and tried to get comfortable. I spent an hour staring at the river instead of my book.

As unfortunate as it was, living in the heart of the Green Mountains, I knew my real hiking days were behind me. In the weeks after my diagnosis, I made one last assault on Camel's Hump with some friends. I fell over a couple of times, but with nothing more than a gouge out of my palm, I had to consider it a success. Later that fall, I got out a few more times on the Nebraska Notch and Long Trails. I was experimenting, waiting on a miracle to show me I could still do some of the things I feared had been lost forever. My uncertainty ended with an abbreviated November sojourn up the bottom section of the Long Trail's ascent of Camel's Hump. In the midst of light snow and distant (deer season) gunshots, unable to jump, I placed a boot directly into a two-foot-wide mountain stream. That would be my last try.

For a while, I liked to (I don't know if I liked to, but I did) drive to a spot by Gillett Pond, near the Richmond/Huntington line, and park the car. I'd walk past the pond, around the blind curves in the dirt road, past the Robbins Mountain sign, and down the steep, paved section toward Jonesville. It was cathartic to use the strength I still had. I'd try to pick up the pace down the hill, shuffling along as best I could. Just a year before, I'd descended Camel's Hump in much the same way. That was a 4,000-foot mountain — the trail was steep, uneven, and covered with rocks. Footfalls occurred at a variety of awkward angles, requiring strong and flexible ankles. Sufficient core strength was needed merely to remain upright. This, by contrast, was a freshly paved road. It was steep, to be sure, but homogenous and predictable. Nevertheless, only seconds into my experiment, I'd begin to lose control, give up and go back to my walk.

I'd arrive back at the car tired and sweaty in the summer heat. My feet felt like long-abused prisoners. I'd sit on the driver's seat, pull off my shoes and socks, and stare down at two red, cartoonishly swollen objects. I'd drive my three-pedal car barefoot, relishing the air on my toes.

I knew all the exercise in the world wouldn't do me any good. On the contrary, the doctors had warned me not to over-exert my muscles or overtire myself. If I caused damage to a muscle or tendon — pulled an overtight hamstring, for example — I had no guarantee it would ever heal. In hindsight, I may have deluded myself into believing that riding my bike or going for long, strenuous walks could do me some sort of good because I needed to hold on as long as possible. As was the case with a whole host of physical activities — from getting on the floor to attempt a few push-ups to descending the stairs without the handrail — I needed to repeatedly prove to myself that I *could* still do it. I woke up every morning knowing that another small piece of me was gone. I didn't want to say goodbye; I wasn't ready.

11.

My second winter in Waterbury was different. I was no longer working, and my walking had worsened. The night came on early; the snow made everything more difficult. I felt like a shut-in, stranded in my apartment above the garage.

I was at home alone one Saturday night; I hadn't gone anywhere in days. My car looked abandoned in the driveway, still covered in six inches of snow from a storm several days past. I was feeling uncommonly antsy after dinner; I needed to get out and do something. I couldn't sit and wallow alone.

My image as a regular at the bars up the street had never materialized like I'd wanted. I was scared to go alone; I wasn't comfortable interacting with strangers. Sadly, those days were behind me. I felt confident with friends by my side; friends felt like the armor I needed.

I tried that night to put my fears in a box and go out on my own. I put on my jacket and boots and hesitantly walked out the door. I stepped carefully through the driveway like I was committing a crime. *Am I really doing this? Damn right you are. Don't be a wuss.* I almost lost my nerve and turned around.

It wasn't just the bar; it was the walk. I had tripped on the sidewalk the previous summer; Laura and Lenny had witnessed me bloody my knee. Now, staring down at the footprints in the snow, I made my way slowly. *Why can't I walk in the street? Why am I even doing this?*

The street was clean; the pavement was bare. But this was Main Street, and there were cars. I saw people joyously sliding — like surfers in boots on a wave — on the last downhill block by the bar. Carefully stepping down the icy sidewalk, I tried to ignore them; I tried to pretend I wasn't seething with jealousy. Repeating my mantra — *please don't fall, please don't fall* — I made it and nervously looked in the window. I pulled open the door to Prohibition Pig and took the first stool at the end of the bar.

I ordered an unfamiliar beer and sipped it quietly. There was a group to my left — three or four guys and a couple of girls — heartily drinking and carrying on. One of the guys looked over and introduced the group. Fresh off a Saturday night at Hen of the Wood — the swanky ski-tourist restaurant up the street — they looked like the typical food service crowd. I would've loved to catch up to their level of drunkenness, stayed until closing, and shared a few laughs. That's what would've happened just a year or two before. Instead — after downing their recommended cocktail — I was reaching my limit. Still afraid of the sidewalks, I said my goodbyes. I lived right down the street; I told them I'd see them again. But I never went back on my own.

I can't help but long for what could've been; my time in Waterbury might've been so much different. On paper, it all seemed so appealing: a newly built apartment to myself, an easy commute, membership at a private country club just up the road, all the hiking and skiing I could ever want within reach, and a walkable village with a number of bars for me to choose from. Writing those words, it seems like a dream. Unfortunately, it never became anything more.

TRYING TO FIND THE FAMILIAR

I've talked a lot about drinking. If I went back farther, to high school and college, there would be a whole lot more. In high school, it was a new and exciting, rebellious activity. In college, it was often irrational, excessive, self-defeating, and counterproductive. But that's what we did, and I certainly wasn't alone. I'm sure many of my contemporaries look back in much the same way.

Drinking is the most widely used social lubricant. I have heard it said — by a comedian, the ultimate truth-teller — that people think drinking gives them courage, makes social situations easier, smooths out the rough spots. But, in fact, drinking only makes people dumber, both in appearance and in reality. And while it is certain that both can be true, the dumbness overtakes the social lubricant after a particular number of drinks. It may never have taken over my life — prevented me from attending classes, or paying the rent — but the college-age ritual of dumbness-level drinking often stood in the way of what could've been a more mature social existence.

A lot of it was only male camaraderie masquerading as a possibility for something more. It turns out it's difficult to leave the party or the bar with a girl — or perhaps, more importantly, think beyond the night itself — when you can't hold a coherent conversation. Don't get me wrong; I'm not going to pretend that a couple of drunkards never find their way into bed, but that's not really what I needed. I'm not sure that I could've seen the bigger picture at that age, that I could've enjoyed more mature relationships, but the fallback of shortsighted heavy drinking only clouded the matter.

Most any gathering I attended in my post-college years — while no longer strictly alcohol consumption themed — included it as an important ingredient. Backyard barbeques, dinner parties, or just a few friends spending the evening together, alcohol — mostly local microbrews, but also hard ciders, wines, and the occasional cocktail — always seemed a crucial element. There were so many times that a few beers among friends — before my diagnosis and after it, just sitting on the couch or around the kitchen table laughing in each other's company — was all the comfort I needed.

I can still drink, and for the most part, it still has the same effect on my brain, but a lot has changed. I haven't had a drink in months. I don't want to. I haven't been in many social situations that call for it. On the occasion that I have — most specifically since I've been wheelchair-bound and have to rely on others for my transportation needs — drinking a beer (only one) has become more of an attempt to hang onto the past than a genuine source of enjoyment. I still enjoy the taste of a coffee stout, pilsner, or the 10,000th iteration of the New England IPA, but I feel like I'm joining in just to join in.

It doesn't bring the same sense of freedom and possibility that it once did; it quickly wreaks havoc on my body. It doesn't accompany and enhance the variety of activities that it used to; it makes them more complicated or impossible. It doesn't help me sleep; it seems to make my heart rate increase, my body more jittery, and relaxing more difficult. It's become only a symptom of the problem, a further impetus to my ability to communicate, walk, and stand without fear. There is no possibility to do the things or feel the way that I used to; alcohol is no exception. As many times as I've tried (and pretended) to recapture a piece of the past — with a bottle of beer or by some other method — at some point, I had to accept the futility of those actions.

Drinking isn't the same anymore. It doesn't have the same physical, mental, or emotional effects. It may seem like it should, but it doesn't. It's just another reminder of the life I now live. I'm always trying to find the familiar; I don't have high hopes.

12.

I spent a lot of weekends crashing at Tom and Katie's place in Winooski. They invited me over for dinner and drinks; sometimes we'd walk down the hill to the bars. It was at their apartment that I first told my news — two days after I'd received it.

I pulled up to the curb in the same spot every time — turned the key, unbuckled the seatbelt, and pushed open the car door. I'd systematically turn my body and place my feet in the little space between the car and the curb. I'd step onto the curb, shift my feet to turn around and throw closed my driver's side door. I'd move to the back door, lean forward, and awkwardly pull out a six-pack or bottle of wine. It seemed every once-routine, thoughtless action had become a multi-step, robotic process in my world.

I always had a bed (it was a futon) there. For a long time after that Wednesday morning in August — even before I moved out of the frat house in Stowe — there weren't many weekends where I didn't spend a night in the tiny spare bedroom off the kitchen. We didn't always do much, but that's what I needed — friends to spend time with, people who knew.

Sometimes on Saturdays or Sundays — with Katie at work waiting tables — Tom and I would eat breakfast, split a French press of Tom's kick-you-in-the-face coffee, smoke some pot, and head out for a walk. The weather always seemed to be gorgeous.

On those mornings, full of an over-allotment of coffee and the highly unusual morning bowl, I could barely get my body to cooperate. On the sidewalk in front of 14 Audet Street, I tried to stretch and shake the stiffness out of my legs. Ingesting two powerful drugs to start my day brought my nerve activity to a ten. It was not an unfamiliar feeling — similar to the bodily anxiety I'd experienced giving a presentation or talking to a (potentially) inquisitive cop. There was no fighting it, but the severity would pass.

We'd head down the hill to the circle, cross the bridge into Burlington, and start the hike up Colchester Avenue. We made it all the way downtown a few times, to Church Street or the farmers' market for a bite, a beer, or a coffee. One time, we walked around the museum-like Champlain Mill, looking at pictures of its long-ago workforce. Time drifted as we carefully examined the black-and-whites of our would-be grandparents as sullen-looking children.

The walks were just something for us to do. After years spent running, and hiking, and golfing, and skiing together, it was something we still *could* do. We both knew even this wouldn't last forever.

Slowly I stopped spending so much time in Winooski. My comforting routine — the safe space Tom and Katie had created — wasn't needed so much. My friends had helped me through an impossibly difficult time. I had a new interest in the spring. A girl came into my life.

CHAPTER 6

NEW LIFE

I've found joy in the sadness. It seems real. I hope it is.

1.

On February 7, 2013, I posted the following:

Dear Facebook,

I have some news I need to tell you. In August of 2011, I was diagnosed with ALS. That's Lou Gehrig's disease. I should have told you all long ago. And I should have told you face to face. I apologize for my inability to do so. I just couldn't handle the overwhelming dread of telling you and the look in your eye when you found out. I still can't handle that look in your eye.

If I've ignored you, didn't call you back, or haven't kept in touch, I'm sorry. I just didn't recognize myself and it's been very difficult to accept that I'm not who I used to be. I guess maybe I thought if you didn't know, then maybe it wouldn't be real for you the way it is for me. I don't know what else to say except that I'm doing fine and I appreciate those of you who have supported me.

A lot of people came out of the woodwork to send me all varieties of messages, most of them simple and supportive. Some didn't — people I'd wanted to hear from. Very little changed in my life; there wasn't a long line of old friends knocking at my door. While I will always appreciate every bit of support, a few stood out to a brain searching for negativity. Allow me to briefly indulge in the George Carlin style of labeling absurdity.

Because I imagine they want to be positive and encouraging, people say things like *You got this* and the like. I guess they're trying to tell me I'm strong enough to endure, adjust, or (as much as it makes me cringe to even write it) make the best of it. As unhelpful as those thoughts might be, they're preferable to the ideas I hear with those words. I don't need a pep talk. This isn't something to work through; there's no light at the end of the tunnel. In fact, there's no tunnel. There's a vice that's slowly crushing me, taking away everything piece by piece. A positive attitude is not going to help; I'm not going to beat this.

One Facebook friend — someone I hadn't talked to since high school, and I'm not sure I talked to *in* high school — sent me a doozy I'll never forget. She told me that this was God's plan — that I had been chosen because of my strength. Sidestepping the simpleminded blanket euphemism of "God has a plan," (What makes you think the words "God has a plan" can be used to explain any situation?! You are choosing delusional comfort.) what struck me was the utter, illogical insanity that this was intended to make me feel better. Am I supposed to feel pride in being a martyr? Martyrs die. I'd like to live.

The most important of the messages came from an old friend from high school. I shouldn't call her an old friend, that was just the way I thought of it at the time. She was actually more of an acquaintance — Kim and I spent one year together on the cross-country ski team. Still reluctant to see anyone who'd known my former self — afraid of the sadness and disappointment that surely would follow — it took me almost six weeks to respond.

Kim had spent five years in Boston after college. She made a lot of friends and had a lot of stories but decided it was time to move home. She was working as a para-educator in Hinesburg. We exchanged a few messages and made plans to have dinner.

I invited her to meet me at Duino! (Duende) and sent a link in lieu of directions. I'd eaten there a few times with friends. It was young, fun, and a little off the map. As I expected, she'd never been. *Perfect*.

I arrived a bit early, parked nearby on North Winooski Avenue, sat facing the door, and ordered a glass of wine. A few minutes later, as she walked through the door, I thought, *She looks the same and completely different*. Of course, she did; it'd been more than ten years. She'd grown up.

Though I really didn't know her or what she'd been up to all these years, it felt safe, familiar — entirely different from the last time I sat across from a girl in a restaurant. This time I wasn't hiding anything; this time, I wasn't scared. This girl knew who I was, had known my brother, grew up around the corner. She knew what I didn't have to say: ALS. Also, this wasn't a date. The cute and cuddly girl I remembered (and had a crush on) as a shy and timid teen appeared before me all grown up. I saw her through the eyes of a friend; it didn't occur to me (in my deep, blinding postdiagnosis depression) that she'd want to *date* me. Nonetheless, I still saw how she looked. She wore a form-fitting wool dress over jeans; she still looked like the runner I remembered. She had dark hair and eyes, a natural, perfect smile, and an ever-so-slightly dimpled, cute-as-a-button face.

I sat there talking with this bubbly, positive person who seemed fascinated, like there was nowhere she'd rather be. We had those same get-to-know-you conversations with ease. I felt like — for maybe the first time outside of my small, inner-circle — I could just *be*; all of my cards were on the table.

2.

She invited me to join her for a show at Higher Ground the next week — her friend's boyfriend played keyboards in a band. We made plans to meet at nearby Jaycee Park beforehand. She'd bring a pizza.

I stopped on the way and bought a bottle of wine at a gas station. I forgot to bring a corkscrew — and glasses. Accompanied by an unopened bottle of wine, we ate a few slices of pizza at a picnic table by the parking lot.

We walked to the Mobil station on the corner in search of a corkscrew — they didn't have one. We crossed the street to Gracey's, and I spent $1.09 on the two-piece, red plastic device we needed. Though only a few hundred yards, it felt like an adventure to my legs. Trying to maintain a steady gait at Kim's side, I kept those thoughts to myself.

In the cool air of an April evening — in the park where I'd played Little League baseball — we drank from the bottle in the oncoming darkness. Kim wasn't the least bit phased by any of it. We could've bought cups, but she didn't care (and I didn't care); we drank from the bottle. When the wine had run out, we got in my car and drove around the corner to the show.

As we stood in line at the ticket window, I struggled to get my wallet from my back pocket with my freezing cold, useless hands. I almost gave up and asked Kim to reach into the back pocket of my tight-fitting pants. That I even considered asking shows how much I'd let my guard down. At the last moment, I got it; we bought tickets, received our "21+" bracelets, and pulled open the door to the ballroom.

When I was growing up, it was Merrill's Showcase 5, an all-too-average suburban theater built in the '70s. Higher Ground — a two-stage music venue — moved into the space from Winooski in 2004. I'd seen countless acts there in the years since.

We ordered Maker's Marks at the side bar. *Wine from the bottle, straight whiskey — I love this girl.* With a drink in my hand and a heavy buzz, time disappeared to the crowd and the music. When it was time for another, I could hardly say no; so, what if I drove in from Waterbury?

On the walk through the lobby after the show, we decided I couldn't drive home. Kim invited me to stay the night at her place in Shelburne and got on the phone to a cab. We stood out in front of the building as the post-show crowd slowly dispersed. A "Green Cab"

Prius pulled into the circle; I tripped on the curb and stumbled my way to the car. *Yup, I'm a little drunk.*

She walked me to the living room couch and told me again — because she felt she needed a reason — that she had just moved, her bed was tiny, and I had to sleep on the couch. (I later learned, in the light of day, that the dark couch was consistently, visibly covered in the hair from two dogs and a cat.) I guess anyone might have expectations in that situation, but I really didn't. I was happy enough she'd invited me back; the couch was already more than enough. As I sat on the couch and she leaned in to arrange me a blanket, we somehow fell into a kiss. She wished me goodnight, excused herself to her room, and I lay back with a smile.

3.

We had dinner at The Spot the next Tuesday. We ate fish tacos at an outdoor table and talked by her car as the parking lot slowly emptied and the manager locked up for the night. She asked me if we could go someplace and talk — she mentioned Overlook Park.

I didn't know what she had planned. Overlook Park felt like a place for teenage pot-smoking and promiscuity. We parked side by side, got out of our cars, and sat on a rock in the dark. The warm, sunny evening had turned to a windy, cold night; in minutes, I was visibly shivering. Though I was freezing — and my body was quickly stiffening to the point where walking would be a challenge — I wasn't about to show her how fragile I was. But she saw my discomfort almost immediately, and together we retreated to my car.

We talked until sunup. We'd built an uncommon level of trust in only a few days. We shared thoughts and memories of my brother, from our days on the ski team to the shock of his death to each of our experiences in the aftermath. She told me stories from her childhood, growing up with her single mother in a Burlington apartment. She opened up about the traumas of her life, from her nonexistent father to a recent and particularly unhealthy romantic relationship. I told her stories from every angle of my ongoing struggle. We had a collective therapy session; we laughed and we cried — together. I think each of us wanted to take care of the other, creating a dysfunctional dynamic from the start.

4.

I invited Kim to my place the following Saturday. We had dinner and drinks and talked on the (legendary) blue couch. Though we hadn't discussed it, I think both of us knew she had no intention of going home. With a couple of refills and more than a few laughs, things moved into the bedroom. I was nervous in the usual, first-time ways, and even more so. But I felt safe with Kim. It *had* been a while, with an ALS diagnosis in between, but I wasn't hiding; I wasn't afraid of being found out. I felt like I'd been accepted. This seemed like the first time of many. I also drank a lot of gin.

We started spending more time together and though we never discussed it, quickly turned into a couple. Because she worked in Burlington and I didn't work anywhere, I spent a lot of weeknights at her place. I'd drive over around dinner, walk up the handrail-less steps to the screen door, and find Kim and her roommate at the kitchen table.

I always stayed over, never intending to drive back to Waterbury. I'd wake up each morning to the sound of a coffee grinder — Vermont Coffee Company dark roast in a French press. I'd stumble into the kitchen, asleep on my feet, as she frantically made for the door. Her hair wet from the shower, she'd kiss me goodbye and tell me to stay. I'd sit in the kitchen — the sunlight streaming through the door of an empty house — and drink the other half of the coffee.

We spent most of our weekends at my place. I couldn't help but think of my landlord seeing her come and go. Finally, I wasn't spending every minute alone, holed up in the apartment above the garage. With Kim at my side, I made it out to all of those places that had been so difficult. We walked up the street to the restaurants and bars. I felt confident, even prideful — happy to be out with my girlfriend.

ON EATING; ON SLEEPING

I don't eat like I used to. I don't lack an appetite or adhere to some peculiar diet, it's mostly my hands. They don't work. There are so many foods that I would otherwise love, except for the increasingly complicated task of getting them into my mouth.

If I'm going to a restaurant, I try to look at the menu beforehand. My choices are not based on taste, but on my perceived ease of use. It's almost like I have food allergies; I'm allergic to foods that will be physically difficult or impossible to eat.

Soup is always out; it's been that way for years. Ignoring the near-impossibility of delicately lifting the liquid to my mouth, I can't even hold a spoon the right way. Unless it's thick enough to stick to the spoon — like anything from chocolate pudding to three-bean chili to oatmeal or curry with rice — it's not making it up to my mouth.

Sandwiches of any kind — especially anything a high-functioning human might call "messy" — are a maybe at best. I'm flabbergasted by how skillfully people routinely slip their fingers under a plate-bound slice of bread, hamburger roll, or taco — oh how I love tacos. Putting aside the sore neck and messy hands that result from a juicy cheeseburger and the inevitability of finishing the meal with a fork, simply getting a sandwich into my hands is always a challenge.

Small handheld items, anything held between a finger and thumb — like a French fry, peanut, slice of bacon, or cocktail shrimp — require workarounds. It's impossible to get a potato chip or cracker, M&M or jelly bean onto a fork. The only way to successfully ingest these items is to adhere them directly to the tongue. I lean forward and stick my tongue directly to the chip, like a cartoon frog. My method — while shamelessly effective alone — is thoroughly awkward (and mostly avoided) among company and absolutely rules out dips and salsas.

Perhaps the easiest are fork foods — things I can stab rather than scoop. The turkey is the easiest thing on the Thanksgiving plate, the cranberry and stuffing the most difficult. Even pastas are workable, though sometimes tedious and messy.

With all of it, at every meal, I gaze in awe at the speed with which others devour their food. One of the obstacles I face — of which I am continually reminded by my nutritionist — is that I will grow bored, tired, or both before finishing my meals. It's not only my fork- or spoon-work, it's my mouth and throat. My chewing and swallowing are far less effective. A lot of people eat with such maniacal speed their stomachs and brains can't keep up; I have the opposite problem.

I don't sleep like I used to. I haven't in years. It's almost impossible to remember what it was like to hit the pillow and hear the alarm with seemingly nothing in between. But those times did exist. The old me slept like a champ.

I know I'm not alone, that many people suffer some form of sleep envy — whether for their partner or a memory of themselves — but mine is a bit different. Some portion is mental — an overactive brain jumping from topic to topic — but largely, it's physical. My body won't shut down — indeed, it never shuts down.

When I lay down to sleep, nerves and muscles refuse to relax. I feel it in my spine, legs, back, shoulders, and face — like little shocks, pinpricks in my body. While most are small and cause only discomfort, some bring violent spasms or deep cramps. I roll over and back, trying to find that ever-elusive calm. I look at the clock one more time.

Every time I turn my body — which is, in fact, a series of small shifts of my hips, torso, and arms — I pull the sheets and blankets with me. Everyone does this — I can almost hear the laugh track from the two-men-sharing-a-bed, all-too-common sitcom scene —

but it's a problem for me. The covers get stuck under my torso, and I can't easily get them out. With a back that won't lift off the mattress, and all-but-useless arms and shoulders, I end up flailing around and trying to kick out the sheets. After several rounds of flopping, I get hot and sweaty, pushing me further from comfort and sleep.

I've always slept on my back — since I had morning neck pain as a kid and taught myself to do so — but that's becoming more difficult. Oftentimes, laying on my back — with the inevitable throat full of mucus that comes with the territory — it's like I can't breathe. Or, in fact, I can't breathe; it's hard to tell. But there are times when I'm in that gray area between awake and asleep, just starting to drift off when I'm jolted awake for a much-needed breath.

The shape of the human torso, with the shoulders jutting out from both sides, doesn't seem to lend itself to laying on its side. My shoulders, not especially bound by the associated muscles, tend to cause problems. The lower often feels crushed and pushed out of place under my immense weight, while the upper, harmlessly draped over my body as it may be, can cause my arm to fall asleep.

I'm never refreshed in the morning; I don't feel rested or ready for the day. I lay still and try to experience the most relaxed version of myself. My nerves and my body are calm, and I relish the feeling. Lying flat on my back in the morning is the closest to normal that I'll ever feel.

5.

We planned a road trip in Canada in July. For several days on my laptop, I charted our course and made reservations. Our plans were ambitious; I was excited.

We'd stay one night in each of eight locations: Quebec City, Parc National du Bic, Kouchibouguac National Park, Prince Edward Island National Park, Halifax, Kejimkujik National Park, Fundy National Park, and finally somewhere in Maine. VT to QC to NB to PE to NB to NS to NB to ME to NH to VT.

It was a lot of driving, a lot of packing and unpacking, and potentially a lot of stress on a new relationship. We were in the car for at least three hours every day but one. My itinerary called for four 5-hour drives. I didn't build in any downtime. As I imagine was inevitable, we often found ourselves in a world of laughter-inducing overtired delirium.

What was most memorable for me wasn't the *what* but the *who*. Kim and I spent every second together, making our way through a number of frustrating experiences — including setting up camp and cooking dinner in the rain, getting inexplicably lost in Prince Edward Island, show-stopping car trouble, and the inevitabilities of traveling with a physically limited person — and kept going. We didn't bicker, we didn't whine, each of us did things for the other. It really felt like we were a team. I liked that.

And she was a trooper; it was like she'd been in the army. She'd done a walking tour of Europe in college that, based on her description, consisted of a group of students, a single large tent, and very little in the way of planning. Responsibility for talking a local landowner into allowing a huge tent on his or her property rotated among the group. She seemed to often draw on that experience with an "it'll work out" attitude.

Pee on the side of the road? Set up a campsite in the rain? Endure several sweaty July days without a shower? Use whatever gas station toilet we happen to come across? Live out of a car and a cooler and cook on an old gasoline camp stove? No problem.

I was continually impressed by her low-maintenance mindset. To be fair, I did more than my share of the driving, and she wasn't afraid to doze off in the passenger seat, but I didn't mind. And I did cook nearly every campsite meal on the Coleman (my uncle lent me his old, bulletproof camp stove, a folding brick of steel with a self-pumping, pressurized gasoline reservoir) but she was always setting up or packing away the site. We were good teammates.

Almost finished with about 2,200 miles of driving, Sunday morning found us packing our Mount Desert Island campsite headed home. Her baby-blue stick-shift Ford Focus had so far been up to the challenge, but soon after crossing into Vermont, climbing a hill on I-89, its engine abruptly cut out. Kim was asleep when I pulled onto the shoulder. I somehow expected a solution to flow from her mouth when I woke her. It did not. Unsure what to do — the wind from passing trucks shaking our little car — we sat there for a few minutes, and she made some phone calls for advice. I don't know what we expected she'd learn. I absolutely did not want to admit that we might have to get the car towed, on a Sunday, all the way home or to I don't know where. Frustrated and low on options, I tried the key. It started right up.

The car died twice more, but eventually, we limped into my parents' driveway for our planned Sunday dinner. Charcoal-grilled steaks were our reward. My parents' reward: a couple of exhausted travelers, sweaty, smelly, and safe.

I walked everywhere on that trip. I waded into the warm ocean waters at Kouchibouguac; I floated on the lake at Kejimkujik. I cooked the meals, crawled in and out of the tent, and got up from the ground. Though my stamina was limited, and watching people bike along the coast of Prince Edward Island broke my heart, more than three years after my symptoms began, I was still able to do most everything I needed.

Kim took all sorts of pictures; one stands out in my mind. I'm standing on the beach at Prince Edward Island National Park, with my arms stretched out in a Y. I'm straining to lift up my arms and hold them in place. That simple pose, as awkward as it looks, was indeed still possible. That picture is perhaps the last evidence that I could ever lift my arms at all.

6.

Kim accompanied Mom and I to one of my all-day ALS clinics later that summer. I was more than happy to have her there, but a cynic might look back on her attendance as more of a fact-finding mission than one of selfless support. (Any ulterior motive, justified or not, didn't occur to me at the time.) I hadn't gained much of anything in all of my doctor's visits; they were just boring tasks to be endured. If nothing else, Kim's presence made my day a little more tolerable.

Though I assured everyone that I was doing fine with the stairs, my continuing inhabitance of a second-floor apartment was becoming a problem. Now there was one more voice in the chorus against me. As would become the case with so many things, I'd say I'm fine; they'd say I'm not. But now that the pressure was coming from so close, it became harder for me to ignore. I talked to my landlord, who'd always been kind and supportive. She asked only that I not leave in the winter. If not for Kim, my stubborn denial would've been allowed to rule longer; I'd have undoubtedly stayed until I was physically afraid of the stairs.

Still only about six months into our relationship, Kim and I started talking about finding a place together. That turned a negative into a positive. It was a big decision, but I was nothing but grateful; everything should be — I felt everything *had* to be — moving fast. I flipped the switch in my mind, and I was on board.

We looked at a bunch of places, all over, some out of (her) pure curiosity. We checked out an old farmhouse in Richmond and a new trailer in Starksboro. We visited a tiny, dilapidated cottage on Monkton Pond and several apartments in Burlington. After watching Kim make endless small talk with dozens of strangers, we'd narrowed our search to two: a ranch-style duplex by the Round Church in Richmond and a third-floor flat in an elevator building off Riverside Ave in Burlington.

We chose the condo, and we chose correctly. Not only was it in Burlington — closer to, well, nearly everything — but heat was included, laundry was in the bathroom, and there wasn't a single stair for me to deal with. Had I been moving alone, it would've even more easily won out.

The new apartment lease was to begin November 1, but as a courtesy to my landlord, I agreed to be out of my place by the end of September. I planned to live at my parents' for the month of October. They were happy to have me but not that happy to host all my stuff, which lived in the garage to be moved yet again.

Kim had a little more trouble. She told me her roommate (and friend since childhood) had gotten upset that she was leaving their rental. They had a big fight; it wasn't going to be easily smoothed over. (With the benefit of hindsight, I can see that it may have been more complicated. I'm not sure how I know this or why I believe it to be true, but I think Kim's roommate had long advised her against letting our relationship get too serious. Her practical advice was unlikely appreciated and indeed ignored. Moving in together seemed to be the final straw and drew a wedge between close friends.)

Things were tense back at the house in Shelburne, and for the rest of October, Kim mostly stayed at my parents' with me. The thought of our new apartment helped the weeks pass. It would have been easier to spend time at her place, but it was time to move in soon enough.

It was a two-bedroom flat with the living room in the center, a galley kitchen, and a washer/dryer in the lime-green bathroom. Each bedroom contained a single north-facing window and an oversized closet. Straight ahead upon entry, at the far end of the living room was a sliding glass door to a small, covered balcony. Other than the kitchen and the bathroom, which were linoleum, and the entryway/dining room, which was laminate oak, the whole place had thick wall-to-wall carpeting. It caused me to trip and fall multiple times; my brain needed some time to adjust.

And so, it began — living together. It didn't feel all that different to me. There were no roommates sharing our space, and yet I wasn't alone. Like any newly cohabitated couple, it felt good to say, "Our place."

I fell into a new routine living with Kim. I bought groceries, cooked dinners, and started writing a blog. I contacted National Life and started working part-time remotely. (On Social Security

Disability, ten hours per week was all I could do.) Each morning, Kim went off to work and I had the day to myself. I was in a new physical place, but it felt like much of the same.

We were both closer to friends on Riverside Avenue, more able to maintain some independence. She could go for a drink after work, I could hang out with Lenny and Tom, and we could do couple things together. I'm glad we didn't choose some place more isolated. I'm not sure I cared at the time; mostly, I wanted to be with her.

FINDING ACCOMPLISHMENT

I started writing a blog for a number of reasons — primarily, I wanted to vent. After quickly and shortsightedly closing the door on my prescribed therapy after one token session, I had no outlet for my frantic and never-ending thoughts. For a long time, that's just what I wanted — to avoid all of my thoughts, feelings, and fears in a semiconscious attempt at maintaining my sanity. But my ignorance couldn't last forever. Things built up even as I chose to push them down, and very slowly, I began to face reality.

I was upset, angry, and sad; I couldn't see the purpose. How was talking to a therapist or communing with a group of terrifying, invalid strangers going to fix this new, life-crushing problem? I didn't want to move forward and try to make the best of my new life. I wanted my old life.

With varying effectiveness, writing has become therapeutic. Though I would undoubtedly enjoy more dialogue, organizing and recording my thoughts has been helpful. In attempting to communicate my feelings with the world, I'm forced to determine exactly what they are. I'd never spent so much time in self-reflection; I think I've learned a lot.

But it has also filled another massive void in my life: it's given me a sense of accomplishment. A wide variety of tasks, large and small, simple and complex, provide people with a steady stream of accomplished feelings. As the years have passed, more of those tasks have grown out of my reach.

It may seem unlikely to miss doing the laundry or the dishes, but I do. You may dread that next snowstorm and the shoveling it brings. I miss that feeling when you're done.

I don't find satisfaction in the work I do, can't find any in athletics as I used to, and in my personal, day-to-day life, it's all but disappeared. I've tried to find accomplishment in a variety of ways, but nothing has proven as significant as writing. There's but one common thread among everything I've written: it was all for me; to help me communicate; to bring to my life even the smallest sense of purpose.

7.

On a Sunday night in January, there was a citywide street-parking ban. Our apartment had two assigned spaces in a lot in front of the building, but I always parked out back. From there, it was a short walk to the garage and its elevator. I wasn't beyond using the stairs to the front door, but it was much easier to avoid them.

When I woke up on Monday, I had an epiphany: my car might be gone. The road inside the condo complex — where I routinely parked — was in fact a public one, subject to plowing and towing. I had forgotten. In my T-shirt and sweats, I rode the elevator down to the garage to have a look. As I had feared, my car was not where I left it.

Having several times seen an otherwise empty lot down the street full of cars after a storm, I thought I knew where it was. I ate breakfast, had coffee, and prepared myself for a jaunt in the snow. I pulled on my heaviest coat, hat, and boots before tediously jamming my hands into a pair of mittens. (I had trouble straightening my fingers; I could never have gotten them inside gloves.)

I walked down Riverside Avenue to the Domino's on the corner and up Barrett and Grove Streets to the lot at Schmanska Park. It was a long, slow slog — a little over a mile on partially cleared sidewalks. It seemed like I hadn't walked in the snow in years; I couldn't remember the last time.

Pushing up the hill on the final stretch, the snow crunching under my feet, my legs grew weary. It was hard to believe this was me; a mile in the snow was almost too much for my body to handle. As I finally approached the group of cars, I spotted mine right away.

I wiped the snow from the windshield with my arm in the fastest, laziest way possible. I pulled off my mittens with my teeth, fumbled around my coat pocket for my keys, pulled the door open, and climbed in. Starting the car, I waited for warmth and let out an audible sigh. My body felt heavy in the seat — spent muscles haphazardly firing in my legs. A few minutes later — though the windshield was far from entirely clear, the wipers still immobilized with ice — I pulled out onto the street.

Snow from the hood dusted the windshield, almost completely impeding my view as I drove. On Riverside Avenue, the wipers finally broke free, spreading water from their icy blades. I fully deserved to be pulled off the road. I was a danger; I couldn't see.

Nonetheless, I made it home safely. Anticipating Kim's reaction, I almost kept the whole thing to myself. But I was a little too proud of my accomplishment. "I could've driven you," she said, lovingly annoyed.

"I know," I shrugged.

8.

The result of the winter blues and a credit from a canceled flight, we talked about taking a trip in February. After a tedious airline research project and numerous discussions, we began to book a week in Puerto Rico. And I began to think about proposing.

I had asked my mom about my mémère's ring and told her about my idea. She, of course, gave me her blessing and — with an eye-to-eye promise (like I was five years old) not to lose it — gave me the ring. She also couldn't help but research and send ideas for our trip.

We'd stay two nights at The Gallery Inn in Old San Juan and five nights in the Pitirres Nest cottage on the island of Culebra. The former was a quirky place in an eighteenth-century building that also functioned as a gallery for the owner's many paintings and sculptures, the latter a one-room structure overlooking the ocean. That was the entirety of our plans.

After a couple of nondescript flights and two trips through customs (we flew out of Montréal), we landed at San Juan Airport. We climbed into one of the waiting cabs — a minivan with a pleasantly polite, Spanish-speaking driver. As with most of our interactions with strangers (and it turns out especially non-English speaking ones), Kim did most of the talking. She loved casually chatting with strangers; I hate most any form of small talk.

The inn was incredible. It *was* Old San Juan — two- and three-story stucco with imposing doorways and varied balconies. *This is why I didn't want to stay in one of those corporate high rises we saw from the plane.* Its multilevel cobblestone courtyard was full of tropical plants and a half dozen varieties of parrot.

I had booked one of the cheaper rooms, and to both my relief and disappointment, it was at ground level off the courtyard. All of those ocean-facing balconies were surely magnificent, but the stone and tile staircases would've been a challenge. Ostensibly to preserve their beautiful, historic appearance, handrails were nowhere to be found.

It was a stunning place to spend time, nonetheless. Filled with Victorian furniture, it was a long, dark room with a massive wood door and high, exposed-beam ceiling. Especially with the door shut, which brought darkness in broad daylight, it felt like our own private cave — in a good way.

We spent the next couple of days exploring the hilly, cobblestone streets of Old San Juan and its colorful buildings and waterfront. We found a few local restaurants (that catered more to locals than tourists), ate the signature local dish, mofongo, and sipped rum drinks. We ate breakfast at the counter in a diner where the fresh-squeezed orange juice — at an exorbitant $3.50 — was the costliest item on the board. Two members of the tourist-filled city's ever-present police force sat down at the bar, drinking coffee and sharing a newspaper.

We walked a half-mile up the hill to Castillo de San Cristobal, the largest Spanish-built fort in the New World. We sampled the self-proclaimed original piña colada at a bar in an indoor/outdoor mall. Kim held my hand as we climbed two separate sets of (hand-rail-free) stairs to the hotel's widow's walk and rooftop trellis.

In the months since our Canadian road trip, my strength had noticeably diminished. I'd walked all over those parks, on trails and beaches, and countless city blocks. It was exhausting, required periods of rest, and my radius was limited, but I did it. In Old San Juan, hiking the hills on the cobblestone streets with the sun beaming down, I quickly grew weary. I looked around at the other tourists, watching their carefree movements. They stared up at buildings, at parked cars, and the feral cats climbing all over them. They stood on the crest of a hill and gazed toward the horizon as they turned to share with a loved one. Instead of merely enjoying the wondrous sights, my mind was focused on every uncomfortable, calculated step. I could walk, and I could take in my surroundings, but truly not at the same time. I was only pretending I wasn't resentful; it was hard to fully enjoy it.

I had to find us a way to Culebra. I knew there was a boat, but I didn't know anything about it. In a few clicks of the mouse, I set aside my practical (cheapskate) ideologies and booked a flight. How better to enjoy a short trip in the Caribbean than aboard a tiny plane?

We were weighed, alongside our luggage, on a freight scale in the terminal, and followed eight or so people through a ground-level door onto the tarmac. The pilot — standing beside a twin-propeller Cessna — gave brief and surprisingly informal instructions to the group. I was assigned the copilot's chair, and with help from Kim and the pilot, climbed my way into the plane.

The flight was a lot of fun; I had an incredible view from the cockpit. We took off and climbed to a few hundred feet — low enough to enjoy the spectacular views — leveling off for the thirty-minute flight. The corner of each front window was pushed open, like a quarter-vent window on a classic car. The wind and engine enveloped me in sound. I felt completely connected to the world around me, like I was riding a bike through the sky.

I watched a tiny island in the distance turn into a landing strip in what seemed like the blink of an eye. My confirmation read, "To check in, please stop at the Carlos Jeep Rental main office and notify the supervisor that you're staying at the cottage." There was no address. We walked into the one-room airport and discovered the sign above one of the service counters.

From a window by the airport's entrance (it resembled a creemee window, for all you Vermonters), Kim ordered us icy, tropical rum drinks as we waited for our golf cart rental to arrive. I was feeling woozy in minutes — undoubtedly dehydrated in the heat. We were instructed to follow a Jeep Wrangler to the cottage.

Midway through our drive, at full throttle on a long straightaway up a hill, my gas-pedal-foot shook violently as we hit several bumps in the road. I couldn't hold my foot in a steady position; the cart jerked, and our bags fell from the back. The Jeep stopped as I did, and Kim ran to retrieve our stuff from the road. That was the last of my driving.

Having seen pictures, we should've been prepared, but I don't think we were. It was beyond incredible: a one-room cottage with a king bed beneath an oversized ceiling fan, kitchen, bathroom, outdoor shower, and deck, set hundreds of feet above the ocean on the western cliffside edge of the island. It was a truly spectacular place to spend time — the perfect tropical vacation locale. *Wow! This is where I'll propose.*

We drove that cart all over the island over the next few days, making every effort to remember all the turns on the road to our cottage. We bought groceries, beer, wine, and coffee and stocked the fridge. We saw nothing but Wranglers, golf carts, and bicycles.

We started each morning slowly in the nest. We made coffee and eggs and ate in the shade of the west-facing deck. We took the golf cart to the famed Flamenco Beach, sipped oversized, plastic-cupped frozen drinks in the sun, and downed generous helpings of rice and beans to soak up the booze. Each night after dinner, we drove back to our cottage in the dark. Though it felt like summer, by six-thirty, the sun had set, and we'd missed that breathtaking view.

Kim went for a run each day as I sat reading on the deck or at the beach. I always tried to encourage her to get out for a run, ride her bike, or accompany her friends on a hike. I knew she needed the physical activity to stay sane, as I once felt the same way. I was happy she had that outlet; I knew it was healthy. But sitting on Zoni Beach, trying to be content with my book as I watched her running on the wet sand in the distance, my rational mind gave way to emotion. A wave of self-pity came over me, and I wanted her sitting by my side. How could we be happy together if I couldn't find a way to be happy myself?

Privately planning my proposal, I was intent on seeing that sunset. On day four, with dinner and drinks in the fridge, I would have my chance. I cooked dinner, Kim made sangria, and we ate on our deck high above the glistening waves.

For hours I repeated a few phrases in my head. I thought I'd written some good lines; I gave myself a mental pat on the back. I stood on the deck, a bit nervous, but really intent on enjoying the moment. Kim had stepped inside for a minute. I called her to join me for the sunset, and more slowly than I would've liked, she came. I built up with talk of the night, the view, the cottage and finally put my focus on her. As the sun hung on the horizon, I looked into her eyes and said my lines. It was perfect.

I tried to read her face as I spoke. She looked surprised. And I imagine she was. For what was only a fraction of a second, but felt like much longer, she paused. *She doesn't want to marry you, you idiot. I should've brought the ring.* But then she said yes, and I kissed her and held her.

I didn't want to risk losing my mémère's engagement ring, I told her. She was disappointed; she was anxious to see it. How could she share the news (post it on Facebook) without a ring? Though there was no symbol for the world to see, we were engaged.

The next morning, Kim was on the phone trying to book a catamaran tour. She got the idea, and the number, from an advertisement on the tourist-map flyer of the island. In no time, she found one — all we had to do was show up at the dock.

We arrived to learn it would be just the two of us. The captain (I'm going to call him John) and his bikini-clad first mate (she reminded me of Dee from *It's Always Sunny in Philadelphia*) were longtime expats living a sort of beach bum lifestyle. After some brief instructions and John and Dee's mental coin flip, we set off to Culebrita, a small cay to the east.

We cruised across the open ocean and before long slowed to a shallow area of crystal-clear aqua water. Another boat pulled up beside, the captains made their greetings, and an athletic young couple stepped aboard. It was snorkeling time.

I didn't want to go on a catamaran tour. I saw the advertisement — boasting of swimming and snorkeling — I knew how my day would go. But Kim was over the moon, and all I had to do was show up and try to convince myself I was having a good time.

John and Dee tried every accommodation they could think of to get me in the water. Three letters stopped them in their tracks. I tried not to sulk on the boat while Kim (who swims like a fish) and the others went off in search of sea turtles. One of them popped up in excitement every few minutes as John yelled further instructions. I tried to act nonchalant, like I was used to this sort of thing. I didn't want our hosts feeling uncomfortable, feeling pity for me; I was embarrassed.

When the snorkeling was (mercifully) over, we floated into the shallow bay of Culebrita. John pulled the boat as close to shore as possible, but for me, it still seemed a long way. With Kim waiting to grab my hand, I climbed down the ladder into about five feet of water as warm and as calm as a bath. Miraculously, I managed to stay upright (at first on my toes to keep my nose above water) and slowly bobbed my way to the beach. (Had I fallen off balance, tried to swim or regain my footing, I undoubtedly would have had to be rescued.) Kim carried our sneakers above her head; we'd be hiking.

After a short uphill walk on an obstacle-free trail through the woods, we came upon the ruins of what appeared to be a small fort. Faro de Culebrita is a Spanish-era lighthouse built in the 1880s that stands in ruins after extensive hurricane damage over the years. The impressive stone structure is wholly without a roof, its glass-topped lighthouse merely a shell. We walked among the rooms and came to the tower's castle-like spiral staircase. About five steps up, there was a big hole in the heavily rusted iron steps. Kim was sure I could jump the gap with her help and climb to the top for the view.

I looked at the stairs for several minutes, trying to rid my mind of the likelihood that I'd end up falling into a hole I could never get out of. *There's no way in hell. You can't jump. Remember the last time you jumped? You almost fell on your face. And that was two years ago! In the living room! No, your legs are tired, the fear has you shaking. You shouldn't even be thinking about it.*

It wasn't going to happen. Defeated yet again and beginning to wallow, I told her to go on without me. She did, and she stayed up there longer than I would've liked, taking pictures, basking in the ocean breeze, feeling alive — and, perhaps, contemplating her life as my partner.

We hiked back to the beach and waded to our catamaran without incident. Kim pushed my butt as I tried to climb the ladder. Soon we arrived back at the dock where John, having watched me all afternoon, gave me the white glove treatment, grabbed my hand and pulled me out of the boat. Besides the return flight on another tiny airplane, which was bound to bear less excitement the second time around, the last of our adventures were over. Before I knew it, we were going through customs and searching Montréal-Trudeau International Airport for my aunt and uncle.

9.

Kim and I had two tasks ahead of us over the summer: planning a wedding and trying to buy a house. Somehow — because we were in a rush with everything — we set the date for September 20. Having already announced our engagement on Facebook — and receiving hundreds of warm, fuzzy congratulations — we sent out save-the-date e-vites. Formal invitations were thereby put off until later. Meanwhile, I put all of my focus on a long and unfamiliar process I hoped would end in a house.

We spent the summer looking at wedding venues and houses — both seemed a foregone conclusion. Eventually, we nailed down the venue — a picturesque barn and hillside on the western edge of Camel's Hump. The property belonged to our high school ski coach, who had become a family friend in the years since my brother's passing.

I didn't fully recognize all that still had to be done as the wedding date approached. I saw the calendar turning, but I didn't address it. I didn't really care about all of the wedding-day details. I thought, *It will get done*, and went back to jumping through hoops for a mortgage.

Because Kim had a seemingly long-term position at Hinesburg Community School, and I worked from home, I thought we should live near the school. I'd commuted to Montpelier for five years; I couldn't help but focus on the time and money wasted. I thought life would be much easier this way.

We looked at a number of houses — in Shelburne and St. George, Starksboro and Bristol, then finally Monkton. I think we were starstruck in Monkton. It was a beautiful summer day; the owner was mowing the lawn; there were flowers and bushes and trees strategically placed in the yard; the peaches were ripe in the orchard; the sunlight was beaming through open windows and doors. It was a postcard house on a postcard day.

For weeks, both before and after finding a house, I seemed to spend every day on the mortgage. I was in constant communication with the bank; they created a new task every day. (I didn't have a regular job, and because I had long since paid off my car and student loans, and hadn't used a credit card since college, had no credit. I was firmly outside the box.) Finally, on August 25, shortly after my friends threw me a bachelor party at a camp on Lake Champlain, I closed on a charming cape by an apple orchard in Monkton.

With Kim (oddly) at work, my parents accompanied me at the closing. As I signed the papers, my dad sat with his dog in his fully loaded truck and trailer in the parking lot. When, finally, we finished, keys in my hand, we headed to my new house and unloaded the truck. With my bed and dresser in place and boxes in every possible corner, my folks left me alone. I stood in the front yard staring in awe — *I own this house.* I walked up the driveway, pulled open the screen door, and walked into the kitchen — *I can't believe we live here.* It felt strange to be relishing those moments alone.

Shortly after pausing for revelry, on an exhaustion-defying organizational quest, I picked up a wooden folding chair. Dragging my feet slowly as I carried it across the room, my over-tired leg kicked the floor. I stubbed my toe on the living room carpet, stumbled, and collapsed onto the dining room hardwood. My arms didn't pop out to save me; I'm not sure it would've done any good if they had. I certainly couldn't have broken my fall; instead, I might've broken an arm.

I landed on my chin with the chair wedged under my ribcage; my arms were still down at my sides. I lay there a second, waiting to feel what had happened, blood seeping slowly from my chin. I was sure I'd broken a rib on the chair, groaning in pain as I slowly rolled over. Flat on my back, I reached up to check on my chin: blood soaked my beard and kept coming. *I have to call Kim; I'm sure I need stitches.* I turned myself over, got to my feet, and walked a few steps to the table in a stupor. Kim answered my call, left work, and came to our new house for the first time. I sat at the table with a balled-up paper towel jammed into my chin until she arrived. She should've been joyous — as I was — in arriving at our house for the first time. Instead, there was fear in her voice as she rushed to my side. I peeled back the towel and presented the damage — we were back out the door in a flash.

She drove me to the doctor in Hinesburg. I walked up to the counter with a bloody clump of paper towels in my hand, told the receptionist, "I fell," and showed her the wound. A needle of Novocain and five stitches later, we drove back to our new house together. No one had to tell me what I already knew: it's not the external — the cut and the blood — but the potential internal damage that's the problem. This wasn't my first experience with a head injury.

As I lay in bed — a trash bin by my side for falling vomit — I thought, *maybe I shouldn't have called her; maybe she didn't need to see this.* I could've called my mom. But I was closer with Kim. I trusted her. She was the one I wanted. I didn't want to worry my mom; I didn't think about worrying my fiancée.

10.

Two days later, while Tom and Katie carried a couch through our sliding back door, Kim took me aside. With my friends thinking we'd snuck away for a kiss, Kim told me she couldn't marry me. Or that the wedding was off. I don't remember the words; I remember their meaning.

✱✱✱

People seem to think that all must have been well if we were engaged and about to start a life together. But it wasn't real. And not because she was planning on getting out for who knows how long, but because it was one-sided. I knew that I had no other option. And I'm sure a lot of people feel that way, but really, I wasn't going to find anyone else. I may have just thought, *I'm in love, this is it,* but driven deep into my existence was the knowledge that I had no Plan B. For perhaps the first time in my life, I didn't second-guess myself. I didn't consider anything else; there *was* no decision.

I realized later what might've been obvious: she'd been pulling away for months — the wedding was never real. I must've seen the signs, the changes in her behavior, but I was willfully blind. Maybe it was never real for her because she was never going to go through with it, but it was only real for me because I didn't see it as a choice. Any doubts I had would never be enough; barring something catastrophic, I wasn't ending that relationship. Did I love her? Yes, of course I loved her. But would I have chosen to marry her if circumstances were different? I'm not so sure. My waffling, hesitant mind would never have been so set.

Obviously, she felt unable to confront me as the thoughts weighed heavier on her mind: *I can't marry him; I need to get out.* Instead, she acted out and pulled away. I think she decided what she wanted then tried to make me feel the same.

Things had moved quickly from the beginning — we knew that; we'd talked about it. I had very little in my life; I dove in. And by all accounts, so did she. It seems obvious that we didn't have a plan, not a real one. Neither of us was inclined to think about the future; I couldn't face the inevitable reality of the years ahead. Instead, we enjoyed each day — me in a fantasy, her, undoubtedly, in denial.

I think I saw it in her eye the moment I proposed — she wasn't all-in; she was scared. The ring — and all that it meant, our future — had to weigh heavy on her mind.

Maybe it's inevitable in a relationship, maybe we got sick of each other, but one day all we seemed to have was a couch and a TV. We'd had such fun together — going to dinner, hanging with friends, endlessly entertained in each other's company. Suddenly, night after night, we were playing the "one more episode" game.

It always ended the same way — me slinking off to bed, Kim falling asleep on the couch. Sometimes I'd feel her join me, but increasingly often, we'd spend our nights a few feet apart, separated by two layers of sheetrock. Several times I voiced my displeasure, but my words seemed to fall on deaf ears. Maybe that's what she wanted.

It's easy to see things more clearly now — there was never going to be a wedding. I let Kim do the planning while I worked on the house. She'd invite friends over, spend hours on one minor task, then neglect everything for weeks at a time. She became obsessed with every detail of the dress while ignoring the more obvious realities of food, venue, seating, and music. Supremely gifted in the art of avoidance, I let the days tick by in silence.

On one particularly memorable Sunday the week of my thirtieth birthday, after taking the gondola to the Cliff House restaurant on Mount Mansfield (a surprise trip for which I was blindfolded with a pink T-shirt), we stopped by the apartment en route to my parents' for dinner. I stayed in the car, with both of our phones and no keys, while she ran upstairs. I don't remember what she was doing, but it should've been quick.

It was not. At the rear entrance by the dumpsters, I sat in the passenger seat of Kim's Focus, checking the time. After a lengthy twenty minutes, I got out of the car and paced around. I had no way in the building.

I walked around front, fearfully climbed the stairs, and waited in the vestibule until someone opened the door. In the third-floor hallway, I knocked and then battered our door. For ten minutes, I pounded and yelled — drawing a door-opening stare from multiple neighbors. Utterly dumbfounded and sweating in the suffocating, windowless hallway, I went back outside and made a few phone calls.

I called my parents to tell them we'd be late — Mom's neurotic mind was sure something must be wrong. I called my landlord — who lived only a few miles away and owned but the one condo —

to try to get a spare key. He wasn't home, but if I could get over there, he told me, I could get into his house and retrieve a spare key. My instinct was to walk to his house; I knew just where it was near the Winooski/Colchester line. With no other plan, I started down the road in my lime-green, omnipresent, summertime Crocs.

At my uncertain, leisurely, and only pace, I'd gone less than a half-mile when reality struck me. I tripped and fell, bloodying my hands and knees on the Riverside Avenue bike path. I had to admit I couldn't make a five-mile round trip; I found an alternative in my phone. I stood on the sidewalk in front of Bluebird Barbeque on what was a gorgeous late afternoon in July, waiting for Lenny to arrive from his house in the New North End. He didn't ask questions — about the blood dripping down my knee or the absurdity of the situation I'd tried to explain. He just drove me to my destination.

Having retrieved the key from an empty house using the garage door code, we stood in the hallway outside my door. We walked into a quiet apartment, and Lenny hung back while I went for the bedroom. There she was, lying face-down on the bed, sleeping — or pretending to.

I wanted to believe that this was all an innocent mistake, that she'd laid on the bed for a quick minute, and exhaustion had gotten the better of her. She was certainly someone who could sleep anywhere, any time. I was embarrassed to consider what Lenny thought.

Whatever it was that had happened — whether she passed out by mistake, an incredibly selfish and oblivious thing to do on its own, or if this was indeed a more sinister manipulation aimed at driving me away — I'll never know. It wasn't my way to yell and scream and demand answers. I never thought people — and she was not *people*, she was my fiancée — were out to wrong me. My logic-loving brain told me to be suspicious — that this person seems to be disappointing you more and more — but I didn't want to believe that. And I didn't want to give up on her. She was all I had.

***

For the next few days, we were in limbo. Kim hadn't broken things off entirely, and my hopes still hung by an imaginary thread. But she was even more distant — sleeping on the couch and treating me like a roommate — and in the house that I'd bought for us, I didn't know what to do. Three days after getting my stitches, I tripped again in nearly the same spot with nearly the same result.

Kim was at Mount Philo with a couple of friends, doing something I couldn't. Sad and embarrassed and afraid, I called her, and the three of them hurried to the house. Though Kim wanted to bring me to the hospital, her friend, a veterinary technician, convinced her I was OK.

A day or two later, she ended things. Now it was real; I couldn't pretend otherwise. She asked to stay upstairs for a few days while she found a place to live. Overwhelmed with sadness that had not yet turned to hate, I allowed her to live in my house. Despite what she had done, I didn't think of kicking her out. I guess I could have; what good would that've done?

I have one vivid memory of those final days: Kim standing nearby trying her best to make things a little bit easier, I see myself crying on my bed. Through tears and mucus, I let it all go, "I don't want to be alone..."

Kim told me it was the look in my eye, the thought of the joy draining from my face, that made it so difficult for her. I wasn't in any place to hear her, but when my sadness and anger had passed, in a small way, I understood.

With time, I've mostly forgiven her. I wish she'd gone about things differently, more maturely, but I'm not sure it would've made much of a difference. There was no right or easy way to end things. It was an unnatural relationship — she had all the options, and I had none.

It's been long enough that I can look back at those times with a level head and dry eyes. Kim and I had a lot of fun together, more than I could ever have reasonably expected at that time in my life. I struggle to extract value from those memories, but I wouldn't change them.

CHAPTER 7

A HOUSE JUST FOR ME

"Wobbly legs and weak arms are a bad combination."

- Neurologist #2

1.

Ten days later, I drove to the doctor's and a nurse struggled to remove the black stitches from among my dark chin hair, now a bit longer. By that time, Kim was gone, moved out when I wasn't around. She took her dining room table, the oversized couch I'd bought for our apartment but never liked, a mountain of boxes, and one of the two cats we'd adopted together over the winter.

Newly single, utterly depressed, and alone in Monkton, I spent my evenings drinking in front of the TV. As each night wore on, I'd stumble around, my legs all the more disconnected from my mind. Drunk and tired, on every trip to the kitchen, or the bathroom, or into my room for bed, I was out of control, just waiting to hit the floor. But I always seemed to catch myself and avoid the violent crash I expected.

After Kim left, the foregone conclusion returned. I didn't think, *One girl liked me and wanted to be with me; maybe it could happen again.* I didn't even think at all; I'd be alone — that's all there was to it.

I didn't try to change that. I didn't try to date. I didn't think, *Today is the best I'm going to look and feel for the rest of my life.* I didn't give up because I was never playing. I simply went back to the broken person I'd been before.

I almost embraced the new low, another shot to be absorbed. I didn't need to do anything; I could wallow for a while. I shut myself down for a time.

I was sad; my friends were angry. They couldn't seem to understand my lack of hate. I didn't look at it that way. I was sad and alone. That's all there was room for.

CHANGING WITH CHANGE

For years, living alone, I never gave up — on anything. I couldn't; no one was there to help. There was a determination built into my mind, a knowledge that frustrations would always come, and I had to get through them.

Every task has a series of smaller steps built in. There's oftentimes a bottleneck: a black-or-white, can-or-can't moment of truth without which you can't go on. If you can't get the lid off the pasta sauce, you better find something else for dinner. If you can't get the shirt over your head, jacket onto your shoulders, or sock over your toes, all of the subsequent steps are irrelevant.

There's the difference in your mind. All of those other things, though they may take far longer than you'd like, you know they'll eventually get done. But the completion of that first step is never guaranteed. You're different every day, your strengths and abilities unclear.

You'd think I'd get angry, kick my feet, and vent my frustrations loudly. On the rare occasion, I do. But I've learned to act differently. With no one to see or react to my tantrum, what's the point? I've grown past all of that — it would be constant if I hadn't — beat down by years of experience.

That's not to say I'm not frustrated. I'm constantly frustrated. I've gotten used to some of it — I know certain tasks will take longer and annoy me — but there are always surprises. It's unrealistic to expect to get used to a body that's constantly changing.

I use an almost infinite number of workarounds to get through all of the tasks in my day. On a regular basis, I find myself unable to do things the old way, the way I'd learned as a child and never considered again. On each painstaking occasion, I find something new, a singular, often admittedly limited technique to accomplish my goal and add it to my routine. In almost every case, I can't remember when my new method began or how things evolved over the years. From the moment I wake up to the time I return to bed, I'm always embracing inventions of my own.

The way I walk, eat, type, sit, stand, and brush my teeth are all entirely outside the norm. Everything about my body, from the way that it looks to the way that it functions, is unnatural. Everything I do has been carefully and sometimes painfully crafted to create function where none should exist. And that function is not guaranteed — an unknowable something is lost every day.

Alone in my house in Monkton, I had to find my own way. I sat in the same place, on the edge of the bed, to pull on my underwear and pants. I kept a chair by the door to put on my shoes. I brought my electric toothbrush to the tube of toothpaste, resting beside the sink. The tube lived in that spot, often uncapped; I never picked it up. (If I made the mistake of buying a twist-off cap, I wouldn't even attempt to get it back on.) I stored my dishes — plates and bowls, glassware, and cups — on the counter; I couldn't lift them into the cabinets.

I've lost my sense of confidence in any physical movement. Each day I wake up slightly different from the day before, a part of my knowledge gone forever. All of the things that I learned, all of the routines built over decades, fade one day farther into the past.

When I lift up my arm to hit the light switch, and I don't come high enough, it's not because I don't have the strength. I don't know how strong I am; my brain isn't sure how much to lift. There is no routine movement, no blocks to build upon, no second nature. Every instance I come to, I must assess and learn anew. It's exhausting being me.

As I've adapted to new ways of accomplishing so many tasks, I've forgotten what everyone else does. So many universal human abilities, from using a touch screen or writing with a pen, to standing on one foot and pulling on a sock, to jogging up a flight of stairs, have become unimaginably foreign to me.

2.

One of the reasons I bought the house, aside from all of the usual factors, was that there were no stairs. There was a second floor, but the master suite was on the first. There was no basement and no set of steps to any of the three doors. The house was only about a foot above ground level — a cement slab at the entryway split that distance in two. I'd been living without stairs for almost a year; I couldn't go back too far.

About a month into my new home ownership experience, Tom and Katie approached me with an idea: they asked about moving in. I was more than receptive; surely, I could use their help. They could have the entire second floor: two big bedrooms and a full bath. They could help with things around the house and with the bills and mortgage. And though I'd grown used to living alone over the years, they'd be good company. From their longtime apartment in Winooski, they moved to Monkton in November.

They filled the house with furniture and set up a second living room upstairs. With winter around the corner, they brought in wood from the two cords my parents had stacked in the yard. And they continued with their busy lives: Tom teaching school, running, and spending weeknights on his laptop; Katie waiting tables part-time, and enrolled in nursing school full-time.

To all of our surprise, this being a dirt road in Monkton, there was a new-to-Vermont young couple a hundred yards up the street. Through mutual friends, the five of us met and started spending time together.

They liked to cook, and though neither had any formal training, always seemed to be dishing up chef-quality items. I ate a lot of incredible meals at their house, sitting on a kitchen stool, chatting, and enjoying a beverage while they cooked. On one occasion, looking to host a number of guests to a semi-formal dinner party, they requested we dress for the occasion.

Having worn a shirt and tie for five years, I had a closet full of options; putting them on would be complicated. I chose for myself a shirt with a button collar, a light sweater, a pair of well-worn chinos, and a favorite tweed jacket. Topped off with glasses and a beard, I'd be going as a college professor.

With several hours to go before our planned arrival and an afternoon nap under my belt, I started preparing. I undressed and got in the shower, still a safe and relatively easy task. I brushed my teeth, combed my hair, sat on the edge of the bed, and pulled on some underwear. I lay my pants on the bed and slowly attached a belt before sitting on the bed to get my legs into them. With my bare feet poking through to the carpet, I stood up and pulled them up and over my butt. Though I'd lost double-digit pounds since their purchase, my sedentary belly had grown, and my finger strength had diminished — the button wasn't happening. As was my routine, I pulled the zipper as far as possible (not with my thumb, but pressing it between middle finger and palm), and tugged and fastened the belt. My pants were about an inch too small.

I'd recently abandoned the pants button. For a long time, on all of my pants, fastening and unfastening was a struggle. The strength in my fingers and thumbs seemed to vary by the moment; I regularly had just enough to get the job done.

In the waning days of my full-time employment, my pants — and truly much of my office attire — had become a problem. Standing in the bathroom stall, sweating, just trying to button my pants. It always seemed like a miracle when I finally got it and was free to return to the doldrums of my desk.

I opened a drawer on my bureau and took out an undershirt. Leaning forward, I placed each hand into it before bringing my head down and arms up to get it onto my shoulders. Next, I pulled and grabbed and shook my torso to unfurl it over my belly and back. From the drawer, I grabbed a pair of socks and walked to the living room.

Since moving to Monkton, I'd only put on socks in one place: the maple-framed, red fabric chair, a sister piece to the (legendary) blue couch. (I was no longer in possession of the couch. It had become a dog bed in my parents' garage.) The chair sat unusually low, allowing me to reach my feet more easily. I dropped the socks — a tan pair with some sort of pattern — on the carpet and dropped myself into the seat. I picked one up, put both thumbs in the opening, and reached forward toward my right foot. Getting the sock onto my toes, like getting the shirt over my head, was the make-or-break action — without it, I couldn't move on.

A few things made the whole process more challenging than it may seem. My shoulders were basically shot, entirely incapable of supporting my outstretched arms for much more than a second. My hamstrings and hips were always abnormally tight, severely restricting my flexibility. My ankles were weak, and my Achilles were tight — with my heel down, it was almost impossible to lift my foot off the floor. My hands, fingers, and thumbs lacked strength and dexterity.

On nearly every other occasion, I wore stretchy cotton ankle socks because I was comfortable and confident putting them on. But knowing that I'd be removing my shoes, I didn't want to be the dork in white socks. I got the end over my toes, and after an extended period of frustration, grabbing, and tugging, one sock was over my heel and up. The left foot wasn't any easier, but as before, it was finished eventually.

I got up from the chair (a significant task on its own; without the oversized wooden arms to hold on to, it may have been impossible), walked back to the bedroom, and took the waiting shirt from the hanger. Holding it in my left hand, I slid my right arm into the sleeve, reached behind to find the left, and with a few awkward jerks of the torso, flipped the shirt over my shoulders. That was the easy part.

I'd been struggling with buttons since before my diagnosis, and as a result, I always wore my shirts unfastened. To help with this everyday problem, I had a helper called a buttonhook. It looks a bit like a paperclip with a handle; it's inserted through the button-hole, slid over the button, pulled back through, and released. As long as its user can physically hold it, reach the buttons, and manipulate it correctly, it's very effective. It does nothing to take the buttons back out.

Holding the buttonhook in my left hand, with more difficulty than I'd remembered, I pulled each button through, leaving the collar open. (Had the buttons been placed on the left, as a women's shirt would be, I'd never have accomplished this task. I couldn't lift and hold my right arm high enough.) Preparing to tuck in my shirt, I used the bathroom once more.

Because my pants weren't — couldn't be — buttoned, and left a visible gap in the zipper, I decided to wear a sweater to cover the space. I followed the same procedure as with any T-shirt, but given its more delicate nature, and the fact that I was pulling it over a long-sleeve button-down that further restricted my movement, it took much longer.

Lastly, with my sweater in place and my shirt tucked, fighting the inflexible fabric, I climbed into my jacket. By the time I was ready to leave the house, I was exhausted. Just for a minute, I lay on the bed, closed my eyes, took a few breaths, and got up to go.

As I did every time I left the house, I sat on the chair in the mudroom and pushed my feet into the only shoes I ever wore, a no-lace pair of Merrill's that lived by the door. (After tripping a number of times, I'd retired my Crocs.) As the last step before the dinner, I drove to Lantman's Market.

Though I was only buying a few things to bring with me, I headed for the carts inside the door. Slowly, one deliberate step at a time, I backed one off the rack, pushing it through the store like a walker.

With a single plastic grocery bag on my back seat, feeling even more like a nap, I drove the five miles back to my house. Tom and Katie were at the top of the driveway on their way to our neighbor's. They approached as I parked, Katie took the grocery bag from the car, and they gave me shit for being late despite the entire day I'd had to prepare.

I didn't explain how long it had taken me to prepare, how frustrating it all had been, or how tired I felt. I never talked about those things; I didn't like to let people into my world. My every day felt like a battle, and I was embarrassed. Giving it life would've been one more step toward defeat.

FINALITY

A sense of finality weighs heavy on my mind. Each day the door closes a little. Each day I say goodbye to another.

So much of my life is buried behind me. The possibilities have turned into memories. Much more is to come in the future; I'll never be done losing things.

I can't revisit the past like the others. I can't choose to pick up a basketball or my saxophone after years on the shelf. There's a growing list of *lasts* in my head. The last hike and the last run; the last bike ride of my life. The last time I lifted my arms up over my head. The last time I stood on my feet — that one's still to come.

There's also a long list of lasts I don't know about. I might see them as maybes and likelies, but who knows what the future will bring. Have I had my last kiss? I don't know.

My long list of lasts has filled up so quickly, it's hard to recognize each one as it goes. There's no celebration, no funeral as each possibility passes me by. It would be never-ending. Instead, I mourn each of their losses alone.

3.

I wasn't the ideal roommate in that I was nearly always there. I learned in college: a busy, independent person makes for a much better roommate than a homebody with nothing going on. My times with Tom and Katie had always been fun: dinners, drinking, road trips, and the like. Now, like newly cohabitated partners, we were sharing all of our time. Tom kept a busy schedule, dominated by his still-new teaching position to which he gave more than I would've imagined. Katie was always at school, at work, or holed up in her room staring into a book with yet another cup of Red Rose Tea, her all-hours accompaniment to nursing school. (I, of course, very rarely ventured upstairs; I only saw the tea in her cup and the stress on her face.) I had very little to fill my time, and with one of my main destinations now having given up their apartment and moved in, one less place to go.

It never really felt like a long-term solution. Despite living under the same roof, we seemed to be hanging out less. In the summer, as they had communicated for months, they moved to a condo in Burlington. Though it was nice to have them around, and I'd certainly need more help without them, I saw the positive: I always liked living alone.

4.

On October 25, 2015, the National Football League's Buffalo Bills and Jacksonville Jaguars played at London's Wembley Stadium. The game kicked off at nine-thirty in the morning and was broadcast on Yahoo. For the casual fan, Londoners included, this wasn't exactly Brady/Manning or Cowboys/Giants. It was a game between two longtime loser franchises with no rivalry and records of 3-3 and 1-5. Buffalo quarterback EJ Manuel, who started for an injured Tyrod Taylor, gave the definitive account of the game, "It was bad football." Indeed.

I'd been living alone almost three months, and since starting regular chiropractic care over the winter, feeling a little better. My movements felt smoother, a bit more function seemed to return to some muscles, and my confidence improved as a result. Perhaps most importantly, in more than a year since the twin falls I'd taken right after I moved in, I hadn't fallen — at least, I hadn't hurt myself falling.

I'd driven home late from Lenny and Laura's the night before, and slept in past nine. In my usual routine, I half-filled a pot from the faucet, carried it to the stove, and turned on the gas. From my Tupperware of fresh-ground, I scooped coffee into my French press. To heat my water or anything else, I never used the microwave. It lived in that familiar spot above the stove; I could just reach into it, my right arm only with help from the left. From the day I moved in, removing a hot plate or bowl was a dangerous proposition.

I placed both hands on my stovetop pot's handle and dumped the boiling water, stirred my concoction with a wooden spoon, and put on the cover. With two hands, I carried the stainless, insulated French press to the dining room table, where my laptop and half-finished glass of water awaited. Typing awkwardly on the keyboard, using a wired mouse in place of the touchpad, I checked my email and fantasy football lineup over a freshly poured coffee.

In Sunday relaxation mode, I sipped on my coffee, stood up to pour another cup (I had to stand up to pour; I couldn't lift my arms high enough), and switched over to Yahoo for the game. Midway through my coffee allotment, I pulled a bag of kale and a carton of eggs from the fridge. With a slab of butter, I put some kale in my eight-inch cast iron and removed two eggs.

I'd developed a very specific method for removing the eggs from the fridge, something I did most every day. I always kept them in the same place, on the second shelf, lengthwise front to back, at about belly height. I'd reach my left hand around back, pull the carton forward, and pin it against my body. With a step and a pivot, the eggs would reach the counter, ready for the next step.

My thumb and forefinger no longer had the strength or dexterity to pull an egg from the carton. Instead, I removed my eggs by holding them between my fingers and palm. That's how I hold most anything.

I cracked the eggs on the counter, opened them into a bowl, and walked the shells to the compost under the sink. I rinsed the egg from my hands, dried them on a dishtowel, scrambled the eggs, and stirred the kale. It needed more time; I walked back to the table to catch a bit of the game.

I walked behind the chair and somehow, turning to face the table with the wall closely behind, began to lose my balance. My body had turned, but my feet hadn't; once I lost my center, there was no coming back. Seemingly in slow motion, helplessly, I began to angle toward the wall. In those fleeting moments, my mind accepted my impending fall and reasoned away any fear of the consequences. *The wall's right there; it'll break my fall; I'll be fine.*

My brain was overly optimistic. I wasn't headed directly for the wall; I was tilting at an angle. I bounced off and started falling to the side. My mind went blank as I braced for impact. Before I knew what was happening, I fell loudly to the floor, smacking my head near the base of the wood stove. I lay there a second or two, my brain suddenly reactivated: *Tell me I'm OK. Please don't be bleeding.*

I was hopeful; I seemed fine. Maybe nothing happened. But the switch quickly flipped; the dam broke — warm blood began to pour from my head. Panic.

I scrambled to my knees, grabbed the hoodie off the chair, and with both hands pressed it against the mess of blood-wet hair above the right side of my forehead. *Holy shit, I'm not OK! Where's my phone? Get the phone!* Kneeling at my dining room table, blood continued to flow as I grabbed at my phone with both hands. Terrified and violently shaking, I tried to unlock the screen of my antiquated physical-buttoned phone with its slide-out keyboard. My thumbs wouldn't do as I needed; it took multiple tries. *Who do I call? My parents? What if they don't answer? 911! Dial 911!*

I propped my right elbow on the table to hold the sweatshirt to my head and jammed at the buttons with my left hand. I pressed 9-1-1, hit the send and speaker buttons, heard two rings, and then, "911, how may I assist you?"

I almost couldn't get my mouth to speak. *Say something! Say something!!* "I need help…I hit my head."

The operator, in the most professional manner, ran through the routine set of questions in what felt like anything but a routine time. I gave my name and address, and told her that I was alone. Her robotic tone struck my ears as nonchalance. I fought to convey the urgency of the situation.

Was the door unlocked? she asked. Yes, I assured her, having unlocked it recently that morning. (I walked out to my car to retrieve something. It may have been my phone; it may have been something else. I can't seem to remember that most vital of details.)

In between questions, I filled the silence with a brain full of blathering fear. "I have ALS…I lost my balance…Please send someone soon." Still on my knees at the table, I peeked at the floor: a puddle stretched from my knee to the wall. I'd never seen such a thing; it looked thick. I couldn't believe it was real; I couldn't believe it was mine. "Oh my God, there's so much blood. I don't want to die!"

An ambulance was on its way from Bristol, ETA twenty minutes. The call went out to the local volunteer fire department, she told me; someone should be there sooner. My heart was pounding. *Am I just scared? Is it my nerves? Or is it the blood loss? Please let my heart be OK.* Still kneeling at the table, I tried to slow down and breathe; she stayed on the line while I waited.

A few minutes later, sooner than I could've expected, I heard the crunch of the gravel driveway as someone pulled in. "I think someone's here," I told the operator. Out of sight around the corner, I heard the entryway door creak open a few inches as a timid volunteer investigated the scene. I yelled something, and he came in.

Help had arrived, I informed the operator, and turned my attention from the phone. The man approached, surveyed the scene, and began unloading items from his bag. With a mountain of gauze and bandages, he tried to wrap my head and slow the bleeding. (He also struck me as reasonably nonchalant. What does it take to rile these people? A crime-drama-sized pool of blood didn't do it.) The whole mess was constantly sliding around; like the sweatshirt before, I held it in place.

I was still kneeling at the dining room table when the ambulance arrived. My knees were sore; my hamstrings engaged and tight; my traumatized body cold and trembling. I tried to explain what had happened.

They went through their protocol, bracing my head and neck as I moved from my long-frozen position. Unsure of the need for a stretcher, they asked if I could walk. I couldn't trust myself even to stand in that state. After a brief explanation that seemed to fall on deaf ears (they all but let out a collective sigh and eye roll), the EMTs went out to retrieve a stretcher.

I was lying flat, my head and body strapped down, as they prepared for a trip to the emergency room. Primary among the group's activities was wiping up the puddle of blood with a mountain of paper towels. (In other circumstances, I would've provided them with any number of towels. The full trash bag seemed like such a waste.)

"Would you like to call anyone?" one of them asked. At my direction, she used my phone to dial my parents. There was no answer.

As my heart rate began to slow, the worst of the panic behind me, a previously buried thought popped into my head: the stove. The gas burner had long been scorching my go-to iron skillet.

"Could you turn off the stove?" I asked sheepishly, as if leaving the house with a blue flame burning was no more than an afterthought. In my mind, in that moment, it didn't seem to matter.

At first, she thought I meant the wood stove, which was on everyone's mind. Turning to the kitchen, she saw the problem and cut the gas, leaving the pan to cool. She put the bowl of eggs in the fridge and returned to my side, asking, "Anything else?"

They carried me out through the rarely used front door and walked me across the lawn. I felt like a victim on display, moving through the onlooking crowd. With my head strapped down, I couldn't see if any of my neighbors were watching as they loaded me into the ambulance. I suspect it was all in my head; there was no one to see. I couldn't help but flash back to that morning at 6 Patrick, twelve years before.

I flew out of the house in a panic. A woman approached as I reached the street — an ambulance parked in the driveway. She asked if my grandmother (her words) was OK. I didn't even look up as I rushed past her. It was seven-thirty on a Friday morning; I had nowhere to go. My brother lay dead in the house.

***

Covered in blankets, I lay in the back of the cold, steel box, visibly shivering in my blood-soaked shirt. Between the coffee, wet shirt, cold air, loss of blood, lack of a desperately needed breakfast, and the highly sensitive nerves of an ALS patient, I felt truly awful. The same EMT who'd called my parents and now carried my phone repeatedly tried to insert an IV in my right arm. Cold and perhaps fearful of losing more blood, the vein retreated, subjecting me to multiple stabs without effect. The IV was protocol, she explained. It was never used.

Unable to see out the window, I tracked our progress to Burlington in my mind, anxiously waiting for the ride to be over. The miles passed slowly, and I tried to let my thoughts drift away. I wondered, had I not been so irresponsible to crack my head open on a Sunday, could I have gone to the doctor's in town?

The scene felt surreal as they opened the doors, unloaded me, and wheeled me into the building. Bypassing the waiting room paperwork, I was brought to a patient room, released from my bonds, and lifted onto a bed. A doctor arrived almost immediately, introduced himself, and peeled back the bloody gauze. "Are you allergic to Novocain?" he asked. With his answer, he filled a needle and jammed it several times into my head. Promising a timely return, he walked out the door while the drug took effect.

It took nine stitches to seal up the gash. From just above the hairline at the far right of my forehead, it stretched back several inches toward the top of my head. "I can add one more if you want double digits," he joked as he finished. I did not want more.

Lying in bed a few minutes later, I picked up my phone from its resting place beside my leg. Still shaking inside, I pressed the buttons and tried to prepare my voice. When I heard a voice on the other end, I didn't know what to say. Choked up and weak, I managed to mumble a few words, "I fell. I'm at the hospital."

"We'll be right there," I heard my dad say.

I lay in the bed, alternating between closed and open eyes, intermittently leaning over to sip water from a plastic straw. I opened my eyes to see Mom hurriedly approaching, a crazed look in her eye.

"What happened?!!" she repeated.

"I fell," I told her, turning my head to show the bloody mess.

"Oh my God," she gasped.

A week or ten days later, I drove to the urgent care center on Williston Road (the former Burger King) to get the stitches removed. I parked my car, climbed out and, with intractable and heightened anxiety, forced one foot in front of the other to the door. I stood at the counter with knees locked, answering questions, unable to beat back the invisible, full-body shakes.

When I finally made it into a chair in a patient room, before anything had been done, I felt thoroughly relieved. Observing the stitches, a PA put some gauze — wet with a skin-softening mystery liquid — on my head, asked me to hold it in place for a few minutes, and left the room. I tried to comply, but my right shoulder didn't have the strength to maintain the position, and I couldn't find an effective substitute.

I'd waited too long, he told me. "Head wounds heal fast; we'll have to try this again. Let's lean you back."

The stitches were pretty well molded to my scalp. After about a half-hour with what amounted to a wet washcloth on my head, he was ready to cut and tug. He got them all out, though not without tearing some thread-attached skin. All done, he told me, and that's all that mattered.

If you ever wonder whether maybe you'd like to die, should it become a real possibility, and you're anything like me, the answer will become crystal clear. Whether it's merely adrenaline, or a much deeper, Darwinian instinct, a powerful feeling came over me when I thought I might die. It was not 99 percent; it was 100 percent: I don't want to die.

Running my hand over the scar, it's the little things I think about: on most days, I made fried eggs or oatmeal. Had I not bought that bag of kale or chosen another breakfast that Sunday morning, none of it may have happened. If there were no London football game, if I'd taken just one step differently, I wouldn't be writing this. What if my phone wasn't in reach? It's too scary to consider. What if the door was locked? I guess they would've smashed it. I try not to think about what could've happened. It's another memory that I have mostly chosen to forget.

I WANT YOUR PROBLEMS — GIVE THEM TO ME

I find myself jealous of other people's problems. In moments of self-pity — which are impossible to avoid — I can't help but compare myself to friends and strangers alike. The grass is always greener in their lives.

I feel jealous of almost anything, any problem to be solved. If the question has an answer — an achievable solution — I stand ready with a response. It all seems so simple. You know the answer to your problems (there *is* an answer to your problems), follow the instructions; do the work.

My friends usually avoid venting to me. They try to be considerate of my feelings — bitter, angry, jealous feelings. I try to draw things out, lend an ear, and pretend to be any other person. It's almost an escape to think about "regular people" problems. Looking in from the outside, the solutions seem obvious. It's kind of refreshing.

Sometimes it's too much for me to listen; I can't believe what I'm hearing. *Doesn't he know who he's talking to? Does he have any idea how minor, how petty, how privileged this sounds?* I keep my thoughts to myself; my eyes roll back in my head involuntarily. My presence doesn't change how he feels. I don't want to bring anyone down by voicing my anguish.

I'm jealous of diseases that people come back from. Cancer's the big one. *Cancer kills people. Like* that! *Every day. You can't possibly wish you had cancer. Don't tell anyone you wish you had cancer. You're completely insane. You could be gone tomorrow.*

But sometimes I do. There's an answer with cancer; there's a protocol to be followed. It may not work — you'll be in for a battle; you may lose — but at least you'll have hope. In time you could put it all behind you — defeat the disease and come out the other side. You could get your life back. Oh, how glorious that must be.

I don't know what it's like to have hope, to be fighting a battle against an enemy. People (those who don't know better) occasionally tell me to "keep fighting" or say things like, "You got this." I don't want to hear it. I don't "got this." And I'd love to be fighting, but I'm not; I'm succumbing.

I hear about addiction, and I just can't feel the pain. I try to be understanding — and I get it, it's difficult — but my perspective prevents me from feeling true empathy. Drugs or alcohol, fast food or sugar, anything that brings both pleasure and guilt. I know this is harsh, but these are choices you've made. A few days in my shoes, and you'd have no trouble changing. I can't help but see them as weak; all the willpower in the world isn't doing me any good.

I have to remind myself constantly: my perspective only matters to me. They can't understand what it's like to be me; I don't know what it's like to be them. My ALS doesn't make your cancer any less scary. The fact that I see your addiction as a choice — from over here, on my high horse — doesn't make your problems any less valid. Perspective isn't fully transferable; it isn't that easy. I've lived my life, and you've lived yours; hopefully, we can learn a little something from each other.

5.

After recovering a couple of days at my parents', I was back at my house. The puddle of blood was gone, cleaned with such stunning proficiency that I found myself questioning my memory. My laptop was asleep on the table, the bowl of egg remained in the fridge, and the unmistakable evidence of bloody paper towels filled the kitchen garbage. Somehow, after the fall, the blood, and the ambulance ride, I convinced my parents and myself that I could still live alone.

I wasn't afraid; it was only a freak accident. That's how I felt; that's what I told my parents, and I think I was right. I remained confident in my physical abilities. Whether I was delusional didn't much matter: my will and independence far outweighed my fears.

I spent the winter holed up alone in my house. I hired a guy to plow my long driveway, and in the case of a big storm, awaited help to dig out my car. My parents piled firewood in my dining room and replaced it as needed. It was a big pile, two rows stacked to my chest; it lasted almost a month with everyday burning.

I developed a steady routine centered around the wood stove. I'd wake up each morning, stir up the remaining coals, add some kindling, and bring the fire back to life. From the stack of firewood that effectively doubled the width of my countertop peninsula, I'd carry each piece with two hands, a few feet across the dining room to the waiting stove. Before bed, I'd build up the fire to last until morning, filling the stove to the top on cold nights. Though the house was equipped with baseboard propane, I set the thermostat below sixty, and the furnace rarely turned on. Instead, every day that didn't reach about forty, I kept a fire burning. (Because I rarely left the house for more than a few hours, I easily maintained a fire for long periods of time. Over the entire winter, I only used a handful of matches; one fire effectively burned for forty-eight days.)

Spring came, and then summer, fall came, and then winter: as the time passed, my routine became stronger. I still saw my neighbors, still drove to friends', still held on to some of the things I'd always done. I tried to get out, sit on the deck, or walk in the orchard. I tried to enjoy the weather.

Partially out of necessity but also borne out of boredom, I started to take naps in the afternoon. I can't begin to explain how utterly unnatural and depressing it feels to lay in bed with the afternoon sun beaming through your window. I'd longingly lay in the sun, overcome with self-pity and the occasional tear. I couldn't stop thinking of all the joy that came with a bright summer day. I resented the sun; *Bring on the rain.* Each passing week looked alike. My routine grew emptier in Monkton.

GOING ALONE

Years into my diagnosis, when invited to a friend's, event, or gathering, I always showed up alone. It was part of the old me: independence that looked and felt like a strength, but was also a hindrance. I always liked to pretend I didn't need anyone. I didn't tag along; I came and went as I pleased.

When my body began to fail, and I couldn't pretend anymore, I started to need people around me. Venturing into a public place on my own became more taxing mentally when it became more taxing physically. If I had people around me, I could fade into the group and feel safe.

In the winter of '17-'18, I was invited to celebrate a friend's birthday at Koto Japanese Steakhouse. I wanted to show up like everyone else, walk in the door, and join up with the group. I felt I could do that: drive the half-hour to the restaurant, park the car, traverse the wintery parking lot to the door, and make my way to the table.

As I approached the restaurant in the car, my mind grew wary. All of those steps were becoming reality and I felt overwhelmed. I slowed my approach but couldn't pull in. I took the next right to loop around and come back. I was kidding myself; I'd already flipped the switch, given up, and forgiven myself. I drove all the way home, walked in the door, and found myself dinner. I texted my apologies; I tried to explain. I couldn't seem to ask for help; for years, I'd had a built-in excuse. How could they understand?

***

In the summer of 2018, I drove myself to the Burlington farmer's market for the last time. I didn't make plans, ask anyone to meet me, or tell anyone I was going — I just showed up; that was my style. I was greeted with a dream spot on Main Street, walked to and around the market, and hung out (and sat down and rested, without which I may have fallen) with Lenny for an hour or two at the New Duds booth. (Lenny and Laura had been a fixture at the Saturday market for years, selling screen-printed and embroidered apparel.) I walked back to the car, ready to go, and stopped short to get out my keys. I stood on the sidewalk — in front of the pizza place that used to be another pizza place that used to be Dunkin' Donuts — as dozens of people strolled past, and for several minutes tried to get my sweaty hand into my pocket. I actually considered asking a stranger to reach into my pants. But alas, I finally retrieved them and fell into the driver's seat.

***

In March of 2019, after yet another winter as a borderline shut-in, I drove to a party at New Duds. It was my first visit to their new location behind Costco in Colchester. I arrived early, parked, and crossed the lot with relative ease. I was there several hours, standing nearly the entire time, and as always, didn't eat enough, didn't drink enough. When I announced my intention to call it a night, Laura followed me out with a bag of leftover doughnuts. It was raining and dark, and the light from the building only reached so far — my car seemed far off and invisible. Laura walked slowly at my side until, unable to see further, I stopped and asked for her hand. She reached over and, unsure of my needs, provided the security blanket I needed. We made our way to the car, she opened the door, and I slid into my seat to start my slow-moving pre-drive routine.

6.

On Sunday, October 15, 2017, Thibs invited me to his parents' to watch some football. Twelve of us had made up a fantasy football league for a number of years, but with busy lives and geographic disparity, we rarely had the opportunity to get together. Thibs was visiting from Boston and asked a few of us to join him for the afternoon. Eager to get out of the house and spend some time catching up, I planned to drive myself to Milton.

Though it'd been several years since my physical and occupational therapists had begun to question its safety, I still regularly drove by myself and with passengers. The Subaru I'd bought a year out of college mostly sat in the driveway, and while still reliable, was starting to feel old. In its early life, we'd logged a lot of highway miles on my commute, but now the car and its driver felt uncomfortable at speeds over about sixty-five.

Recognizing the house from its Google Street View, I pulled up to the curb. I swung my arm up to pull the door release, turned my body and pushed open the door with my knee. Turning further to put both feet on the ground, I shimmied to the far edge of the driver's seat. Leaning forward over my legs, hands on my knees, I used my momentum to push forward, locking my knees when I'd reached the vertical. The first try didn't always work; sometimes I'd fall back in the seat and start over.

With a hodgepodge six-pack of beers from my fridge, I stepped carefully across a freshly mowed lawn to the open garage. I put down the beer, reached forward, and knocked on the door to the house. An older woman answered, introduced herself, and went off to find her son. Unable to safely climb the two handrail-less stairs, I waited for help.

Tom and Thibs came to the door, asked how they might best assist me, and provided two arms for me to grab to hoist myself into the house. After using a dining room chair to sit and remove my shoes, I gripped the handrail and, in my socks, descended the wooden stairs to the basement. I turned my body slightly toward the railing to my left and took each descending step with my right foot, pausing to reposition my hand with each step. (My palms were perpetually clammy, unable to slide down a handrail.) I reached the bottom to reveal a massive flat-screen accompanied by couches, chairs, and a pool table in a carpeted basement.

I plopped down in the empty chair nearest the stairs and was offered a beer. The guys had an endless assortment of bottles and cans, pouring each among the group. I couldn't drink beer from a Solo cup in a recliner; I asked for some sort of table. From a nearby closet, Thibs removed a TV tray, set it up in front of me, and poured a few ounces of whatever beer had been opened. Sitting upright on the edge of the chair, I reached my arms forward and propped them on the wobbly tray. Using both hands with all the finesse of a cartoon ape, I lifted the cup to my mouth, denting the plastic on both sides.

Each time the guys finished a communal beer — which happened quickly with five to a pint — I was offered another pour. I wanted to be a part of the group, and I was enjoying the multitude of new beers, but the mechanics were making it nearly impossible. I wanted to sit, relax, watch the game, talk and laugh with my friends, and maybe have a beer and some food. Instead, I found myself preoccupied with the beer on the table in front of me: tipping back a plastic cup to pour out the last ounces, leaning back to accommodate a set of arms that would raise up no higher, all the time trying not to crush the cup, spill its contents, or knock over the tray.

Trying not to drink too much, I took a couple of rounds off and perused the food table. After watching everyone climb the stairs to the bathroom and waiting as long as I could, I announced my need to the room. I grabbed the rail and paused at each step, my right foot always leading the way. Thibs followed close behind, pointed me in the right direction, and at my request, filled me a glass of water. Hoping to remedy the light-headed feeling, I stood by the kitchen sink and drank down the glassful.

Under a watchful eye, I returned to the basement and had a few more bites from the food table. I tried a couple more beers but slowed my consumption for the drive ahead. Before long, the Patriots/Jets game was long over, my fantasy team was dominating its matchup, and it was time to head home.

With a helper on each side, I descended into the garage and crossed the lawn without incident. I got into a hot car and pulled the door shut. Lifting my hand with my knee, I guided the key into the ignition and turned it forward to engage the battery and open the windows. Unable to extend my fingers as always, I jammed my knuckles onto the door-mounted switches and hoped for a breeze to cool the cabin. Using the power controls, I brought back the seat until I could retrieve the seatbelt with my left hand, slowly pulled it across my chest, and after several adjustments, was finally able to latch the buckle.

Finally in position, with my friends' cars long gone, I once again propped my hand on my knee, lifted my leg, and grabbed onto the key. Instead of holding it between thumb and forefinger, I lay my hand over the top and, with middle and ring fingers, pushed it into my palm. With what little strength I had left in my wrist, I pushed my hand forward and felt it slip in my palm. *Damn it!* I wiped the sweat from my hand and tried again. I didn't have the strength to start the car. (Though it didn't much matter at the time, this begs the question: if you can't start the car, should you be driving?)

I tried over and over; I couldn't get a grip on the key. I felt like I was opening a jar, desperately in need of one of those rubber grippers. As I sat in my car, playing out scenarios in my mind — *What if I can't get it started? What will I do?* — I saw Thibs load a bag into his truck for the drive back to Boston. He didn't look in my direction. Surely, I had to leave before him or face the embarrassment of explaining why I continued to sit, unmoved in my car. *Maybe I should just yell out, call him over and have him start the car. I can't do that. What if I have to?* If I didn't move quickly, I was certain he'd come back out of the house, approach the car, and discover the truth.

With all of this running through my head, I turned the key one more time, and as if there had never been a problem, the car started up. Thrilled, I pulled away and out of sight, to the end of the cul-de-sac to turn around. I thought I could turn a circle in one broad motion and moved hand over hand on the wheel as quickly as I could. It wasn't close. I stopped short of driving onto a lawn, jammed the stick into reverse, and tried to pull the wheel back the other way. I was exhausted. The seemingly mundane day at my friend's, and all of the little things that'd gone into it, had left me exceptionally weak, struggling to turn my car around on an empty street.

I drove slowly on the highway as the sun went down; it was dark by the time I got back to Monkton. I pulled into the driveway, relieved to be home, and saw the wind whipping through the backyard cedars in my headlights. I turned off the ignition, popped open the door, and swung my legs to get out. I got to my feet and paused for a few seconds to gauge the wind, find my balance, and stretch my legs. As I began to move toward the house, a few feet away, I carefully turned to shut the car door.

I pushed it shut and started to turn back toward the house when a gust of wind hit me in the chest. My delicate balance was thrown: my knees locked up, and I began to fall backward. *Oh, shit. It's happening.* There was no remedy to try, no way of regaining control; I just had to let it happen. Like a felled tree, I tipped over slowly and crashed violently onto my butt.

Following an impact that left my tailbone sore but head unscathed, I found myself in the driveway, lying neatly between the car and a flower bed. *Shit.* I turned myself over in the gravel and prepared to get back to my feet the only way I knew. With my chest in the dirt, I tried to bring both arms forward and plant my palms beneath my shoulders. I arched my back, straightened my arms, and locked my elbows. Unable to lift my torso, all I could do was keep my elbows locked and pull my knees forward until they were under me. Grunting and shaking, I dragged each knee through the gravel — I couldn't lift either; I would've tipped over. I might've made it on a carpet, but my knees were digging into the dirt — I couldn't move them. Holding too long, one of my elbows gave out. I fell back to the ground, face in the dirt. *Fuck.*

This wasn't the first time I'd had this experience. In the years since I moved to Monkton, I'd fallen a lot, in and around the house, alone. I fell in the driveway, in the yard, in the orchard, by the woodpile in the snow, and countless times for countless reasons in the house. I fell half in the house and half out, lying face down over the threshold, the screen door jammed into the backs of my ankles. Each time, with an increasing level of difficulty (and resulting uncertainty), I managed to find my way back to my feet. Whether that meant turning onto my back and pushing my body across the room onto the carpet, using a table, or chair, or car, or tree for balance, I'd always found a way.

I also knew that the first try was always the easiest. My energy was already low before all of this crawling around in the dirt. I lifted my head, locked both elbows, and tried it again. I caved under my weight, much faster this time. *Fuuuck fuckfuckfuckfuckfuck.*

I rolled over, looked into the sky, and tried to collect myself. Walter the cat, out for the day, tiptoed on by toward the door. A thousand thoughts ran through my mind. *Maybe I could just fall asleep. I have to get something to eat. At least the weather is nice.*

As frustrating as it would've been to dig my cell phone out of my pocket and get into some sort of position to dial it, I could've tried to call for help. I could've called my parents. But that would've been a submission. No, I wasn't ready to give up.

As had long been my process when confronted with an impossible task, I tried to think of alternatives. *If the back door is unlocked, maybe I can get into the house* without *getting up.* I wasn't confident it'd work, but I was going to try. Lying on my back, I began to push myself toward the back door. (If, by chance, you wish to recreate my experience, get on the floor and push yourself across the room on your back. Feel every inch of movement on your spine. Don't lift your head off the floor. Next, go outside and do the same across your lawn.)

Inch by inch, I pushed my body to the top of the driveway and over a couple dozen feet of lawn. I came to the back deck in the dark, unsure of how I might hoist myself onto its surface. Though it was only the height of a large curb, I could see only one way up. Laying at its base, with all the strength I could muster, I lifted my head and pushed with my legs, driving the sawed-off square edge into my neck and back as I slowly passed over. I found myself lying face-up on the deck, stunned I'd made it this far.

I pushed a bit further and wriggled around to turn my feet toward the door. I reached up with my feet and slid open the screen door. Relatively certain (or perhaps irrationally optimistic) it was unlocked, I wedged my outstretched foot under the handle to the sliding glass door. It popped open a few inches, and Walter stopped short of jamming his head through the tiny gap. Repositioning myself, I got hold of the door and pulled it wide open.

Turning once again, I began to push myself over the threshold. It had that sharp metal housing you see at the base of a sliding door. It dug into every inch of my spine as I snaked my torso into the house.

Over another hurdle, I took a minute to breathe on the dining room floor. *I can't believe I made it. I'm in the house; it's over. I did it. Well, it's almost over.* Exhausted and ready for a heavy sigh of relief, I still had to get to my feet. With the back door left open, I began to push my way to the carpeted living room.

In most circumstances, throughout my time in Monkton, I was able to get to my feet on the carpet. So, I tried the same way I had in the driveway. Not even close. Much worse than in the driveway. I simply didn't have the energy. But I had an alternative in mind; this had happened before.

I rolled onto my back once again and pushed myself over to the oversized leather chair and ottoman. I was going to do this the same way I'd done everything else — on my back. I lay on the floor with my head at the base of the ottoman and tried to lift up my head and push with my legs. I got into a sitting position against the ottoman and continued to push, flopping my body further up the chair and into an almost-seated position. Squirming around on my back, I kicked away the ottoman and planted my feet on the floor. Using my legs and the sloping back of the chair, I made it to a sitting position. Leaning forward with my hands on my knees, I readied myself to stand up.

I thrust myself into the standing position and stood still, trying to find my center and calm my nerves. I felt incredibly unstable, every nerve in my body on ultra-high alert. With equal parts care and fear, I stepped deliberately toward the back door, pulled it shut, sat down at the counter, and gulped from my ever-present water glass. *Time to find some dinner.*

My keys were in the driveway. I didn't get them until morning.

I LOOK AT PICTURES

I look at pictures, on Facebook and otherwise, from the years since it began. All of the weddings, road trips and vacations, get-togethers and parties — throughout all of it, one thought comes to mind. There are so many memories, so many of the events in my life, connected by a sinking feeling, a dominant force: ALS.

My friends see old pictures and call themselves babies — how much they've grown up is obvious. They see themselves before marriage, before children, before houses and newfound careers. They see an incomplete picture, an immature version of themselves. If I scroll back far enough, I see myself: I only exist in pictures and memory.

It's so easy to see; I could never forget those feelings. I can almost *see* what's on my mind. I remember what it was like, in 2010, 2011, before anyone knew — before there was anything to tell. Those first times — when the life was sucked out of me — I can see myself going through the motions without joy.

At the Connolly wedding, looking fat in the face and holding a beer. I remember the feeling: knowingly avoiding the problems, overseeing a tug-of-war in my mind. At the reception and the house party that followed, I was merely a visitor. They asked me to dance like I used to — I knew how, but I couldn't move my body that way anymore. I couldn't be all-in. I couldn't live in the moment; I didn't even want to try.

There are the pictures of all of us at Johnny's, helping to assemble his post-and-beam house. I see myself reaching high to help move a ceiling joist into place, climbing the ladder, and standing tall upon the beams. I remember lunch and the beers that accompanied. I felt disturbingly woozy afterward.

I can see us partying on New Year's Eve, the first since my diagnosis. I'm posing in my tweed jacket, Sherlock Holmes tobacco pipe between my teeth, gold pocket watch in my hand. They were gifts from Lenny and Tom, given after I'd told them the news.

There's the trip to Maine in the summer of 2012. Everywhere I look, from Portsmouth to Vinalhaven to Acadia, I can see it in my face, a mustachioed grimace that seemed unwilling to go away. In every picture, at every venue, amongst the group, I can only see the way it felt: like I wasn't really there.

Every picture bears a tip: a beer can crunched between uncontrolled fingers; a newly arrived little belly pushing out under a T-shirt; everything from a bearded face to my footwear and posture. I can't ignore any of it. I'd like to remember those moments as an oasis apart from the monster that was gathering strength, but I can't.

And there are the later ones, where everyone knew; I can't take my eyes off myself. I'm always front and center, arms hanging in front of me. I can see it: I'm forcing a smile.

I see all the weddings: at the start, when I was carrying the burden all on my own, to a guy in a wheelchair with his friends gathered around. I relive the memory of each day, all those times on the sidelines, watching my friends cover the dance floor. In all of those times, with the bride and groom beaming, it was all but impossible to see anyone but myself.

The scenes at the beach, the group shots and selfies: there I am, in shoes and socks with curled fingers. The stone set of stairs built into the hill, with multiple turns and uneven heights. Climbing those stairs, with Tom holding me up the whole way, I was as scared as any time in my life. The entire way up, I was shaking with fear — I could see myself tumbling to near-death.

Though I know they existed, it's hard to remember the good times. I can't look at those pictures, and see all the signs, and think of anything else.

7.

Soon after my diagnosis, one of the clinicians said something that struck me. "So, it seems like maintaining your independence is very important to you." I thought it the most preposterous of queries, like, "I hear you enjoy bringing air into your lungs all the time." Is there anything more central to the human experience? Implied in her question are a variety of alternative systems of value. Some folks might not mind slowly (or not-so-slowly) turning back into a child, helpless and dependent on others. I could never have let go so easily; my freedoms would have to be ripped from my grasp.

I did everything I could to hold onto my independence; I couldn't imagine the day when it would end. My mom would mention, casually in conversation, some aspect of my future at their house, and I'd brush it off. My brain still refused to face reality. The same brain whose determination had guided me through every daily challenge for years, continued to hang on, wouldn't give up.

Having neglected the ALS clinic for several years, I agreed to see my family doctor to check in. On a Wednesday morning in July 2018, I drove myself to her office — Mom met me there. Aside from the usual items, she wanted to make sure I was OK. She asked about everyday tasks, and while I tried to downplay my struggles, Mom interjected. As she'd been saying for years about all sorts of things, "I don't know how he does it."

"I drove myself here today. I got up; I made coffee; I made breakfast, eggs, and toast; I got dressed, and I drove here. I didn't shower, but I don't usually shower first thing in the morning."

She nodded. I'd made my point; the subject was effectively closed. Tilted logic, biased examples, and purposeful omissions were enough to at least take some of the worry from her head. It felt like a victory; I needed a victory.

My world continued to shrink. I was still holding on as fall turned to winter. I walked a few steps from the house to the car and nowhere else. My driveway was plowed, car cleared off, and entryway shoveled. My mail was delivered to my dining room table and my firewood stacked in the house. I went days without seeing or talking to anyone. I lived like a shut-in, and for the most part, I was.

A HOUSE IS PERMANENT

I always assumed that when I bought a house, it'd be permanent. I'd paint walls and hang pictures, buy furniture and make improvements. I wouldn't just be passing through — on another one-year lease, unsure of the next thing — this would be mine.

I never really felt like I moved in to all of the apartments over the years. Because I knew they were only temporary — and perhaps, I must admit, because I'm cheap and lazy — I didn't make much of an effort to create a home for myself. I thought I could finally change that with the house; maybe I could grow up.

My picture of permanence started with Kim and the apartment we shared. I felt at home the day we moved in. Though I knew the rental wasn't forever, "our place," wherever that may be, felt like it was.

We were barreling ahead toward the permanence — and the comfort and contentment that came with it — I'd lacked for so long. Neither of us wanted to admit or discuss what that meant. There are so many questions we didn't ask, from the practical to the personal to the overwhelming.

Do we want to, and can we, do all the work to maintain a house? Should we buy a condo? Where do we want to live? What will my health be like in five years? Or ten years? Might I even live that long? Will we have kids? Who will take care of them? Will I need someone to take care of me?

I don't know what I expected to happen. I guess I thought we'd figure it out together in our new house. My comforting dream of permanence ended before I had the chance to find out.

My house in Monkton was just another way station, another temporary place to hang my hypothetical hat. I didn't paint the walls, plant a garden, or even buy a couch. I made no effort to meet the neighbors; I didn't make small talk at the country store a stone's throw away. I couldn't do most of the things that I wanted, but even if I could — build a woodshed, tend to the apple trees, tear up the linoleum — I didn't want to; it wasn't permanent.

8.

I'd been walking the same way for years. I'm not even sure when it started or how my transition occurred. While my right foot could land flat and behave somewhat normally, my left foot could not. Because of tightness and inflexibility in my ankle and Achilles, my left heel never made it anywhere near the floor. Often barefoot, I walked around the house with an uneven gait, as if my left leg were prosthetic. At times — when I'd had something to drink or was otherwise moving too fast — it felt like a controlled fall, like my momentum was out in front, my legs just trying to keep up.

I'd grown very comfortable with my walk. It got me around the house and the yard, in and out of the car, up and down the grocery store aisles, and any reasonably short-distanced place I needed to go. It'd been years since walking had been second nature. Though I longed for those days, and tried to imagine how it felt, I couldn't remember a time when I didn't have to think about every step. I'd come to a place where carefree walking seemed like a winning lottery ticket, only much more meaningful.

It wasn't that I hadn't fallen, because I had, in all sorts of places with all sorts of excuses. Many times, I felt nervous, uneasy as I willed myself forward. But I almost never felt scared. I hadn't lost confidence in my walk, and as long as I had that, I could continue with my stubborn independence.

On a Saturday morning in late February 2019, I got out of bed, and as I always did, walked to the adjacent bathroom. Still half asleep, with my first step onto the linoleum, I stubbed the big toe on my left foot. There was no recovery from such a mistake, no possible way to regain my balance. Like an inanimate object, my momentum brought me quickly to the floor. Not a single part of my body had any reaction until it was too late. I believe my nose was the first thing to hit the linoleum and the cement slab underneath.

In a few seconds, the shock wore off; blood trickled from my nose as I turned myself onto my back. Angry (but not entirely surprised) that this was the way I was starting my day, I pushed myself out of the bathroom and onto the carpet alongside my bed. I turned myself back onto my stomach and, with equal parts confidence and surprise, managed to plant my arms and get onto my knees. With both hands gripping the bed sheets for balance, I used my (stronger) right leg to push myself up.

Both shaken and proud, I took one calculated step at a time back into the bathroom to look at my face in the mirror. The bridge of my nose looked flat and swollen; blood dripped into my beard, soaking my chin. Incredibly slowly (I felt both bored and annoyed midway through), I stepped across the house to my usual perch at the kitchen peninsula. For the first time, I called my parents without hesitation.

That may have been the end of my walking. It wasn't that I'd lost the strength, but almost overnight, I lost confidence. I found myself in the house alone, taking one step at a time, pausing for balance before proceeding. I couldn't seem to make myself imitate the steady gait I'd long mastered. I couldn't seem to shake off the fear.

Everything seemed to be happening at once in the spring of 2019. I lost the ability to walk in any reasonable way, finally agreed to sell my house, and my falls became dangerous. I tripped again in the bathroom, went barreling into the tub, and slammed the side of my head into the plastic-encased shower wall. I fell in my parents' kitchen on Easter Sunday, and seeing my car in the driveway a short time later, asked, "Did I drive here today? How did I get here?" And I lost the ability to routinely step in and out of the tub.

For nearly five years, I'd been using the vertical grab bar mounted at my chest above the eighteen-inch wall of the tub. Holding tight on the way in and out, I'd never had a problem lifting my feet over the rim. One day I grazed my foot on the tub, lost my balance, and ended up on my knees on the floor. I tried sitting on the rim and turning to get my legs into the tub, but its efficacy was questionable at best; I was asking to tip over.

As was the case with my walking, an unconscious switch had been flipped in my head; a mental block appeared where routine had long ruled. Each time I tried to get in the shower, I stood with one foot on the floor, one in the tub, shaking with my legs glued in place. On one such occasion, standing wet and naked with my left foot on the bathmat, I tried to lift my right but got caught on the edge. I tried to hold myself up with the grab bar, but that was asking too much, and I slowly slid into the bathtub. I found myself lying on my back in the tub. This was the nightmare scenario. I'd imagined it happening, and hadn't dreamed up a solution.

Somehow, on my back, I used my legs to push (against anything — the floor, the faucet, the wall) my body slowly and painfully out of the tub and onto the floor. Despite my shivering body, I then got to my feet beside my bed as before. I'd dodged another bullet, escaped from another set of chains. But the fears were gaining momentum; the *What Ifs* were beginning to win out. Even to me, it was obvious: I could no longer live alone.

NUMB

I've become a chronic under-reactor. Everything that I've been through — all of these years of getting kicked around — has caused me to shut down. If it seems like nothing matters, like I don't really care, it's because that's the only logical response.

I have a hard time feeling anything; there are no ups and downs. I think back to college — of all those times that we let loose — and I see things differently. People love to say that they "work hard and play hard," and while more often than not, those are just words, it's easy to see that balance is important. Hard work brings the need to let loose; letting loose allows us to refocus. There isn't any break from my life.

Sometimes, in moments of martyrdom, I welcome the next punch in the face. Every setback brings pain, but it also brings strength. Deep in my soul, I always know I can take it, and there's a little pride that comes with getting back up.

People will say that I have perspective, that I've changed in a way that most couldn't imagine. It's easy to see the positives, but my perspective comes at a cost. All of the little things don't bother me; it's easy not to sweat the small stuff. But nothing seems to matter, and sometimes, it would be nice to feel something.

9.

After the Easter incident, I was out of my house for good. All of the preparations were well underway, the appraisal completed, the photos taken, and the boxing and moving begun. I stood in the living room looking at a lifetime of stuff, ready for disposal. The solid cherry dining room table I bought on Craigslist five years before. Chris had carried it in on his back like Atlas carried the world. The red leather chair I took to my first apartment and the resulting radiator imprint on its back. The three maple end tables and red chair that dated from the '50s and once accompanied the (legendary) blue couch at 6 Patrick. The pine cabinet and heavy oak chairs I bought with Kim. Most of the plates, silverware, cups, pots, pans, and utensils that'd forever be associated with my mémère and pépère. Even Walter the cat, my first and only pet, the only company I had for so long. (I wanted to keep Walter, but he struck fear into my parents' dog, and there's no telling what he'd have done to their indoors-for-generations Maine Coon. He lived his first year as a stray — he was an outdoor cat, killer of mice and birds, and I was his human.) So much of my life would be left behind.

In the middle of May, finally finished with the Craigslisting and Goodwilling, I sat at the kitchen table of my new residence and put 182 Rotax Road on the market.

CHAPTER 8

GIVING IN

*I feel the need to carry a picture of myself. When I'm
introduced to someone new, I'd like to show them. And
tell them. I can explain that this is who I was. I can make
them understand that it wasn't always this way. I used
to look different. I used to be different. I have proof.*

1.

For a couple of months, selling the house was a full-time job. Had
I a family and a career, it would've been overwhelming; I may have
thrown in the towel and hired somebody. Between the aforementioned Craigslisting, the house listing, and the unending checklist
of maintenance items that inevitably accompany a sale, I've never
spent so much time dealing with phone calls, texts, and emails.

It seems a lot of people just like to look. I guess we should've
had an open house and knocked them all out in an afternoon. As
it was, nearly every day, Mom and I were driving back over to the
house and giving a tour.

My walking was almost untenable. All of the recent falls had
irreparably damaged my psyche. The ten or fifteen steps from car
to door required a hand-holder. A few times, the buyers (or lookers, as it were) were waiting in the driveway or poking around the

yard as we pulled in. "You're not supposed to see this," I joked as Mom and I edged our way slowly toward the door.

The first offer suffered a slow death because the buyers wanted the town's pre-approval to build a garage and needed it quickly to sell their own house. Their chipper, smooth-talking realtor assured them it would be no big deal, but when the town of Monkton gave them a six-week review timeline, they pulled their full-boat, too-good-to-be-true offer. A week or ten days later, I received a call on a Sunday that turned out to be the first step in the last battle to sell the house. A few dozen texts and emails, another lawn-mowing, and a perfunctory visit from an electrician to change out (all of) the kitchen outlets, and we were only signatures away from a sale. On a hot, sunny day in the middle of July, in a conference room on the top floor of the Hickok and Boardman building overlooking the lake, we signed the papers and immediately drove the check to the bank.

In place of a house and a yard, I had numbers on a page. On my thirty-fifth birthday two weeks later, my license expired and I didn't renew it. A couple of months later, after spending $600 on a variety of items for the inspection and sale, I watched with sentimental eyes as my thirteen-year-old car — my first real, adult purchase, full of memories spanning both of my lives — drove down the driveway and disappeared around the corner. In its place, I held $2,000 in an envelope.

MY FACE IN THE MIRROR

I think the world sees me better than I do. I don't often want to face my full self; it scares me. In the days after my disturbing barrage of falls, I took a rare occasion to look in the bathroom mirror and think about what I was seeing.

My eyes appear tired; they're telling the truth. My head doesn't naturally stay in one place; I'm continually, consciously readjusting. My cheeks and chin aren't as full as the image in my head. There seem to be permanent lines on my forehead.

The bridge of my nose has a red scar. My left cheek is yellowed. There is a very unnatural swelling at the top of my jaw, just under my left eye. The eyelid and under-eye are dark purple. A thought crosses my mind, and I am thankful to have a full complement of teeth. There's also what I cannot see. The hairless scar on my chin that took five stitches. The longer one above my hairline that took nine. It's easier to see myself in my memories.

2.

Everything changed the day I moved in. All of my household tasks — most impactfully making my meals and cleaning up afterward — were gone. Everything that living alone had meant, the frustrations and the independence, was gone. I felt like I'd given in, like all my determination, all of the mental grit it took to keep things going, had finally run out.

It seemed like another loss all at once, but actually, I'd finally reached the end of a long, continually descending road. It still felt like I was standing on my own, but I'd had so much support. For years — truly from the day I moved in — my parents had helped me in ever-increasing ways. What started with mowing the lawn, digging my car from the snow, stacking and bringing in firewood had also become weekly visits from my mom. She always did more than she needed. She'd vacuum and clean the bathrooms, change the sheets, and check up on Walter's litter box, food, and water. (He had plenty of food and water; I kept the food a few feet away and carried a pitcher to his bowl on a regular basis.) She did the laundry start to finish, went grocery shopping with me, put away the groceries, and, if need be, emptied the dishwasher. No, I wasn't living on my own.

Life could have been so much easier, I thought; maybe I should've given in long ago. It could be so freeing, so luxurious to be served my meals and have help with my socks. That part of my mind, ever-occupied with questions and frustrations — *Will I ever get this shirt over my head? What if I can't get up off the floor?* — will be free. And my world shrinks further — I wonder what I'll do.

I haven't cooked a meal since I've been here. I've barely opened the fridge; I have to ask what's in there. Three times each day, I arrive in the kitchen to a plate or bowl, fork or spoon, and feed.

I don't need to fight to get dressed or exhaust myself in the process. My clothes are neatly folded, laid out, and ready when I need them. If I need help with anything at all, I only have to ask.

TRIPS TO THE GROCERY STORE

A lot of simple tasks changed over the years. Running errands — to the grocery store, the bank, or the gas station — became more difficult or disappeared altogether. I tried to find ways to continue as long as possible. Let me explain.

Years ago, like a lot of young men, there was one way to buy groceries: with a hand cart and a free hand for a large item, nearly always beer. I'd lift the cart onto the conveyor, unload from there, and carry the resulting bags out the door. I continued with this method as long as I could, through my diagnosis and well into my Waterbury years. One day I gave in: upon entering the store, I pulled a cart from the pile.

Like a mom with a couple of bratty kids in tow, I placed both hands on my new crutch and walked slowly down the aisles. I came to the register to unload my items and despite my best efforts, the cashier was left waiting. I was cold and nervous; my hands didn't work in the cold. I couldn't grip anything with one hand, but had to use both for each item. I never asked for help and no one offered.

When I was finished, I pushed the cart to my car, using both arms to lift the heavier bags out of its deep metal cage. I got in the car, and as was becoming customary, paused to enjoy the pleasure of sitting before driving away. Though I hated to do it, I didn't walk my cart to the pile.

In Waterbury, I had to carry my bags up the stairs. I needed one hand for the railing; it always took more than one trip. When I moved to Burlington, there was an elevator. In the beginning, I'd park and carry the bags into the garage. At some point in the next eleven months, I began to pull the car up to the elevator in the garage (where I did not have a parking space), unload the bags, drive out to the lot, walk back in, and press the button. In multiple trips, I'd move the bags past the doors as they tried to close. I did the same at the third floor, moving to a resting place in the hallway before the last leg into the apartment.

All of these steps may sound tedious, but the reality was much worse. Every movement I made — in my life, beyond grocery store runs — was awkward and forced. There was no ease on my face; everything felt like a war.

At some point, living in Monkton, my mom started grocery shopping with me. It made things much easier. She could reach everything, take a jar from the shelf without fear of collateral damage, and deal with the checkout process. All I had to do was walk, choose my items, and drive. I liked to drive.

The day came when I could no longer walk the aisles. Now, if I go to the grocery store, I sit in a chair. I don't pull items from shelves; I don't carry or push a cart; I don't drive. I sit and look around and, pointing with my eyes (because I can't reach out my arms), say what I want.

3.

I'm thirty-six years old and I live with my parents. I should've known, from the day of my diagnosis, that it was inevitable. Among all of the thoughts in my head, moving back in with my parents should've been high on the list.

Mom always seemed to see my future with a level head. From the start, she's been preparing in a way that I never could. I think the people around me have seen the changes (and oftentimes accepted them) more easily than I. I've always lived in the moment, often paying little attention to the bigger picture of my life. My mom is a cut-and-dry, this-is-the-way-things-are-done planner through and through. But I also think I've been blind to what's happened.

At times it's been hard to see; at times, I've been unwilling to look. The human brain is a powerful instrument, and sometimes, I think, to continue to move forward with some kind of sanity, it uses some tricks. We all do it with various items for various reasons. We use euphemisms, make excuses, draw illogical conclusions, and deny what we like — all to get ourselves through each day. When life gets difficult, our brains try to make things a bit easier. It's superficial at times, and we know it — one look at my arms or in the mirror and it's easy to see the truth — but those are the tricks of the trade, and I'm very good at them.

My parents were having the house built in 2011, an empty-nester's dream in the country. They located some land, formed all their plans, and watched hopefully as things began to take shape. Before the first swing of the hammer, the house site merely a hole in the ground, everything changed — their son in a wheelchair was now in the mix.

If you were to think of moving in with your parents, in your thirties, I can guess what you'd say: you'd never be home. It'd be a place to crash and nothing more. And it would be temporary — you'd be plotting a way out from the very beginning. You'd do your own laundry, make your own meals, and come and go as you pleased, treating your parents like roommates — with respect and without need, except for the roof.

None of that applies to me. The mere act of moving in with my parents meant that I could no longer enjoy any of those freedoms. Unlike every other person in their thirties, moving back in with their parents, my reason was not financial — it was everything else.

I can't make my own breakfast, wash my own sheets, or drive my own car. All of the routes a person could take to escape from the horror of cohabitation are unavailable to me. I don't have my own space; I don't have my own life; I don't have a say.

Of course, I feel trapped. I've felt trapped for years. But it's gotten much worse and will only continue.

ASKING FOR EVERYTHING

If I want it done right, I'll do it myself. You may not be in the habit of saying it, but I think everyone knows it. There's a big difference between what you would do yourself and what you would ask others to do for you.

Asking for help (of any kind) has always made me uneasy. Whether a ride home from school, a question in class, or even a mechanic to look at my car, I've never wanted to ask anyone for anything. I'm indeed the classic, closed-off male in this way. Somewhere along the line, I learned not to show weakness. I could move through my life like I had all the answers, like I didn't need anyone at all. But we all need people, and I should've asked questions. I only denied myself an honest opportunity to grow.

I need so much these days. I'll never have things — I'll never be in control — the way that I'd like. It'd be impossible and impossibly annoying. Think of all of the things that you do — from the way you like your eggs to the way you make your bed, drive your car, or whether to open a window — and how much they would change if they were done for you. Maybe it sounds freeing, and sometimes it is, but it's a constant reminder of vulnerable need and the imperfect (though appreciated) solutions of others.

The small, nitpicky things — the types of OCD behaviors and pet peeves that may seem so important — I've learned to give up on them. Sometimes they weigh on me — five feet of the desk to my left is covered in clutter — but realistically, there's only so much I can ask. I'll never have the control that I want. I've had to give myself over to asking for everything.

4.

Almost from the beginning, the neurologist was worried about falls. Though my legs showed plenty of strength, it was the "tone" that worried them. There's a jumpy, inflexible quality that makes fluid movement nearly impossible. More than once, they brought me a walker, sat back, and watched me complain while trying to use it. It only added to my difficulty. It felt like yet another encumbrance, like I was pushing a grocery cart. Maybe I'd have gotten used to it, but walking around the big room at the clinic, it felt like a nuisance and a danger. I knew if I spent my days leaning on and pushing that thing around, I'd constantly worry about it getting away from me. I could see myself leaning forward, my arms pushing the walker further away from my body, dangerously unable to stop. A walker is meant as a safety net, to provide reassurance and prevent falls. It felt like a liability, like it would do nothing but cause me to fall.

In June of 2019, I got a wheelchair. It was not so much for use around the house, but in public, for distances beyond the reach of my newly-adopted hardwood floor sock-shuffle. My dad, ever-prepared, had already built a wooden ramp in place of the stairs from the garage to the house. I hadn't walked with what anyone would describe as ease in several years, and it obviously hindered my ability to get out and do things, but I looked at a wheelchair like I looked at a lot of the changes in my life: it was another loss. It was another step, and a big one, away from the person I wished I could be. However inevitable the less delusional part of my brain knew that it was, I couldn't see crossing that bridge until absolutely necessary.

It's a strange experience to be in a wheelchair — I've learned a few things. Walking is exercise, sitting is not. Walking gets the blood flowing, brings energy, and enlivens the body. There are no benefits of sitting; slouching is bad for the spine.

I'm already tired of the over-the-top apologies. Yes, you are in the way. No, you didn't see me. You don't need to apologize like you ran over my dog.

I felt both hugely conspicuous and invisible those first times in the chair. I'd long noticed people's eyeballs drawn to my unnatural walk, but this was entirely different. I imagine some portion was in my head, but I seemed to garner two distinct reactions: some folks smiled kindly, which made me feel like a dog or small child; others ignored me entirely, perhaps as they would with a dog or small child.

The world sees me as an invalid; there's no way around it. I sit in a chair, my arms resting lifelessly on my lap; my voice is weak and often hard to understand. It has become obvious that I'm not seen or heard as the intelligent human being I know that I am.

It's difficult to feel that you are not respected like the others around you. I don't want to be treated differently; whether you think you're doing the right thing doesn't matter. When I was still on my feet, and my voice was stronger, they may have seen the awkward limp and bony forearms, but still, I was seen as a functioning human. In the chair I'm talked down to; I'm a wheelchair first, a grown man second.

It was a manual chair, and there was never the thought that I had the strength, dexterity, or coordination to operate it on my own, so I was forever tethered to and relying upon another person. In the early going, I realized I'd see the chair in two ways: I'm able to get out and move around without worry or exhaustion, and, I'm a useless lump of shit. If only because I had no other choice, I began to try to accept the former.

I wish I'd been able to embrace the chair earlier; I spent so much time with limited mobility. For almost five years in Monkton, and even beforehand, I allowed myself to succumb to needless restrictions. Yes, I could walk, but walking is not black and white. I could walk where I had to — around the house, to my car, and even a few blocks — but not as I wanted. The days of my long walks with Tom were well behind me. It was purely utility; there was no pleasure — only fear — in my walk. It could've been so much easier; I could've been out in the world so much more if only I'd accepted the inevitable.

The manual chair, and the driver it required, was not a permanent solution. It was a stepping stone, a stopgap to prevent further injury. I was also fitted for a power chair. I spent more than two hours with my physical therapist and a wheelchair salesman in the big room at the ALS clinic, taking measurements and answering questions. Using the left-handed joystick (with my higher-functioning left arm) and changing the speeds and modes, I cruised the hallways and spun circles with ease. Maxing out at 6 ½ miles per hour up and down the hospital corridor — with the PT running beside — felt pretty fast. As impossible as it was to admit in the face of being dragged kicking and screaming into a new wheelchair phase of my life, it could be kind of fun.

The new chair was delivered a month later. I was still walking around the house, and I didn't have any way to transport my battery-powered conveyance, so for the time being, it mostly sat in the corner of my room. I could roll up the driveway and the dirt road beyond; I could circle the house on the lawn, but unless I dropped a big chunk of change on a new vehicle, that was all it was good for.

MY NECK IS GETTING WEAKER

My neck is getting weaker. For weeks I've been feeling the muscles fire at random. I sit at my desk, and they're jumping; I lay down at night, mercifully rest my head on the pillow, and the action won't quit.

It's hard to remember a time when I wasn't constantly feeling the weight of my skull. Sitting or standing, it sits like a bobblehead, precariously holding its place. It's a strange thing to be so acutely aware of one's head and neck. It's exhausting.

Nearly every time I tip my head back, I hear a pop, a series of small cracks, or a grimace-inducing grinding noise. On the more severe occasions, I feel a light-headed rush as the blood, or whatever other essential bodily force, moves into or out of my head. I've never learned a name for that occurrence. I imagine the muscles are no longer strong enough to hold everything properly in place.

The neurologist used to have me lay on the table, face up, to test my neck strength. I'd lift my head off the table and hold it in place while he watched for my neck to grow tired and give. After five or ten seconds, to further measure my strength, he'd push down on my forehead and watch me resist. Satisfied with the results, we'd move on. I can no longer lift my head off the table at all.

Almost every day for the last several years, I take an afternoon nap. It serves a number of purposes. Primarily — or so I tell myself — I'm tired and need rest. But it also serves to break up the mostly long, empty days that have become so common in my life. And beyond both of those unquestionably legitimate purposes, taking a nap is a break for my neck. Whether I actually fall asleep or not, I rise with newly refreshed muscles.

There will come a day in the not-so-distant future when my neck needs help. I've seen the ALS patients with their halos and headrests; it seemed like I'd never be that guy. Soon I'll be one step closer to an amorphous blob.

5.

For years I'd been edged toward buying a wheelchair-accessible van. Over the winter of '19-'20, I began to look. I was finally ready to begin to accept my inevitable future.

It's what you might call a specialty item — there aren't dozens of local dealerships vying for your business. In fact, in this area, there's only one. I learned very quickly that these things are not commodities. Not only are there a variety of automobile brands, but a number of conversion companies and styles; each individual vehicle I came across was different from the last. Buying a handicapped-accessible van was looking more like finding a house than a car.

There are any number of vehicles available that can accommodate a wheelchair: full-size vans, the occasional SUV, and a whole lot of minivans. The latter have all been converted: floors cut out and lowered, suspension modified, power and manually operated ramps added, and seats (including, in some cases, the driver's seat) altered or removed. Instead of the stock carpeting, most floors resemble the indestructible black rubber of a school bus.

I learned that there are two basic designs of converted minivan: side entry and rear entry. The side entry vans are more complex and expensive: a power operating ramp — replete with a hunk of electronics and secondary battery — emerges from the second row sliding door. The rear entry models are simpler: a section of the floor is cut out, and a manual folding ramp extends from the tailgate. I didn't know which would be better.

Most people want to see, touch, and experience a new vehicle before arriving at a decision. Even if it's not the exact car they're buying, even with a thousand YouTubers for advice, they at least like to take it for a spin. From the start, I realized that could prove difficult.

I was referred to a network of dealers with an office in Essex, where I could purportedly peruse some vehicles. Like anyone, I wanted to demo the features of each van in my chair. In order to do so, I'd have to get my chair to the van, or, as I found out, the van to my chair.

On two separate days in the middle of February, in the snow and ice of our gravel driveway, the vans came to me. Not surprisingly, they're set up for this; they schedule showings at potential customers' houses. With very little effort on my part, I learned nearly all that was needed to narrow my search.

Both of the vans — the first one a power-operated side-entry Dodge Grand Caravan ("DGC") that we deemed to have too little ground clearance (thanks to the floor having been lowered) to reliably navigate the dirt, mud, and snow just beyond our doorstep; the second a manual-folding rear-entry DGC that more piqued our interest — were used, seemingly overpriced, and had accidents in their past. I wasn't looking for anything new, or even newish, but if I'm buying used, that's what I expect to pay for. I don't know if it was the result of a limited supply, but I couldn't help but think these vans didn't depreciate. You're paying for the van, but you're also paying for the conversion, and that's the part, it seems, that drives the price.

I've always been into cars. In another reality, my mid-thirties could be the time to finally buy something fun. For years I've spent too much time looking at cars online — realistic cars, cars I could actually afford and see myself buying. I longed to drive my new car — shift through the gears of its essential manual transmission, crank the music with the windows down, take a road trip with a friend, just sit in the driver's seat and bask in the glory of my new companion. I couldn't help but dwell on my circumstances: buying a car was supposed to be fun; it felt like only another in a long line of surrenders.

I thought back on the cars that I'd owned in my life — there were three. The '93 Saab 900 I bought in the summer of 2000, months before I'd had Driver's Education and a license; the '90 Audi Coupe Quattro I bought midway through college, a cry for help if ever there was one; and the '06 Subaru Legacy with which I commuted to work, perhaps the most sensible choice of my life. I remember those times as pure joy: cruising up the beltline in the Saab, a freshly minted driver's license in my wallet; sitting in the black leather passenger seat of the Audi, watching the previous owner take it up past 100 on the highway; watching my Subaru roll into the parking lot, delivered on my lunch break at work. All of those things were so clearly behind me; I could no longer drive and was buying a minivan.

Having decided what I needed (a rear-entry converted minivan), and thoroughly disappointed with the inventory at the recommended dealer, I scoured the Internet and made some inquiries. Eventually, I found a number of vans I considered acceptable. Then the coronavirus lockdowns entered our lives, and, like nearly everything else, my quest for transportation was put on hold.

Finally, after resuming the process a couple of months later, my van arrived on a transport truck from Kansas. Accompanied by my mom, I drove (I still don't know whether "drove" is the correct term) my chair to sign the papers at the end of the driveway. (The behemoth automobile transport truck couldn't make the turn onto the private road that becomes our driveway.) Pending pandemic-era Vermont registration, which was completed by mail and took almost two months, I had myself a new mode of transport.

In the summer of 2020, I bought a leftover 2018 Dodge Grand Caravan with fourteen miles on the odometer. It has a manual liftgate, manual fold-out access ramp, a system of tie-downs on its school-bus floor, two folding aftermarket second-row seats, and everything else you'd expect in a base model minivan. A wheelchair can be tied down between the second-row seats or in place of the third row at the back. Two crisscrossing aftermarket safety belts hang from the ceiling. Loading and unloading can be a bit of a process.

Mom and I spent a few hours in the driveway familiarizing ourselves with all of the components. I realized that I needn't sit in the chair itself, requiring the use of those cumbersome belts. Instead, for the time being and as long as I am able, I could eliminate some hassle and make my way to the second-row jump seats. With a freshly printed paper plate scotch-taped to the rear window, Mom and I took our maiden voyage down the road.

EVERYTHING IS HEAVY IN MY WORLD

Gravity pulls a bit harder with each passing day. As muscles shrink, their burden grows. The numbers on a scale have become all but meaningless.

I stand in the shower and wrap my fingers through the handle on the wall. I slide my feet a few inches at a time to turn my body. My knees strain under my weight; I'm afraid soon they'll give up.

It feels like their burden has doubled, like I'm carrying an extra hundred pounds without their knowledge. A rare look at my lower half in a mirror makes me cringe and look away. It's still hard to believe those withered muscles and crooked, bony knees belong to me. They look like a picture in a medical textbook: this is what happens when things go wrong.

Of course, it's not just my knees or even my legs. Every piece of the body allowing me to stand is growing tired of the most human of actions. My core is holding on, less visibly affected, but altered, nonetheless. I regularly feel the strain of the muscles wrapping my torso — muscles you may not know exist. It's not only the abs — the glorious symbol of fitness — but the back. My balance is a casualty of a weakening core.

I would work out with dumbbells in my days at 6 Patrick. They were twenty-five-pounders and belonged to Tyler; he never used them but liked to collect junk. I built up a tolerance and began to enjoy building new muscle. But at some point, my wrists seemed to lose something; though my biceps were up to the task, my wrists — surely an afterthought in weight training — had unexplainably weakened. Soon, twenty-five pounds was too much to support. I tried to hang on in denial — altering my exercises to accommodate my new shortcoming — but it didn't last long. I left the dumbbells in their place in the corner and moved on.

In the spring of 2012, I accompanied friends on a short hike to the cabin at Sleepy Hollow. I tried to pull my weight and carry a gallon of water. About halfway through the mile, my fingers gave way. I'd already switched arms and grips a number of times, but there were no fixes. A gallon of water weighs eight pounds; it felt like fifty.

I don't try to carry anything anymore; my weight on its own is enough. We're not meant to notice these things: the weight of our arms and our skull. We're meant to run free, seeking purpose.

6.

I still try to move my body in the little ways that I can. I've always been encouraged to use light exercise to help maintain, rather than regain, strength and flexibility. At times it seems pointless, and I can't be certain it has ever bore physical fruit, but in the least, it's helped me hold off an entirely sedentary existence.

I bought a recumbent bike on Craigslist in the summer of 2012. It's an old steel and plastic machine with a hand-crank tensioner; it came from an old guy's musty basement. By some miracle, in two pieces, I managed to drag it upstairs to the spare bedroom of my Waterbury apartment. It'd followed me with each move since, getting regular, if diminishing use. It lives at the foot of my bed by the window.

I've seen a number of physical and occupational therapists since attending my first ALS clinic. They've come out to my house — in Monkton and Hinesburg — to observe and evaluate my living space. For six weeks in the summer of 2018, a woman — several years my junior, though I never asked — came by for an hour at a time, instructing me on a variety of stretches and exercises. She was a go-getter; I liked her energy and, frankly, her company. As with every evaluator I'd seen over the years, I couldn't help but see every task as a competition. At every opportunity, I tried to impress her.

Certain assumptions are made when a medical professional visits or hears of a patient who lives alone. Namely — and this is assuredly a primary subject of the evaluation — that he is capable of safely doing so. She asked me to walk across the room, get in and out of chairs, and, most importantly to me, get myself up off the floor. Confident in my well-worn method, I was more than happy to demonstrate.

I do find myself discouraged by exercise. It'd be impossible not to. I think of all of the regular, healthy people who abhor exercise; I get so angry with them. It's that satisfying feeling of well-earned sweat and worn-out muscles. If only I could feel that again.

In the summer of 2020, following an appointment with my family doctor, I had another series of visits on the calendar. Physical and occupational therapists came to advise on my day-to-day tasks. I knew it would be déjà vu — I'd been hearing the same sorts of things for too long. But I needed to listen this time; the nonchalance era had passed.

One of the first things the physical therapist did was acknowledge my situation. As I sat awaiting instruction in my chair, she looked me in the eye and said, "First, I want to say I know how much this sucks," and continued from there. Very few people in the medical community (or in my life) bother to make that concession. It was refreshing to hear.

They showed me a few exercises to perform from the safety of my bed and put down my bike. The woman couldn't believe I could get in and out of its seat, about a foot off the floor. She extolled the importance of stretching every fiber of my body — something I'd been hearing for years — and, with my back on the bed, moved me through an extended, purportedly daily routine. But more than any of that, each provider came to see how I moved around and interacted with my house.

They wanted to know if my wheelchair fit in the bathroom. Sort of. They wanted to watch me sit down and stand up from the toilet and see how I got into the shower. They asked about meals, where, how, and what I was eating. They offered the same suggestions I'd (mostly) ignored in the past. We went to my bedroom and talked about dressing and the danger of sitting on the edge of the bed.

I'd long found ways around a lot of my limitations — I knew how to drink from a glass and get into bed — and they mostly applauded my methods. People are always impressed with my adaptive inventions. It's almost as if they don't understand, like other people just throw up their arms and ask for help. I spend every day with me; I've learned a few things.

Though I may sound difficult, and you'd be right to think so, I did open my ears long enough to take a few things from those visits. One lesson stands out. I've always been instructed to stretch my shoulders, to bring my arms above my head and out to the sides in whatever way possible. I used to lay on my bed and, hands together, painstakingly lift my arms and hold onto the slats that made up my headboard. It was meant to maintain range of motion, to prevent my shoulders from locking downward in place.

But I was given a new reason: stretching my shoulders helps prevent that classic hunched-over elderly look. And while that may not have been enough reason alone, there was another: it helps the lungs breathe. That one sold me.

7.

Our house is out in the country at the end of a dirt driveway off a dirt road. It's an old road with a few houses still standing from more than two centuries ago. The names on the stones in the old cemetery are often familiar — Baldwin, Beecher, Bostwick, Bissonnette, and Hines — from street names, farms, and in the case of Hines, the town itself.

It's still mostly open land, hayfields, farms, and a plucky little golf course mixed with hundreds of acres of new-growth forest dotted with barbed-wire fences from a bygone era, rock outcroppings, and ravines. There's a hiking trail through the town forest, its parking lot a stone's throw away. It's a peaceful, bucolic existence at the end of Nick's Run, with only one neighbor in sight. But I don't like it.

I've been out in the country for more than six years; it's a different place without a car. We're more than a mile from pavement, State Highway 116, and nearly three miles from the center of town. It's not a walkable, or indeed, power chair, distance.

I look out the window at the kids next door, playing in the backyard and the driveway, and I wonder what it would've been like. The older boy rides his bike around the yard and up and down the driveway, looking like a dog on a chain. He's not allowed on the road, and while I would like to think — for the sake of the child and his bike — that his parents are overprotective, I very much understand. This isn't a quaint suburban cul-de-sac with sidewalks and speed bumps. It's a dirt road with no shoulder, full of blind hills and corners, and while most folks are local — slow, smile, and wave — the speeding pick-ups also abound.

I imagine myself in the chair, living in downtown Burlington, in an elevator building right on the sidewalk. I could cruise around town every day — look in the shop windows, sit in the park, meander down to the lake — I could make it up as I went. Even at our old house, in post-war ranch-land suburbia by the airport, there was pavement and a sidewalk — I could get out.

Mom and I go for walks up the road. We usually make it about a mile south, through the woods and up the hill, around the corner past the pig farm and silo-turned-houses. We've taken alternate routes — visited both graveyards (one very old, the other mostly new: the hilltop resting place of my big brother, Nick) and gazed up at the towering black locusts and stately old maple — but mostly we have a well-worn and increasingly boring routine. It's not ideal for the chair: the passing cars, bumpy dirt road, and quicksand shoulders don't always make for the pleasant stroll I picture. I've already been stuck, spinning the wheels of my 370-pound chair, freed only with the help of a passerby.

I've been out on the road on my own a few times. I speed through the dark patch of woods (where I might not be seen), cruise up the hill and into the wind. I cross and enter the grassy overlook through its open gate. Slowly (I put the chair in Indoor mode for the bumpy grass), I consider my route and crawl up to the crest of the knoll. There are only a handful of graves; almost all of its multi-acre grounds are empty, an exquisitely maintained hilltop lawn bound by rustic, merely symbolic wooden fences. I sit in the sun and ever-present wind, staring into the yellows and oranges of the hillsides to the east.

I have plenty of time to think, and alone time abounds, but not really. I'm not often alone in the house and far less out in the world. I don't have the drives and walks and bike rides that I used for so long. I feel trapped in the house. It's peaceful up on the hill; I have a chance to breathe deep and simply exist in the surroundings.

Outside of the warm and dry conditions of summer and fall, the road is all but impassable in my chair. My parents like the peaceful freedom of the home they built. Nearly everywhere you'd need to go is merely a short drive away, while the feel is one of a country cottage, away from the overheard conversations and prying eyes of ever-encroaching neighbors. I don't see it that way. It's not an ideal location for life in a chair. I feel trapped.

AN ALTERNATIVE PERSPECTIVE

I try to consider all of the ways in which I am fortunate.

I have parents who love me and take care of me. (The details of "take care of me" are indeed quite extensive.) I have a roof over my head and plenty of food in my belly. I have friends and family to talk to, spend time with, and share laughs. I have money in the bank and don't, thus far, struggle to pay my bills. The progression of my disease has been unusually, odds-defyingly slow.

I live in a time when so much is available to me, of historically unprecedented understanding. Social Security Disability insurance exists; Medicare exists. I'm privileged to have worked five years for an employer that provided private disability insurance. I'm able to work part-time from my house on a computer.

Medicare — along with the supplemental insurance that I pay for — bought me a battery-powered, technically advanced, joystick-operated wheelchair. In this way, I've been able to maintain some semblance of independence. I was able to purchase an accessible van to transport my conveyance. I'm fortunate that these things exist.

I live in the age of computers, of easily and endlessly available knowledge and entertainment. I'm thankful for all of the modern methods of communication, to help me feel a little less alone. I'm lucky for pen and pencil alternatives: the mouse in my hand and point and click on-screen keyboard. It's impossible to imagine my life in an earlier time.

It's easy to forget all of these things, and usually, I do. But I have to remind myself of the good things and try to give them some weight in my mind.

8.

Living with a battery-powered prosthetic transportation device has proved both wildly beneficial and woefully limiting. As with every other "solution" I've been presented, sometimes it seems worse than the problem. It has given me freedoms I'd long gone without and introduces an upsetting number of roadblocks.

It didn't take long to get used to driving in and out of the back of a van. It's strange to be tied to one vehicle, but if I could drive it myself, I would have only good things to say. Having to be chauffeured around makes me feel like a dog on a leash.

There's a lot to consider when doing anything in the chair; some things are just not going to happen. One single step, snowy or sandy or muddy or wet or uneven grassy terrain, is often enough to turn me back. There are a whole host of obstacles few people ever know exist.

I've seen less of my friends since I gave up my car. They've been a comfort since the beginning, and despite growing families and geographic distance, I still saw them regularly when I was still driving. A drop-off requires twice as much driving; my chauffeurs require reasonable hours.

I don't have a way into anyone's house; even a standard set of front stairs is impenetrable. There are portable ramps — I have a foldable aluminum one — but they're only intended to traverse a couple of feet. If I need to climb a few stairs, a manual chair and some muscle are required. My 370-pound friend, and its freedom-enabling joystick mobility, has to be left on the sidelines.

The transition into yet another new life — one in a wheelchair, at my parents' house, without my own transportation — feels more life-altering than all of the changes before. While for years things have been slowly taken away, with the flick of a switch, I watched so much independence disappear. I'm still trying to figure out my life in this place.

EVER-PRESENT AND IGNORED

I hardly talk about it — with anyone. It almost always makes for awkward conversation, for which very few people are prepared. It's not that they don't want to know how I'm doing; they might want the knowledge without the pain they assume questions will cause me. I don't mind at all — it's mostly matter-of-fact to me — but I don't bring it up on my own.

It's entirely different with my parents: they know everything on the surface; I usually avoid going deeper. I don't talk about the mental and emotional struggles that plague my day; I don't want to harp on the obvious and cause them more pain. They don't often ask how I'm feeling, what I'm thinking, or what I would like out of the rest of my days. We don't talk about the future; I'm not sure I could.

I've tried to make it a point, in my post-COVID-19-lockdown life, to try to reconnect with old friends. I've left a lot of people in the dark since my second life began. They look at me with caring eyes and ask how I'm doing. I shrug, tear up a bit, and silently nod. I'm unable to fit all of my answers into a tidy little answer. I have nothing and too much to say all at once; we move on and talk about their lives.

Some of my bolder friends focus on the details, ask specific questions, and tell me I seem as strong and healthy as the last time. I talk about my changes and the struggles of the day. They might even challenge me further and ask deeper, more complicated questions. They ask what I want out of life, if I'm prepared for the future, and the like.

It's always interesting around strangers: I'm not sure what they might think; I'm certain they'll never ask. It'd be almost refreshing to confront a few moments of honesty, to be asked the question on everyone's mind. "What's wrong with you?" might be too blunt — for them, not for me. If only there were an easy way to start, I'd be more than happy to relieve their curiosity.

I'm not sure why it all needs to be so taboo. I know I have ALS. It's been ten years; I can talk about it. Maybe there's only one question: maybe three letters put an end to it. Or maybe they'd rather pretend those letters didn't exist.

9.

Most every day seems the same. Following an often fretful, sometimes overtly frustrating night of sleep, I awake between eight and nine. My bedroom door is closed, and the room has cooled — the heat from the woodstove cannot penetrate my door.

I turn to an ancient clock radio to decide whether it's time to get up. Using my legs, I push the covers down off my body. Sometimes they're pinned under my back and I have to kick harder. Shifting my hips an inch at a time, I turn onto my side and prepare to get up. I sleep on the left side of my queen mattress; I'd never be able to get out of bed on the right.

Using my right hand, balled in a fist, I push my left elbow away from my body, roll myself onto it, and prop myself up. My core is growing weaker; it's getting harder every day. I brace my right leg against the edge of the mattress for balance and leverage, push down with both hands, and, if all goes well, sit up on the edge of the bed. Sometimes, like getting up off the floor in the past, my process takes more than one try.

A pair of sweatpants and dirty socks lay on the floor at my feet. If I'm so inclined (increasingly often, I'm not), I put pants on for breakfast. I slip my right foot into the waistband, prop my leg on my left knee, grab onto the fabric with my hands, and pull my foot through the bottom. I lean forward and pull the bunching pant leg past my left foot, stand up, bend over, and with a series of herky-jerky motions, coerce the waistband to its proper resting place. The actions themselves take several times longer than reading my protracted description.

In my T-shirt, sweatpants, and sockless feet, slumped forward with my head down to maintain my balance, I take a few careful steps to the door. Like a lifeless pendulum, I swing my left arm to land on the institutional-style horizontal door lever. I force my curled fingers around the handle, push down, and carefully pull the door open. I take a series of backward mini-steps, pausing to release the handle, and fall into my bedside wheelchair.

I take the chair through the doorway, turn right into the hall, and stop in front of the pocket-door bathroom at my left. I fold up the footrest with the back of my right heel, inch and lean my body forward, and with several preparatory motions (one...two... three), pop to my feet. I step onto the tile floor, edge to my right to swing my left hand to the light switch (it often takes multiple arm swings to hit the right spot), and turn to the nearby toilet. I lift its seat with my left hand, dig my right thumb under both waistbands, push down my waistbands, and, you know, pee.

I drive out to the kitchen, get back out, and position my high-back wooden stool (I have my own stool, without cushion or upholstery, that's easier to get onto) a precise distance from the island counter. Standing alongside, I place both palms on the counter, lock my left elbow to bear weight, and slide myself onto the chair.

With both palms and curled fingers, I lift the waiting plastic cup of water to my lips multiple times, pausing to breathe in between. Beyond the long peninsula in the living room, my mom is finishing her morning YouTube yoga. She'll be right there, she promises.

In minutes she's in the fridge getting eggs and asking me questions. Scrambled or fried? Bagel, toast, sausage, banana? Minutes later, there's a plate of hot food placed before me.

When I've finished eating, I turn to my right, carefully rise from the stool, pivot, and fall into my wheelchair. I stop again at the bathroom, get up, inch my way in, and with my left hand supporting my right wrist, pull shut the door for my morning constitutional.

After I've finished, I slide open the door and utter my catch-all beckon, "Eh mama." She's never far and always confirms with a response. She sets in place the shower-floor-covering no-slip mat that she recently cobbled together and grabs the towels and floor mat from their hooks. She pulls my shirt over my head and leaves me to get started. Standing with both hands strategically latched onto the bathroom sink, I carefully step out of my underwear. Turning my body, I cautiously place each foot on the mat, swing my left hand up to the shower-side grab bar, and lift each leg over the three-inch-high lip into the stall shower.

When I moved in, I was unwilling to accept help in the shower. Unable to lift either arm above my head, in Monkton I developed a makeshift method to get shampoo into my hair. I propped my left elbow on the horizontal handrail and bent my head down to reach my hand. Despite my best spine-twisting efforts, for several years my hair and scalp were never perfectly clean. I kept my hair short to lessen my burden. We washed my hair thoroughly over the kitchen sink after I moved in. Using a washcloth and liquid soap from a pump-action bottle, I washed the rest of my body myself.

Both of my parents continuously reminded me of my inevitable need for help in the shower. I was perfectly happy to continue my half-assed shower technique, but eventually gave in and allowed my mom to — fully clothed, of course; this isn't a horror story — wash my naked body. I still maintain control over my delicate regions.

By the time I'm dressed, it's usually past ten. I read a few pages from my book and (in recent weeks) sip a cup of green tea delivered by request. I turn on my laptop, check in on a daily routine of websites, and log in to work for an hour or two. I drive back to the kitchen for lunch around one.

I take an hour-long nap most every day in the afternoon. It's often preceded by ten or so minutes on my recumbent bike, a few bed-top exercises, and/or a short stretching routine with assistance from my mom. It didn't take long to grow addicted to my nap.

I've been doing most of my writing — for my blog, for this book, in emails, or for myself — in the hours before and after dinner. About every other day, we have a family meal, usually cooked by my dad. I'm summoned from the office precisely at six (as precisely as, say, a bus schedule), and my plate is set before me, fork or spoon on the left. I'm always served first, and despite both of my parents bouncing around the kitchen before and sometimes during the meal, I always finish last, by a long shot. It's usually polite to remain seated until everyone has finished their meal; in my house, that would be more than impractical. By the time I'm done chewing, Mom's well into clean-up and Dad's getting ready for bed.

When I've finished, if I need to wash my hands, I slide my way across the kitchen to the sink. I'm always dripping butter, or sauce, or whatever happens to be at the end of my fork or spoon, onto my fingers — because I don't lift my hand, but rotate the food up to my mouth. Mom, already planted there in dish gloves, holds my hands, applies a drop of soap to a palm, and turns on the water. I could wash my own hands in the bathroom, out of her way, but I need my left hand for the joystick, and I'd like to keep the joystick clean.

I live in my headphones after dinner or any time I need an escape. They're a noise-canceling Bose model, and whether it's music, a podcast, or something visual, they block everything out. Sometimes, when I'm feeling particularly anxious, hopeless, or annoyed, some all-encompassing music feels like a drug, quickly delivering my brain to another world.

Because I can't reach my head with my hands, I had to devise a way to get them onto my ears. I stand in front of the waist-level wood slab and, with each hand wrapped around an earpiece, bend at the waist and jam my face into them. Because my shoulders won't allow me to lift them off the surface, I turn my head back and forth to hook my ears in, arising once they're acceptably in place. I sit, prop my left (always the left, my right shoulder lacks the ability to rotate in this manner) elbow on the slab, raise my forearm, and adjust the headset to the proper position. Grabbing my right wrist with my left arm, I raise my hand and unfurl my index finger to slide the button forward and turn them on.

I push my laptop-shoebox toward the wall around nine, drag the waiting plate from my right, and dig into my awaiting fourth-meal. I shut it down around eleven, push myself to my feet, turn off the lamp with my left hand (holding it steady with my right), and fall into my chair. I brush and (usually) floss my teeth — using two hands on both my electric toothbrush and toothbrush-style floss-stick — empty my bladder and waddle head-down back to my chair.

I drive down the hall and into my room, turn around slowly at the end of my bed, and park the chair for the night. My parents have long been asleep, and for that reason, I only wear a few types of shirts. I never wear anything I have to pull over my head. (On one or two occasions since moving in, I've slept in a button-down.) I stand by the side of my bed and wriggle my way out of an open-front flannel, tossing it on the floor when I'm free. I sit on the edge of the bed and, with each big toe, pry off my socks before standing to pull down my pants.

The bedsheets are pulled open, the overhead light on. I turn the handle to shut the door quietly, move slowly back toward the bed, and lean over the bedside table for the light. Instead of swinging an arm out in front, I turn off the slider with my head. With clammy bare feet that stick to the hardwood, I get myself in position and perform a long-perfected trust-fall back into bed. Using my legs more than arms, I pull the covers over my shoulders; sometimes, I struggle.

It's January. I get out more in the summer.

FULL OF REGRET

I have a lot of regrets. A lot. They are large and they are small; they are real and they are imagined, represented by questions long-answered and unanswerable, by could'ves and would'ves at best. They exist in my mind, from yesterday and a lifetime ago, without resolution.

One of my questions, the things I cannot know, is whether I would've resolved them — whether I *could've* resolved them. I like to think if things had gone as I had imagined — if I wasn't dealt this particular card — I wouldn't have so many. But there's no way of knowing.

I never had the chance to grow up — not really. I don't think of myself as an adult — how could I? I was just getting started, a few short years out of college, when I lost my way. I look back on a life full of mistakes — only now have I learned from them. I can't go back to the person I was, and I can't bring his abilities forward. If only I could combine the two versions of myself.

I think of the fear, indecision, inaction, and avoidance that so often dominated my life. I never knew what I wanted — in school and career, in my social life, and surely most regrettably, with women. I look back and see someone rarely compelled to pursue anything real.

I never tried to answer life's most difficult questions. I never took real time to consider my path; I certainly never talked with anyone about it. You saw my confidence; I acted like I had all the answers, nonchalance personified. I was a child; I didn't.

These are the things that I can't help but dwell on. The things I didn't do; the chances I didn't take; the opportunities I missed out on because I was scared. There were a lot of them.

I lay awake thinking about the girls that could've been part of my life but weren't. I think of the memories that we could've shared. Why did I need to be lonely? If only I opened my mouth, said and felt something real, and to borrow the biggest cliché in this book, put myself out there. Far too much of my life seemed to be things that happened to me; I'm not sure how much was my choice.

I want to tell people, anyone who will listen, not to drift through life in this way. Don't take the path just because it lay at your feet. Don't run away from your fears; they're scary because they're significant. Make choices in your life; don't allow life to choose for you. Talk about the big things with someone you trust. Learn to communicate your thoughts and feelings. Don't let your fear of embarrassment make decisions in your life. Learn to listen; don't be afraid to ask questions — you'll be better for it. Talk about your fears with your family and friends; bring them out in the open and see if they are real or imagined. Spend every day learning, and take time to reflect. Ask yourself, *Am I happy? Is this what I want?* And then do something about it.

Unable to reinvent myself in the way that I'd like, I want someone to learn from my mistakes.

EPILOGUE

It's impossible that it's been more than ten years. Everyone tells me how great I'm doing, how slow my progression has been. They can't believe it. I could have — maybe they imagined I would have — stopped breathing a long time ago. I know that I'm different; I'm not sure I deserve any praise. It certainly doesn't feel like a gift. I can't appreciate what it feels like to rapidly shrivel up and die. I remember what it felt like to live.

I fantasize about getting it all back; I can't help but think of all that I'd do. I think of how easy it would be to live life as the old me and new me combined. I think of all the big things — where I'd work, where I'd live, how much money I'd have — and know none of it would matter in the least. I'd have everything I needed, just being whole again.

I daydream about having that chance. I replay memories in my head, little moments and lost conversations that feel more significant with the passage of time. I never remember the details — the meaningless drivel that undoubtedly poured from my mouth. I replace my words with something better; I can hear myself speaking — meaningful words from the heart. I always remember my feelings; if only I could've expressed them.

My mind doesn't go to the obvious — the physical activities I used to enjoy. Maybe they've become too foreign over the years; it's hard to remember what they were like. Or maybe I've learned — no matter how much I might've enjoyed all of those glorious, athletic pursuits, the camaraderie and competition, that addictive rush of endorphins — they're not as significant as they seemed.

Those things aren't necessary to lead a fulfilling life. Don't get me wrong, I would miss them. They made me feel alive in a way I might never recapture. But I'm more interested in the simpler things — I just want to be capable and independent. I think about walking casually down the street with my mind somewhere else. I relive the joy of driving and the freedom I felt. I want to have an easy conversation, to bring the words in my head out into the world. I want to be clear and concise, quick-witted and eloquent. I don't want to trip over my tongue and have to repeat myself to be understood. I don't want to sit back in silence.

I want to be seen as a man and not as an invalid. I want to bring smiles, and not smiles of pity. I want to be the adult that I never grew into.

I dream of the confidence I'd surely have. I'd see everything much differently than before. I'm smiling and talking with strangers; I'm living in a place of my own; I'm out in the world, enjoying my life. There'd be a bounce in my step that might never fade.

There'd be no room for fear and inaction. What could I possibly be afraid of? I'd enjoy every moment, the good and the bad. It's only a dream, but I can't help but get lost in that place. It may not be possible, but it would be perfect.

***

I don't have a bucket list. I'd like to, but so many things are no longer possible. I'm not sure that it matters; it's impossible to find joy where I know it should be.

Merely seeing the sights of the world doesn't do it; I don't want to sit on the sidelines. Actions would be on my bucket list. The feeling those actions would bring — that bucket list feeling you all can imagine — that's what I want more than anything.

I don't know what the future will bring. I know too well what they've told me, but it's hard to imagine nonetheless. My changes are gradual; new challenges only become clear as they confront me.

They've had me planning from the very beginning. Still in my twenties, the end of my life was under discussion. Health care directives and living wills and impossible decisions — they meant nothing and everything at the same time.

I just got a CPAP (Continuous Positive Airway Pressure) machine — I'm to use it at night. It comes with a mask and a tube, and a plugged-in device to act as my lungs. I've known it was coming for what seems like forever. My lungs have grown weaker; I'm told they're at half their original strength when I'm laying down.

The first, shoebox-sized model proved more than a challenge. It's hard to hand over to a machine such a fundamental function of life. Resting breathing is not an active pursuit; unless paying particular attention, we're not even aware that it's happening.

With a mask over my nose and mouth, and a machine pumping air at predetermined intervals, I quickly found it impossible to exist, let alone sleep. I was actively breathing — inhale, exhale, inhale, exhale — for over an hour. Snot built up in my nose, mucus in my throat. I was breathing far deeper than normal, but I seemed to be suffocating, hyperventilating in some way.

That's the way everything goes — the solution seems worse than the problem. They pretend that it's simple and easy, but the troubleshooting starts right away. We tried different masks, tubes, and settings; I used the machine sitting at my desk. It seems I just have to get used to it.

I found out there was another (purportedly much better) option and gave up on the shoebox. The replacement machine immediately wowed me — not because of its superior ease of use but because it came rolling into my house. A gray plastic box perched atop a steel rail on wheels, it belongs in a hospital room in every way.

As much as I'd like to report otherwise, its use has not gone smoothly. On multiple test-runs during my afternoon naps, I began to drift off only to feel air bubbles in my esophagus. Swallowing them down, trying to ignore the problem and fall asleep, I emerged from my nap with a belly full of air that was painfully headed to the intestines.

I no longer sleep horizontally as a result. There's a five-inch wedge beneath my mattress to try to prevent stubborn air from choosing the wrong direction. It's been somewhat effective, but after a week, I can tell you it has made falling asleep all the more complicated. I feel like I'm always falling off the pillow and climbing back up. One day it will all be replaced with a hospital bed.

We talked of a feeding tube on my last clinic visit. Though I can feed and hydrate myself just fine at the moment — and presumably will be able to for several years, at least — the surgery requires a minimum level of lung function. I'm to decide whether I want a permanent hole punched in my stomach before it might be too late. There's no way of knowing when that might be.

There's a new ALS drug on the market; its promises are similar to the riluzole (the only other prescription drug) I took for five years. You won't notice any changes, they tell me, but it's shown to slow the progress of the disease. The original price I was given, based on Medicare and my supplemental insurance, was $36,159.12 out of pocket per year. Somehow, more recently, I've been told that the costs would be covered. When I have that in writing, I'll try to believe it.

The cost — though completely disconnected from its stated effectiveness — isn't my biggest concern. It's the way it's administered. It's an intravenous treatment, given daily, at the hospital. A "port" (a permanent hole in my chest) is surgically installed to connect the IV. It's given in a cycle: fourteen days on, ten days off, with no end in sight. Forever. For the rest of my life. I'm not going to spend every day commuting to the hospital in hopes of some unknowable and marginal improvement.

The day will come when all of my function is gone, when I can't stand on my own, can't chew and swallow, can't hold up my head, when speaking is only a memory, my lungs have given up, and my hands are entirely useless. Nearly every imaginable human function will at some time be lost. The brain in my head will one day be all I have left.

With all of the fears of my future, I think of my purpose. I'd like for my life to have meant something. I don't have a family to live on after me and feel proud of. I'd like to leave something behind.

***

I've met a few women in the last couple of months. For a very long time, a friend has been trying to get me to "put myself out there." I dismissed the idea as absurd. *What woman could possibly want me? The last one walked out on me, and that was before I was using a chair, gave up my car, and moved in with my parents. How will I even begin to describe my circumstances?* "And, by the way, I have a terminal disease; you'll have to pick me up and sign the check." *Insane.*

Nevertheless, she convinced me to try. As we discussed, "put yourself out there," means Tinder. One afternoon, I created an account, posted a few pictures, and scribbled a quick bio. *How much should I say? What should I show them? I can't tell them everything; no one would ever respond if they knew the full truth.*

I've switched up my profile a number of times. It said "ALS" and "wheelchair" in a couple of versions. I even posted a photo in my 370-pound monster for a while. But I decided that was too much. *Maybe I should ease them in slowly.*

It's awkward to ask a date to pick you up at your house. More so when your mother answers the door, chats with your date, and shows her how to secure your wheelchair to the floor of your van. I'm equal parts compliments and apologies from the beginning.

If, at the very least, I text with and meet some interesting people, so be it. It goes against my instincts, but I'm trying to stay positive and not look too far ahead. I'm trying to embrace the idea that possibilities might just exist.

***

I don't know that I've ever accepted the ALS diagnosis — the death sentence — I was given ten years ago. I don't know how I could; it's too much to take. How could I understand? No one understands.

It's not that I'm still in denial — I'm very aware of what's happened. I don't get to live like the others; my life has to be different. I'll always be sad; I'll always be angry; I'll never move on; I'll never accept.

I think from a distance it's possible. You're given the news, and with time it sinks in. You go back to your life; a new reality comes into being.

I don't get to go back to my life. I don't get to escape. I don't allow myself to hope for a miracle.

Though reluctant at every step, I *have* gotten used to it. (As much as anyone can get used to continual loss.) I've gotten used to using a wheelchair and the death of my right arm. I've gotten used to my hands and my neck. I've gotten used to life in this body.

It's the big things that are the problem. I've never married; I've never had children; I don't own a house; I don't have a career. I don't have a partner in life. I don't have a life of my own.

I separate my life into segments, a moment in time divides each in two. Friday, June 6, 2003, my brother was gone. Wednesday, August 31, 2011, my life was left behind. They don't stand on their own; one's piled on the other. There isn't any healing from either.

ACKNOWLEDGMENTS

My life would not be possible without my parents, and not just in a "they gave me life" sort of way. I owe both of them tremendously.

A number of friends suggested that I write a book. At some point, their ideas sank in. Thanks to all of you who have supported my writing. I would never have gotten this far without your encouragement.

A big thanks to Howard Lovy, my editor. There was a lot of rewriting to get my work where it is. Many of the changes were the result of your questions and suggestions. You got me to put more of myself in my writing, adding much-needed depth to the stories. I learned a lot in the process.

Another big thanks to my cover and layout designer, Marko Markovic. We exchanged over a hundred emails over the course of my project, and you were always polite, professional, and responsive. Every person who puts their eyes on my memoir will see the high level of quality of your work.

To Torrey Valyou, photographer and friend. Thank you for not only taking my picture, but for your advice and support with the design of my book.

To my proofreader, April Kelly. Your fine work will go unnoticed by design, but I appreciate your attention to detail. You have increased the level of professionalism of this book.

The 911 operator, volunteer fireman, EMTs, ER doctors and nurses who all played a part in rescuing me on that Sunday morning in 2015. I wouldn't be here without you. You save lives; what could be greater than that?

All of the medical professionals I've seen over the years. Despite my frustrations and resultant unflattering portrayal, you've always been kind and resourceful. I've known some of you over a decade, and you've been on my side all the way. Each of you is a credit to your profession.

To the people of National Life, for rehiring me after I quit without notice, and for their compassion and understanding over the years.

To all of the names in this book, thank you for playing a role in my life. And to those closest to me, I appreciate your longstanding support over the years.

To my readers, Tessa, Scott, Erica, Andrew, Lucy, and Rachael, I am thankful for your time and valuable feedback.

ABOUT THE AUTHOR

Nate Methot grew up in suburban South Burlington, Vermont, with his mother, father, and older brother, Nick. He attended public schools and earned a Bachelor of Science in Business Administration from the University of Vermont. He began a career at a securities broker/dealer in Montpelier after college and currently works part-time for the firm.

Before his ALS diagnosis, he enjoyed running, hiking, skiing, camping, golf, and basketball, as well as playing and listening to music, and spending time with a group of fun-loving goofballs.

He lives with his parents in Hinesburg, Vermont, and spends much of his time reading, writing, going for "walks" in his motorized wheelchair, and importantly, eating.